Victor Meignan

From Paris to Pekin over Siberian Snows. Russia and Siberia

A Narrative of a Journey by Sledge over the Snows of European...

Victor Meignan

From Paris to Pekin over Siberian Snows. Russia and Siberia
A Narrative of a Journey by Sledge over the Snows of European...

ISBN/EAN: 9783744756907

Printed in Europe, USA, Canada, Australia, Japan

Cover: Foto ©Andreas Hilbeck / pixelio.de

More available books at **www.hansebooks.com**

PREFACE TO THE ENGLISH EDITION.

EMBARRASSED readers, who delight in books of travel, whether for the recreation or the useful information they afford, are not relieved of their difficulty when the title of the work, instead of indicating the nature of the subject, only presents an enigma for them to solve. How, for instance, is the reader to gauge the nature of the contents of "Voyage en Zigzag?" It might mean the itinerary of some crooked course among the Alps, or, perhaps, the log-book of a yacht chopping about the Channel, or the record of anything but a straightforward journey. Again, "By Land and Sea" might simply be the diary of a holiday trip from London to Paris, or a *réchauffé* of impressions of a "globe-trotter," who went to see what everybody talked about that he also might talk about what he had seen. Then there are a host of others, such as "Travels West," "The Land of the North Wind"—which one has to discover vaguely by ascertaining first where it does not blow,—" Loin de Paris," " Dans les Nuages," " On Blue Water ; " all of which might be strictly applicable to the metropolitan area if the water were only just a little bluer. But "Voyage Autour de ma Femme" is still less intelligible. Is it a book of travel at all, or only a romance, or a *comédie-vaudeville?* It may not be a *fantaisie* like " Voyage Autour de ma Chambre," nor even the record of a journey necessarily performed within four walls, for—though I have not looked at the book—it may be the narrative of an unsentimental journey, in which the tourist had taken a holiday trip all around picturesque Europe and his wife, leaving her at home; or it may be a sentimental journey as touching as Sterne's—a kind of circular tour *en petit,* circumscribed by the ordinary length of the apron-string; in which event, a very subjective turn of the *impressions de voyage* would be evident; and consequently would not suit readers who decidedly prefer to regard what is presented

PREFACE.

The reader will naturally discover from the title of this book the traveller's course, but he will at the same time, no doubt, desire to know something of the character of the book.

It may gratify him to be told that essentially it is a personal narrative, that cannot fail to interest those who like in a book of travel a tale of life full of incident and adventure: it is one in which his sympathies will be awakened and sustained in following the traveller in his movements from day to day and from place to place, his imagination being vividly stirred by the illusion that the participator is, as it were, in the changing scenes and events passing before his eyes like the tableaux of a diorama. And yet it must not be supposed, because the writer's chief object has been to give an interesting personal narrative, that it is deficient in useful information: far from it; but, instead of overcharging his book with minute details, he has seized the more salient features of men and things. These are presented from his own point of view as the result of intelligent observation or discriminating hearsay.

The traveller, who is evidently a most genial

companion, passes lightly and rapidly over the well-known route from Paris to St. Petersburg and Moscow in the short space of thirty pages. After taking a glance at the wonders of the Kremlin and the monastery of Troïtsa, probably the richest religious community in the world, with its heaps of precious pearls and various gems, he passes on to the famous mart of Nijni-Novgorod, along the frozen Oka and the Volga, through the country of the Votiaks, and across the Ural Mountains into Siberia. Posting at full gallop over the snowy way, sleeping, living altogether in fact, in his sledge (for the luxury of beds is unknown in Siberian hotels), he falls in with a series of adventures, sometimes amusing and sometimes even tragic, in his progress over that vast territory that presents so many strange races, and, in winter, so many remarkable scenes. At one time he is in imminent peril of being lost in a snow-storm on the steppe of Omsk, and at another on the frozen surface of the Baikal. He makes an excursion on the way amid the wild Kirghiz, gets a peep at the life of the Polish exiles, and at the gold miners and the people of Irkutsk in their amusements and occupations.

The grand scenes of nature, particularly at this season, are all duly depicted with the emotion of one alive to the beautiful and sublime: the wonderful atmospheric effects of light at a very low temperature, the novel and changing aspects of the steppes; the startling spectacle of the frozen Angara and Lake Baikal, the grotesque aspect of the snow-capped forests, and then, later, the picturesque, verdant valleys of China. In the course of his journey through Mongolia, he enables us to get a glimpse at those strange people the Mongols, their tent life, their city of tents, their incessant prayer-turning as a chief occupation, and the fearful character of some of their ceremonies. Then, after a caravan journey of eighteen days across the trackless Desert of Gobi, he arrives at the great Wall of China, and finally at Pekin, where he contemplates its curiosities, its works of art, its people, their institutions and their daily life.

Having thus given an outline of the book and its contents for the reader's guidance, I will proceed to explain why I have thought it advisable to depart from a close imitation throughout of the original, and to present, in fact, a modified version rather than a strict translation.

The style of the original, though simple and unadorned, is frequently slipshod ; and the author—contrary to many French travellers, who often make, and perhaps still oftener attempt to make, the subject of their narrative a vehicle for epigram and sparkling and spirited diction—has evidently thought more of conveying a truthful picture to the reader, than of the mode of expression by which this could be most effectively done. In many novel and interesting descriptions, for example, the effect they are capable of producing is almost wholly lost through the want of a more just co-ordination of parts and subordination of minor details, and, occasionally, through the want of sufficient expansion, lest the reader should not have time to contemplate and realize a quick succession of fleeting images.

These, consequently, are some of the chief points I have attempted to correct; though in making the attempt, I hope I may not have exposed myself to an unpleasant suspicion, in the first place, of having assumed too much assurance in undertaking uninvited to revise the writing of another, and, in the next place, in certain *tableaux*, which would be unattractive if obscure or colourless, of having indulged in a taste for fine writing, when the sole object has been to place the matter before the reader as lucidly and vividly as possible.

But it will probably more concern the reader to be assured that the truthfulness of these descriptions, such as represented by the traveller, has not been distorted in this manner of treating them. On this point he may readily satisfy himself on taking the trouble to compare some of them with those in the original edition. He will find, I hope, that my work has not been in vain, and that I have contributed something towards rendering more attractive this interesting narrative, chiefly relating to that land over which Madame Cottin, Xavier de Maistre, and other writers have thrown a glow of romance.

WILLIAM CONN.

CONTENTS.

CHAPTER I.

FROM PARIS TO ST. PETERSBURG.

En route by rail—Berlin—Annoyances at the Russian Custom House—First aspect of European Russia—An evening on the banks of the Neva - - - 1

CHAPTER II.

ST. PETERSBURG TO MOSCOW.

Letters of recommendation for Siberia—M. Pfaffius, frontier commissary at Kiachta—Russian music—Arrival at Moscow - - - - - - - 19

CHAPTER III.

MOSCOW—NIJNI-NOVGOROD.

The Kremlin—Equipage and visits of the Virgin of In-verski—Origin of Christianity in Russia—A few words about Troitsa—A travelling companion—Purchase of furs—Passage of the Oka in a sledge—Feeling of terror on first travelling in a sledge over a frozen river   30

CHAPTER IV.

FROM NIJNI-NOVGOROD TO KAZAN.

The Volga in winter—Varieties of podarojnaia—What is necessary for a long sledge journey—Departure from Nijni—Posting relays—A momentary thaw—The snow—Arrival at Kazan - - - - - - - 51

CHAPTER V.

KAZAN—JOURNEY TO PERM.

The Virgin of Kazan—Russian manner of expressing disapproval—Dining with a grandee—His description of the enfranchisement of the serfs—The Tartars—Journey in a sledge—Caravan of exiles—The Votiaks—Aspect of European Russia - - - - - 73

CHAPTER VI.

PERM—THE ROAD TO CATHERINEBURG.

Hotel accommodation in Siberia—A councillor—Opinions and examples of Russian administration—National music—The passion for aggrandizement of territory—Entry into Asia - - - - - - 98

CHAPTER VII.

OUR PARTY ON THE ROAD TO TUMEN.
PAGE

Trade and manufactures at Catherineburg — Carolling cherubs—Christmas at Kamechlof—Grand gala at a posting stage—Tumen—Its situation—Its gipsies—Fruit preserved in ice - - - - - - 113

CHAPTER VIII.

A PERILOUS NIGHT ADVENTURE ON THE STEPPE OF OMSK.

An ostentatious Siberian custom—The steppe — The cemeteries—Omsk—Its situation—Its society—The emancipation of the serfs related by a citizen—M. Kroupinikof—Visit to an encampment of Kirghiz—Masquerade at Omsk - - - - - - 128

CHAPTER IX.

THE COLD ON THE WAY TO TOMSK.

The intense cold—Its inconveniences—The fine effects of light at a very low temperature—The baptismal fête of Christ on the Obi—Tomsk—Its commerce—An evening on the banks of the Tom   156

CHAPTER X.

THE GOVERNMENT OF YENISSEISK AND KRASNOIARSK.

Wretched aspect of the villages of this province—The

country at last becomes hilly—The night watchers at Krasnoiarsk—M. Lovatine's three collections—A Polish exile's ball - - - - - - - 171

CHAPTER XI.

KRASNOIARSK TO IRKUTSK.

Social position and education of the country people and citizens—Uselessness of Siberian forests—Journey to Irkutsk — A pack of wolves — Cleanliness of the villages—Congelation of the Angara—The government of Irkutsk—The college—The prison—The fire brigade - - - - - - - - - 184

CHAPTER XII.

IRKUTSK.

The gold miners—Their luxury; their wealth; their wives—A few words about the clergy, and the code of religion—The Polish exiles—Travelling maniacs—A dinner *en famille* - - - - - - - 202

CHAPTER XIII.

ATTEMPT AT ESCAPE BY A POLISH EXILE.

Why the Polish exiles cannot escape—Narrative of an attempt by M. Bohdanovitch—Encounter with a bear—Sanitary arrangements in Siberia—Wolf hunts—A blue fox—Different values of furs—A few words on the passion for displaying riches - - - - 222

CHAPTER XIV.

IRKUTSK TO LAKE BAIKAL.

PAGE

The natives—The Olkhonese—Shamanism—The Buriats—The Tungus—The Samoyeds—The Carnival at Irkutsk—Pablo—Adieu to Constantine — Another perilous night on the ice of Lake Baikal - - 244

CHAPTER XV.

LAKE BAIKAL TO KIACHTA.

Observations on Eastern Siberia and its inhabitants—Their dream of independence—Motives that might contribute to independence—Example of the Chinese—The Yakuts and the inhabitants of Kamtchatka - 266

CHAPTER XVI.

KIACHTA TO MAIMATCHIN.

The tarantass—Tea merchants—Their competition—The Sienzy—Aspect of Maimatchin—A dinner at the Chinese Governor's—Preparations for crossing the Gobi desert - - - - - - - - 285

CHAPTER XVII.

MAIMATCHIN TO URGA.

First Stage in Mongolia—The Mongols—Their tents;

their life—How they steer their way in the desert—
The Caravan—A Sacrilege—The Russian Consul at
Urga—The Koutoukta - - - - - - 304

CHAPTER XVIII.

URGA AND THE ENTRY INTO THE DESERT OF GOBI.

Urga—Mongol religion—Praying wheels—Burial ceremonies—The Holy Mountain—My travelling companions in the desert—Departure from Urga—First halt—A Mongolian repast—Easter Eve. - - - 321

CHAPTER XIX.

CARAVAN ACROSS THE DESERT OF GOBI.

A Mongolian Prince and his Court—Prayer turning—Our life in the desert—The sandy plain—Want of water—Lunar mirage—Three executions—A traveller astray in the desert—Arrival at Kalkann and the Great Wall of China - - - - - - - - - 341

CHAPTER XX.

FROM THE GREAT WALL TO TCHAH TAO.

First view of China proper—Last Russian hospitality—The Palankeen—The streets of Kalkann—Travelling along the Great Wall—The Secret Societies—Chinese art—How order is maintained—Origin of the tress—How the titles of Chinese nobility become extinct - 362

CHAPTER XXI.

TCHAH-TAO TO PEKIN.

PAGE

An exciting incident—The Pass of Nang-kao—Picturesqueness of the gorge—A young married couple—The levy of taxes—Toun-cheh-ouh—The last solitude—Entry into Pekin—Arrival at the Legation - - 379

CHAPTER XXII.

PEKIN — DEPARTURE.

The Marble Bridge—The Tartar City—Objects of Art—Japanese lacquering—Interments—The Observatory—The Imperial Palace—The Temples—The four harvests—Kinds of tea—Departure from Pekin—Tien-tsin—The sea at last - - - - - 395

NOTES - - - - - - - - - - 417

FROM PARIS TO PEKIN.

CHAPTER I.

FROM PARIS TO ST. PETERSBURG.

En route by rail—Berlin—Annoyances at the Russian Custom House—First aspect of European Russia—An evening on the banks of the Neva.

WHEN I had quite made up my mind to pass my winter in Siberia and to proceed in the following spring to Pekin by Mongolia and the Desert of Gobi, my friends, hearing of my project, were incredulous of the steadfastness of my resolution; they shrugged their shoulders, quivering, perhaps at the prospect of frost-nipped limbs, and wondered what could induce me to quit the comfortably warmed salons at this season merely to brave the boreal blasts of so rigorous a climate. So far as it concerned me, however, this anticipatory cold was not at all catching, for, indeed, my resolution was then too firmly set to be shaken by a quivering void of sympathetic influence, or to yield to the allurements of the most inviting Parisian *cercle* or boudoir.

Having therefore already well considered my project, I had decided on attempting to accomplish it for this reason: I had seen Syria and Nubia, lands of the Sun, in their full-blown summer radiance and glory, and I now longed to gaze on Siberia, the region of snow and ice, in its wondrous winter garb. When I am in the humour for a tour, I like to visit countries in their typical season, just as one likes to see a man in the exercise of his proper vocation. There is, undoubtedly, a feeling of satisfaction in contemplating the animate or inanimate world merely in its habitual phases, in so far as these are the normal and appropriate expression of a condition of established law and order — the harmonies of nature as well as the moral fitness of things. Siberia, as it is pictured to our imagination, is vividly associated with the stirring incidents of a rigorous arctic winter; it is in this, its most characteristic aspect, that we delight to regard it and muse over it; moreover, in winter only is it so remarkably dissimilar from the nature we are accustomed to see in milder and more genial climates, and in this season alone, with its mighty ice-bound rivers and boundless snow-capped forests, does it present to the wondering eye of the stranger the interest and attractiveness of a striking novelty.

I was in excellent spirits from the exhilarating anticipation of so much adventure, as the reader may imagine, and, busy with final preparations, my friends seeing me thus occupied, amused me with their diverse questions and suggestions. Every one puts questions in his own way according to his habitual ideas or occupation. The doctor with a grave look asks, "Are you sure your constitution is robust enough to bear so much cold?" the druggist, whether you have a good supply of quinine or chilblain ointment, or somebody's magic pills—some comprehensive remedy for all human weaknesses, corporeal and mental, excepting, of course, the incurable one of belief in its efficacy; then ladies suggest a good supply of warm worsted stockings and knitted comforters ; then others inquire whether you have a passport duly *visé*, a six-shot revolver, maps, a telescope, letters of credit, a belt for gold, and I really don't know with what they would not considerately provide me. Some perhaps might have gone so far as to suggest a warming pan; and for my part, I think that a warming pan would not have been the least useful article suggested, inasmuch as it might serve as a stewing pan, and then I should be assured of a hot supper and a warm bed; then in inns its sonorous capacity might supply the want of bells, and on a journey serve to scare away the wolves, and finally, having no further use for this accommodating vade mecum, I might sell it in Mongolia, a land of honey, for a purpose to which, I have heard, it is sometimes applied in England, that is for swarming bees with its deep musical note, and this failing, at all events, dispose of it in China, on taking out the handle, as the latest novelty in gongs in *articles de Paris*.

But not one of my friends, not even the druggist, who sells *mort aux mouches* and other insect killers, thought of the *chasses* one is occasionally, though not so often now, obliged to devote himself to in foreign inns; probably they were not lovers of the chase, at least of such small game; but when one has once been *bien mangé*, the *piqures* leave their marks on the memory when they have been long effaced elsewhere, and not knowing what sport I might fall in with, I took care to secure the completeness of my *gréement de chasse*, and having at last made all my arrangements, I was ready to start.

Accordingly on the 25th of October, 1873, at eight in the morning, I left the Gare du Nord, and no sooner had I taken my seat than inquiries recommenced in another form by a talkative traveller. This traveller was a Belgian, and Belgians are generally loquacious and free in making acquaintances. "Where are you going, monsieur?" said he. "As for me, I am going as far as Cologne; it is a very long journey, you know, and I like to have some one to talk to, to pass away these twelve long hours in a carriage." "And so am I going to Cologne," I replied. "Oh! you are going to Cologne, are you? Is it to buy horses? That is what I am going there for," he explained. "I am accustomed to buy my horses in Prussia." "No," I said, "I am not going to Cologne for that." "What for, then?" "Well, it is to start again from there, for I go to Berlin." "Oh! you are going to Berlin? Why then are you going to Berlin? Nobody goes there, neither tourists nor men of business." "I go there to start again, for I go from there to St. Petersburg." These questions succeeded one another in this way from stage to stage, till the moment we had finished the tour of the world. His simple Flemish countenance then took a curious expression of droll astonishment. He could say no more till after the lapse of some moments, and then it was to exclaim, opening his large mouth as wide as possible and vigorously thumping the cushion with his heavy fist, "Oh! Ah! Then you are really going round the world. Dear me! round the world!" "Yes, almost," I replied, smiling, "and therefore when I want horses I must buy them elsewhere than in Cologne."

As soon as Cologne and the Rhine are passed, a little favoured spot of this dull country—at least, as it appears to the traveller *en route*—you traverse an endless plain, neither picturesque nor interesting. Berlin redeems with no artistic beauty its sterile situation. But a Parisian could not be expected to find much attraction in Berlin, and accordingly I found it very dull. Its streets are badly paved; enormous gutters, separating the roadway from the pavement, expose carriages to danger and exhale noxious odours, filled as they are with filthy water and refuse of every kind.

What strikes one in this city is a general aspect of gloominess. They have tried in all the public buildings to imitate the Grecian Doric, and have only too well succeeded in it. I do not understand at all why the Prussians have adopted this cold style, more sepulchral even than the Egyptian, under a sky so dull, and almost as foggy as that of Old England. In the places of amusement, in the interior of the Opera for instance, they have replaced the Doric style with the Corinthian, that is to say, mourning with half-mourning. The national colours, white and black, profusely distributed everywhere, complete its funereal character.

The finest avenue, Unter den Linden, leads from the Museum to the exterior promenades, but the colour of the houses bordering this boulevard spoils the effect; it suggested a mixture of iron and saffron or something like the sickly hue of jaundice. The general impression is anything but cheerful. One is almost disposed to say to every one he meets: "Frère, il faut mourir!" but I said to myself, "Il faut partir," and, after a short halt, I accordingly took my departure.

The following day the express train, without any incident worthy of note, took me to the Russian frontier.

Though there are custom houses at the frontiers of every civilized state, their character and methods of proceeding have not, in spite of the levelling tendencies of railways, yet arrived at much approach to uniformity; and since these characteristics differ widely from China to Peru, they frequently give some sign of the political and social status of the people into whose country one enters.

At the custom house of this colossal empire of Russia, with a national budget so overcharged, the treasury is especially solicitous of filling the imperial coffers. Money is sorely needed.

The stranger there must first prove his identity by producing his passport duly *visé* at the consulates of all the places he has passed. The passport is returned to him, bearing a word written on the back. This word leaves every uninitiated traveller in complete ignorance of its meaning or object; it is written in Russian characters, and, moreover, badly written in a language which, in conformity with good taste, one is expected not to know.

When I received my passport marked with the mystic word, my embarrassment was painful. I walked up and down the waiting room, showing the word to every one I met. They all looked at me with astonishment, and kept clear of me without offering any explanation. I, at last, heard some one speaking French near me; it was a gentleman whose moustaches of immoderate length and dark whiskers white at the tips, something like the fur of the blue fox, indicated him to be of Northern nationality. I hastened to be enlightened, and at once learnt that this important word was the name of the officer appointed to examine my baggage. After some difficulty, I found the functionary, who, fortunately, spoke

French. "Monsieur," he said, "qu'avez-vous à déclarer?" "Rien," I promptly replied, with all the freedom of innocence; "what I bring with me is for my personal use, and if some of the packages appear to you very bulky, it is because I am on a very long, a very distant journey." "Be good enough to open them." I accordingly began, feeling assured that everything would go on well and soon end. "It is my personal clothing," I explained; "there is nothing but clothes in this trunk. Here is a pair of trousers that seems new; I have had it these three years. It looks, however, new; that is to my credit; you see, I do not wear out my clothes much," I remarked merrily. "But," he rejoined, "it seems too new; we will weigh it; this will be paid for." My mortification was about to begin. He commenced putting into the scales all the clothing which he considered had not been worn. "What are these?" "They are memorandum books." "Is there anything written in them?" "Nothing yet," and then they also go into the scales. But he was not disposed to end there; far from it; I was obliged to open the chest I had got packed in

Paris with the greatest care, containing my sporting equipment and many things for use only in Siberia. Perceiving that he was inexorable in his determination to turn out everything, I entreated him to put the case, just as it was, into the scales, preferring to pay more to having the contents turned upside down in the greatest disorder after they had been so artistically arranged. But I was much deceived, for this gentleman was too much of a Cossack to forego the pleasure of examining Parisian objects. Everything was turned out, and, if possible, inside out, and put into the scales. I was enraged.

In the midst of this intolerable annoyance, there was for me a gleam of malicious satisfaction. I had brought with me an enormous box of vermin-killer in powder, which was considered to be invaluable for my long journey through Asia. The box could not easily be opened; far from it. The officer tried in vain for some time, but at last, the cover yielding suddenly to his efforts, the powder was violently flung into his face, penetrating into his eyes, his nostrils, and mouth, and completely covering his coat. "What is this?" he demanded.

"A very violent poison," I replied, with an affectation of terror, to add to his discomfiture, which had due effect. He turned pale, and, at once, fixed the duty on my effects at the highest possible rate. But I had some unexpected sport with large game, and, my revenge having afforded me full satisfaction, I drew from my pocket my louis d'or.

But, alas! Russia, the country that produces at present so much gold, is the one where it has the least currency. I was obliged to go and change my twenty-franc pieces for paper roubles; and thus I paid at this custom house more than a hundred francs, merely to pass my old clothes—this sum being as much as they were worth—and my memorandum books, which I could not make up my mind to abandon, because they were my only companions to be entrusted with my *impressions de voyage*.

Before getting into the train, I observed a newsvendor on the platform. "Have you the *Figaro*?" I asked. "Yes, sir." "How much?" "Thirty kopecks" (one shilling). "Then give me a newspaper of your own country printed in French." "Here is one, sir, the *Journal de St. Pétersbourg.*" "How much?" "Fifteen kopecks." "But why is it so dear, printed in Russia?" "It is, sir, because here there are enormous duties on the manufacture of paper." This kind of tax, in my opinion, is, for one thing, to be fully appreciated. The Russians should thus be guarded against a propensity for scribbling, which, alas! is so rampant in France. And then again, when universal suffrage is to appear in Russia, who knows whether the exorbitant price of paper will not hinder the candidates from distributing the voting papers, and the electors from procuring them at their own expense? The exercise of this new power will then be the cause of a fresh charge and become consequently an obstacle. Such a state of things perhaps will cause universal suffrage to succumb and disappear —an institution apparently just and attractive in theory, but amusingly droll in practice to those who have witnessed its working, especially in the country districts. This first experience reconciled me with the administration of this vast country, almost even with its custom house, and I climbed up into my carriage, where two stoves, though it had not yet commenced to freeze, kept up a tropical heat. There I installed myself in one of the immense easy seats with which it was furnished, and which was transformed at night, with the aid of a mechanical arrangement, into a kind of bed, where one may be tolerably comfortable, and there I waited the signal of departure, prepared to observe the aspect of the country through which I was about to pass.

The part of Russia between Wilna and St. Petersburg is simply melancholy. When I passed over it, the absence of snow, of sun, and leaves on the trees, rendered this character, which is proper to it, still more striking. Unlimited forests, that are no longer copse and not yet arrived at full growth, and as impenetrable as a jungle, especially in autumn, from the swampy nature of the soil; a long undulating range of land, of an outline the ocean would assume in the monstrous swell of a tempest, sending back the horizon to an enormous distance; the appearance of a few habitations, at long intervals, and whose presence at all in such a spot suggests utter desolation more than absolute solitude :—this is what is presented to the traveller on entering Russia, immensity, impenetrability, and silent gloom.

It is true that autumn is the least favourable season for visiting Russia; it is, in a certain way, the period of inactivity for the whole race, a people scattered over an immense space, whose special character needs a rapid and continual locomotion. The land in autumn becomes too swampy for wheeled carriages, and travelling in sledges has not yet commenced. Soon, however, the snow, falling probably in abundance, will permit the Russians their favourite mode of travelling; and the intense cold, dissipating the clouds, will give to its white mantle unparalleled purity and brilliancy.

We will hasten to arrive at St. Petersburg, of which, however, as well as of Moscow, I will say but little, because I have to describe regions more remote and much less known. When one has a long journey before him, he should not linger at the first stages, for fear of feeling too sensibly the difficulties of the enterprise, and consequently of being tempted to abandon it in spite of a brave resolution at the outset.

I alighted at the Hôtel de France, and, almost immediately, went out afoot. It was six in the evening and quite dark. A mild and refreshing temperature was inviting to a walk. The sky was serene, and the moon shone brilliantly. It was one of those fine evenings described by Joseph de Maistre, although we were still in November. Chance led me towards the Neva, and I was much delighted, for, from the bridge of boats thrown across it, I was able to contemplate a spectacle truly magnificent. It is not a river, but rather an inlet of the sea. Four or five times wider than the Garonne at Bordeaux, this piece of water makes a bend in the middle of the city; and along its banks is exposed the principal architectural magnificence of St. Petersburg. The Emperor's palace, the Senate, the Fortress, the Hermitage, the Academy of Fine Arts, are all along its banks, as well as an immense number of churches, each surmounted with five or six Byzantine domes.

At the moment I was there, the moon's rays were reflected from all these gilded domes, and again these glittering beams were flashed like dazzling fireworks from the surface of the water; the gilded cupola of the Cathedral St. Isaac rose majestically above the others, and surpassed them in splendour. Black barges, resembling somewhat, at this hour of the night, Venetian gondolas, passed to and fro, leaving their luminous trails glittering on the surface of the water. The great mass of water of Lake Ladoga was gliding onward in its full flood with rapidity, but without noise, for nothing opposed its passage. The bells, which gave an idea of enormous size from their deep, solemn, and prolonged tone, alone broke the religious silence of the scene by the call to prayer. It was grand, solemn, and inspiring. This night at St. Petersburg, God revealed Himself to man by the splendour of the heavens and the mystery of the hour, and man's thoughts were drawn to God by the imposing towering of His temples and the awe-inspiring sound of the bells.

Though I was much moved by this scene and its associations, I knew I could not adequately enjoy Russia in its aspect of the mild season. A little later, however, the Neva would be arrested in its course by the frost, the domes of the churches, as well as the land everywhere, would be dressed in a thick mantle of snow, and then I should no longer behold this country as it now was, but buried under its winter shroud. I remained therefore long contemplating this spectacle, the real beauty of which was enhanced in my imagination by the reflection that it was to be but of short duration.

CHAPTER II.

ST. PETERSBURG TO MOSCOW.

Letters of recommendation for Siberia—M. Pfaffius, frontier commissary at Kiachta—Russian music—Arrival at Moscow.

DURING my sojourn at St. Petersburg, I went of course, and more than once, to see the curiosities with which the city is filled, but it was necessary to remember that I had set out for a much longer journey, and that my chief occupation at St. Petersburg was to search for a *compagnon de voyage*. With this object, I availed myself of all the letters of recommendation I had obtained in Paris, hoping thereby to secure the useful as well as agreeable society either of a tourist or of a functionary returning to his post in Eastern Siberia.

In the first *réunions* where I had the honour to be invited, I invariably spoke of my intended journey, hoping thereby to find a travelling companion, but in doing so, I was always answered with a frown or met with a deaf ear.

The reason was this: at St. Petersburg, it is not in good taste to travel in the direction of the East. The inhabitants of this city of pleasure seem to regret their origin; this society, so ·fastidious and refined, appears really to fear being still taken for a horde of barbarians. Women in the highest social rank have said to me sometimes: " Whatever I may do or say, you will nevertheless have your own opinion of me; you will regard me as a Cossack." Everything associated with Asia is in disfavour, and, perhaps, those who exaggerate the sentiment would willingly cede Siberia to the Chinese Government, in order to have nothing in common with the East. To speak French is indispensable; when you are French and are received in society in St. Petersburg, it is surprising to see how much France is *à la mode:* French is habitually spoken, and read in newspapers and books; the *cuisine* is French as well as the costumes, and so are many of the plays at the theatres. It is quite the *ton* to have arrived from Paris, Luchon, or Trouville, and to have brought the latest *cancans* from the *boudoirs à la mode.*

As soon as the frost appeared, I began busying myself with the arrangements for my journey. I was aided in this difficult task by M. Bartholdy, then *chargé d'affaires* at the French Embassy. This obliging Frenchman succeeded with the Imperial Government in enabling me to traverse Siberia in a manner somewhat official, and the ministers accordingly gave me letters of recommendation to the governors of the various provinces I was about to visit.

I obtained also from M. Michaelof, the contractor for the posting between Nijni-Novgorod and Tumen, a circular order requiring each postmaster on the route to give me the best horses at the shortest notice.

Many persons recommended me to their friends in Siberia. In less than a fortnight I was provided with thirty-two of these recommendations, but I had not yet found either a companion or a servant.

The frost, however, was becoming every

day more severe. The thermometer varied between 10° and 12° Centigrade below zero (14° to 10° Fahr.).*

The canal of the Moïka, which my windows overlooked, was already half frozen; enormous blocks of ice were drifting on the Neva; the snow, though not yet very deep, fell often enough to lead me to hope for sledging very shortly. I was about to decide to start alone for Moscow, when I received a letter from the head of the Asiatic Government.

This letter informed me that the Russian frontier commissary at Kiachta, M. Pfaffius, was at St. Petersburg at the Hotel Démouth, and was about to join his post.

Without losing a moment, I gathered up all the letters, those even the addresses of which I could not read, and hastened to the Hotel Démouth.

I did not yet know what it was to travel through Siberia; I had not the least idea of many things that were required, nor that so many things even were necessary, and was therefore not a little surprised, on my

---

* See note 1 at end of book.

entry into M. Pfaffius's apartment, at the sight that there awaited me.

In the middle of the room lay on the floor a heap of pillows, furs, mattresses, blankets, and ropes. This was not all, for I soon perceived also a loaf of sugar, felt boots, a bottle of brandy, and bags and sacks of every shape and size.

The functionary, wearing a ring on the second finger of his right hand, a sign of his office, was seated at table breakfasting. At his side stood a Buriat servant, with half-Mongol, half-Tartar features, clad in a *touloupe* of offensive odour, watching his master's slightest gesture to satisfy the most trifling desire. As soon as I appeared, the commissary ordered a chair for me, but since unluckily, perhaps through accident, no chair could be found in the room, it was necessary to search for one elsewhere. I was obliged to remain standing some moments while rage became apparent on the countenance of my host, who, however, as I afterwards found, was gentle enough. He became red and pale alternately. When the Buriat returned he rated him pretty smartly in words almost inarticulate, though of perfectly intelligible significance, and finished by raising his hand to strike him.

Accustomed as I was to Oriental manners, I anticipated the scene that was about to take place, and took little notice of it, when, to my great astonishment, the servant raised his head, and looking sternly at the commissary, addressed him in these simple words: "You forget then, sir, that I am *a subject of the Emperor!*"

This man well knew that an article of the decree enfranchising the serfs interdicted landowners and functionaries, under penalty of disgrace and even imprisonment, from having recourse to blows against any subject whomsoever of the Emperor, whether naturalized Russian or native of a conquered country, like the Kirghiz, the Buriats, or the Samoyeds.

These words were sufficient, in fact, to cause the lifted fist of the official to drop harmlessly by his side. What passion, indeed, is there in a Russian, when roused even to exasperation, that would venture to offend against the will of the Czar?

When this little scene had ended, M.

Pfaffius became again perfectly calm and self-possessed,—quite a man of the world. I showed him my letters of recommendation. As soon as his eye caught the seal of the Imperial Ministry—and this for a Russian official was much more than was required—he showed me the highest consideration. One of these letters was personally addressed to him. I was accordingly from that moment his friend, and we resolved to travel together.

The reader will learn, from what took place later, that this plan was only partially carried out, in consequence of my having made at last an acquaintance at Moscow. Being unable at this moment to anticipate the number of travelling companions that subsequently presented themselves, I regarded my commissary as a great acquisition. He had to go to Kiew before the organization of the sledging took place. I allowed him to depart only after every precaution taken to ensure our rendezvous, and, filled with enthusiasm, I set out on my *visites d'adieux.*

I will speak of one of them only, which took place in a box of the Russian Opera, not so much on account of the very agreeable people who had invited me there to see the Opera, as on account of the character of the music and the manner of the representation of which I was a witness. It was the chef-d'œuvre of Glinka—*Life for the Czar*.

Without, however, detaining the reader with the details of the manner of the representation, which probably would interest him but slightly, I will give my impression of the character of the music.

The Russians, who are not an inventive people, have, however, a national music of a kind special and original.

Those who appreciate French operas, even plaintive, would feel little interest in listening to long lamentations and mournful melodies, so characteristic of this music. It may, however, move very much amateurs of grave music, especially in the country where it originates.

The phrases of Glinka's opera, gloomy and lugubrious, as uniform as nature in Russia, as profound as its horizons, succeed one another monotonously without ever seeming to reach a distinct solution. At the moment when the impatient ear at last waits to dwell on the fundamental note, a renewed expression of grief comes forth unexpectedly, and the phrase is prolonged without changing its character. I cannot better compare Glinka's inspirations than with the permanent efforts of the sea to assume its desired repose in struggling against the incessant succession of waves. This music therefore is void of the attraction of gaiety, and, on account of its uniformity, does not give rise to lively emotions, but it has all the charm of melancholy and vague reverie.

The flow of soul seems to wander and become bewildered and enervated in the prolonged thrilling notes of this endless melody; all the past comes back to the memory, and when the last note dies away, one wakes up, as if from a touching dream, with a tear starting in the eye.

I had postponed my departure from day to day, notwithstanding the snow that was falling and the hard frost so favourable to my journey, but having at last quitted the Russian capital, my thoughts returned to it in this way. One prefers, no doubt, the first enjoyment of a pleasure to the mere remembrance of it, and yet, perhaps, one separates himself less willingly from the souvenir than from the reality, because he feels that when this prolonged pleasure ends, it has vanished both from the senses and the memory.

When I left St. Petersburg, it was the 20th of November, and on the 21st, at ten o'clock in the morning, in a frost of 24° Centigrade (11° below zero Fahr.), I made my entry into the holy city of Moscow.

The temperature I had to bear this day was very moderate in comparison with that which I subsequently experienced in Siberia; I could, however, appreciate some of the effects produced by intense cold. You feel that everything shrinks, tightens, and contracts. The horses that perspire, on account of the rapid pace at which they are driven, have their coats covered with congealed perspiration that resembles a petrifaction. The drivers' faces are puffed, spongy, and repulsive-looking. The sun, in the absence of snow, seems alone to rejoice or enliven what it touches. Under its caressing beams, the houses, with their varied hues, assume a brighter and more joyous aspect, that strikingly contrasts with the hooded personages afoot. I took care at once to provide myself with the usual winter clothing of Russians. I bought goloshes to march over the snow without suffering from cold or humidity; a *bachelique*, a kind of hood in camel hair to protect the ears and neck; and, finally, a cloak of *jenotte*, a fur not at all expensive and yet elegant.

The choice of fur is an important matter, especially at Moscow, where one's individual value is appreciated by the value of the animal's skin he wears. There is indeed a Russian proverb that seems to discredit this observation: "On vous reçoit selon votre habit, et l'on vous reconduit selon votre esprit." But this apophthegm rarely serves as a precept in a society fond of showiness and imposing magnificence—a society that is closed against the most cultivated mind if the body be not decked in the skins of certain beasts.

CHAPTER III.

MOSCOW—NIJNI-NOVGOROD.

The Kremlin—Equipage and visits of the Virgin of Inverski—Origin of Christianity in Russia—A few words about Troitsa—A travelling companion—Purchase of furs—Passage of the Oka in a sledge—Feeling of terror on first travelling in a sledge over a frozen river.

I CANNOT better compare the disposition of the streets of Moscow than with that of the series of concentric threads in a cobweb. Straight streets parting from the Kremlin, as a common centre, intersect all the circular arteries, in such a way, that it is impossible to lose one's self in the city, notwithstanding its immensity.

Each Russian city has its kremlin. It is an enclosure that contains generally a fortress, a residence for the Emperor, and one or many churches. The Kremlin of Moscow is much celebrated on account of its vastness, its historical souvenirs, and the wealth of its sanctuaries. It is relatively modern, having been rebuilt since the conflagration of 1812. One may still visit a little relic of the old building. It would be difficult to say to what style it belongs; there may be found there a mixture of many of the Asiatic varieties, between the Byzantine and those of the extreme East. Walls of extraordinary thickness; a series of little chambers, vaulted or rising in a point; narrow windows, permitting only the penetration of a mysterious light, sifted through stained glass; low doors surmounted with a Moorish arch; walls, gilt from the ceiling to the floor, on which are drawn figures of saints, having only the head and hands painted or enamelled; here and there Chinese monsters; doors opening occasionally to the height of the first story, and consequently suspended stairs to pass from one floor to another—this is the ancient Kremlin. One wonders, on roving through this intricate labyrinth, whether he is in an oratory or a salon, in a place of amusement or in a torture chamber of the Inquisition. The new dwelling of the emperors is quite different. Although of very doubtful taste, it is at least in harmony, on account of its vastness, with the empire of which it is the seat. Space has not been spared. The hall of the throne is quite a steppe to traverse. Its dimensions are monstrous. What was my astonishment on finding there several statues and portraits of the Great Napoleon! The Russians, far from bearing any enmity towards our military hero, like to render homage to his glory. To admire thus genius, wherever it may be found, even when the admirer has been the victim, is at least the mark of a liberal mind and high sentiments.

I had finished my first visit to the Kremlin, and, muffled and wrapped in furs, I was being comfortably driven to my hotel, musing carelessly on the way, when my coachman suddenly turned round, and with a silly smile, lifted my fur cap, and at the same time raised his own. Obtaining no intelligible explanation, through my ignorance of the language, I fancied myself the object of some practical joke in which coachmen indulge, and, consequently, being unable to rate him well as he deserved, I subdued my rage and smiled also. I demanded my cap, however, by gestures, to which he responded with three bows, as many signs of the cross, and sanctimoniously smiled again. I was just going to recover my property by force, when I perceived we were under the Spasskoï gateway, and that every one was bareheaded.

The proceeding was now intelligible: this gate is surmounted with the picture of the Virgin of Inverski, the favourite virgin of the Muscovites, the miraculous virgin whose supernatural power had been equal to arresting the conflagration of the Kremlin—the conflagration lighted by Rostopchine, a personage much less popular in Russia than Bonaparte.

Nobody, therefore, should pass the Spasskoï gate without lifting his hat. Old men relate that a violent wind forced even the great French conqueror to submit to this law when he intended to pass it unobserved.

The Virgin of Inverski is invoked by everybody; still she does not make herself so cheap to everybody, for a widely spread custom consists in vicarious visits by representations.

In order to obtain miraculous cures, they send for the Virgin of the Assumption, and more special favours, for the Virgin of Vladimir; and when one goes on a long journey, he generally prefers a facsimile of the Virgin of Kazan. But extraordinary circumstances must exist to demand a visit from the Virgin of Inverski.

When the metropolitan considers that a family is worthy of such an honour, four monks and two dignitaries of the Church proceed to the Spasskoï gate in a carriage with six horses. Every spectator bows low and makes the sign of the cross as the picture is lowered from its accustomed place, and prostrates himself completely, in spite of the snow and frost, at the moment it is installed in the bottom of the carriage; the two priests then place themselves on the box in front, the monks act as drivers and footmen, and thus they proceed to the privileged house, whose members do not receive the honour of such a visit without very liberal offerings.

The individual ritual practices in the streets, on the promenade, and everywhere, and at all hours, constitute certainly some of the special characteristics of Moscow. One meets at every step people kneeling and reciting prayers, though nothing apparently calls for the devotion. The worship of pictorial representations is exaggerated almost to idolatry

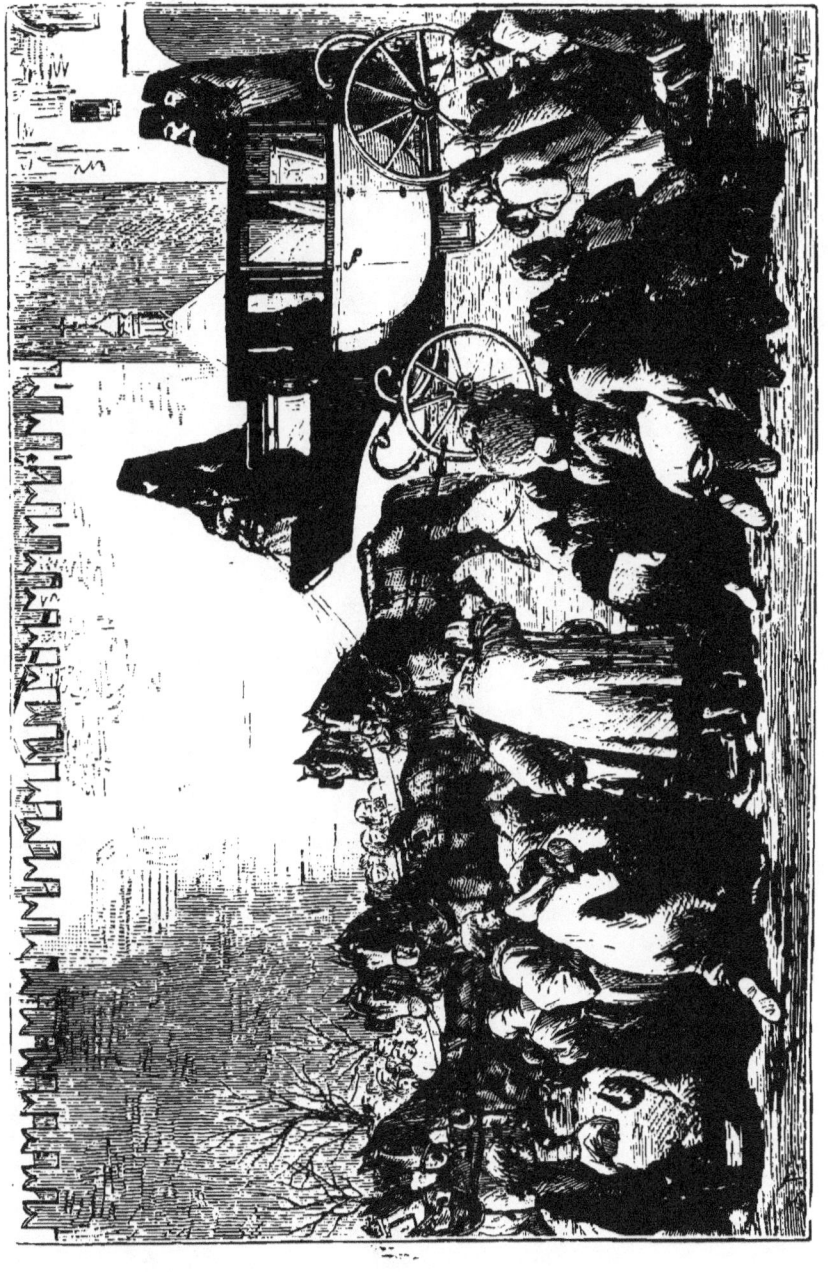

CARRIAGE OF THE VIRGIN OF INVERSKI.

[*To face p.* 34.

even by the more enlightened portion of the community. But then the higher class, though almost wholly Nihilistic, condescends to observe these popular forms on the one hand, merely through a servile deference to the authority of the Emperor, and on the other, an unwillingness to reproach by neglect the superstition of the lower class.

The orthodox religion is well known to be a faithful reproduction of the old Greek worship of Constantinople. About the year 1000, the chief of the horde that was then to become the embryo of the Russian nation—a thorough barbarian in daring and cruelty, in brute force and ungovernable impetuosity—constituted himself the promulgator of the Greek religion in the country subject to his rule.

This Vladimir—such was his name—hurled defiance at all the neighbouring peoples, and subjected to his will nearly the whole of the actual limits of European Russia. He is alleged to have had—if certain fabulous chronicles may be trusted—five legitimate wives, eight hundred concubines, and a multitude of children, whom he sacrificed to the gods. But just at the moment he was about to sacrifice his first wife, the partner even of his throne, he was seized with remorse.

Intent on forming into an entire nation all the hordes he had conquered, he nevertheless understood that this could only be accomplished by means of a national religion. With this object in view, he sent ambassadors into different countries, in order to study their respective religions, and these from their reports enabled him to choose which seemed to him the best. Mahomedanism is said to have displeased him, because the Koran forbade the use of wine, a precept that would not have favoured his indulgence in this habit. Romanism was rejected on account of the celibacy of the priesthood, and especially on account of the obedience it would exact towards an authority other than his own. Judaism, a religion without national coherence, was not favourable to his project of becoming the founder of a homogenous and solid empire. The Greek worship, however, imposed on his barbarian mind by the magnificence of its ritual; he therefore adopted it, and Russia became a Christian nation of the Eastern Church.

Though its dogmas differ but little from those of the Romish Church, the Russians have inherited the old hatred of the Greeks towards the Romans. They would willingly put into practice the ancient injunction of the Byzantine bishops at the time of the expedition of Frederick against Jerusalem :—" To obtain the remission of sins, the pilgrims must be massacred and exterminated from the face of the earth." *

They derive also from the devotees of the ancient Church their idolatry, for the indulgence in which these sacrificed their lives. They are the true disciples of those Byzantines who, at the time of the Latin conquest, overthrew with rage a statue of Minerva, upbraiding her with having called hither the barbarians, because she looked towards the west with outstretched arms.

During my stay at Moscow, I visited the monastery of Troïtsa, near this city. This monastery was founded by St. Sergius in 1338. It would be more correct to say that at this time the pious hermit of the forest of Godorok

---

* Michaud.

became a cenobite in imparting to a few zealous souls like his own a taste for poverty and the renunciation of all worldly things. But inasmuch as the united resources of these devotees were barely sufficient at first to provide for them a shelter, the convent was not constructed till later.

His fortune was indeed changed when St. Sergius, at the moment of the great Mongolian invasion, prevailed on Prince Dmitri to march against the barbarians in the plains of the Don. This prince having become victorious over the fierce Mamaï, overloaded the new community with presents. In 1393, Troïtsa was partially pillaged and burnt by the Tartars, and St. Sergius perished; but his body, recovered as if by a miracle from the heap of ruins, continued to be an object of veneration. The czars, the princes, the boyards, successively bestowed important largesses on the convent, whose wealth then became legendary in Russia. In the middle of the last century, Troïtsa possessed, in addition to an almost incredible heap of jewels, immense domains and a hundred thousand peasants. Then even the wealth of the monastery was estimated to be over forty millions of pounds sterling. Its fortifications, which still exist, defended it in 1609 against the Polish invasion, and sheltered from danger the young czars John and Peter Alexievitch during one of the revolts of the Strelitz Imperial Guards. Besides the buildings serving the community as habitations, it surrounds with its walls nine churches, whose riches excite the wonder rather than the admiration of the stranger. All the painted and enamelled portions of the representations of saints are set around with rubies, emeralds, topazes, and diamonds, of enormous size. The tomb of St. Sergius is in gilded silver; the canopy is of massive silver, and supported by four columns also of silver. The chasubles, worn by the priesthood in the exercise of their worship, are covered with fifteen, eighteen, and even twenty-one pounds of pearls. The spectator is at first dazzled at the sight of so much magnificence; but since all these things are wonders only on account of their immense value, one at last becomes indifferent to the spectacle of a mere heap of precious things. As other writers, more able, have already fully described Troïtsa, I will not fatigue the reader with further details. My guide led me to see everything: the chapels, the treasury, where may be seen *twenty gallons of fine pearls,* which are consigned to a glass case, the authorities not knowing what other use to make of them. When I had seen all these treasures, my guide led me to one of the outer doors and held out his hand. This movement, I must admit, embarrassed me, for after having visited the monastery of Troïtsa, a donation of a thousand roubles even seems a mere trifle. Before taking leave of this devotee, I asked permission to visit the library. "We have none," he replied. This poor fellow then seemed to me really poor, and I was sorry I could not offer him a gratuity of a kind I would have bestowed with more pleasure. M. de Custine says the monastery has a library, but that the regulations do not permit the public to see it. I only hope what M. de Custine says is true.

On returning from this visit, a young man called Constantine Kokcharof came to see me. His complexion was a yellowish brown, and he had prominent cheekbones like the Mongols, crisp hair and full lips like an African, a short stature, and yet great muscular strength. He seemed to hold a place between the native of the North and that of the tropical forests. If he would only have made researches into his genealogy, I am sure he would have traced his origin to the Mongols after the race had passed through some change in India. He said to me on entering: " May God, monsieur, bless your journey!" Then he gave me his name and held out his hand according to the Siberian custom. In Russia it is thought to be impolite not to offer the hand immediately on making an acquaintance.

"Monsieur," added Constantine, " I am the friend of M. Sabachnikof, whom you have met at the house of M. Pfaffius, the commissary of Kiachta. I am returning to Irkutsk, where my parents live. I had written to M. Pfaffius to ask him if I might accompany him into Siberia, and he replied by giving me your address. Will you take me for your travelling companion? I will serve you as interpreter, and with me you will have the advantage of travelling as fast or as easily as it suits you, and, moreover, of taking the route that would be most convenient to yourself."

I showed him my letters of recommendation;

and among them he found one for his father and another for his uncle, both being imperial functionaries in Siberia. We settled the business at once, and I then occupied myself solely with preparations for departure.

My young companion was most valuable to me, because he was thoroughly acquainted with the route we were to take.

He was going to traverse, for the sixth time, the immense space that intervenes between Moscow and the Amoor river. He had made the journey in summer and in winter; he was therefore fully competent to advise me as to what arrangements had to be made, and what precautions it would be indispensable to take against cold and fatigue. He informed me that, in the sledge, besides my *jenotte* fur, I should roll myself up in a *dacha*, a kind of mantle, furred inside and out, in which the wearer, being muffled from head to foot, disappeared altogether. The one I bought the following day was lined with white hare skin, and covered again with elk skin, the hair of which was short, but thick. These two fur dresses not being considered sufficiently *à la mode*, I was obliged to set off with collars of beaver.

Swaddled in this manner, I innocently imagined I could face with impunity the most rigorous cold of Siberia.

I have met, in the course of my travels, many a sharper and with many an impudent attempt at extortion, but never with a demand supported with such unscrupulous reasoning as that of the interpreter at the hotel at Moscow. "Monsieur," he began unblushingly, "you owe me at least a recompense of three hundred francs. I will show you in what way. You had urgent need of a Russian companion to go through Siberia. When M. Kokcharof came to ask for you, I could easily have told him that I did not know you, and in keeping on talking with him, have found out his address. Then I might have come and said to you : ' I have just found the man you want, but I cannot promise to let you know his name and where he may be found unless you give me a thousand francs.' Now, monsieur, *you know, I have not done such a thing as that*, and you ought, indeed, to take it into consideration."

My rage made me forget for the moment the article in the decree of the Emperor—the interdiction to strike a subject. I was about to raise my hand, but I raised my foot instead, and, in this way, speedily dismissed the barefaced impostor. I found out afterwards that this man was a Pole, a circumstance that enabled me to calm my conscience, for could the decree be meant for these convicts? Having finally secured my trunks, I went, in company with M. Constantine Kokcharof, chatting with him all the way, to take the train for Nijni-Novgorod.

Nijni-Novgorod is the last station of the railway before entering by road into Siberia.

To get from the railway station to the city, it is necessary to cross the Oka river, at about a few hundred yards before it falls into the Volga. When I arrived at Novgorod, on the 15th of December, the winter passage over the ice had begun. The surface of the Oka was furrowed with the passage of sledges coming from Irkutsk, from Nicolaefsk, from the world's end, in fact, and bringing to the railway all kinds of Asiatic provisions. Every river in Russia and Siberia freezes in a different way. Some even have an aspect so special as to enable one, at a mere glance at the ice, to say which river it is. This peculiarity is caused by atmospheric conditions, by the nature and form of the shores, and especially by the rate of movement of the stream at the time of congelation.

The Oka, when frozen, presents on its surface a series of great protuberances, in form something like a succession of mounds and consequent dales. The untravelled foreigner sees in his imagination the rivers of the North, during winter, presenting a surface like plate glass, whereon skaters make long excursions at a rapid pace, and thus accomplish long journeys. Except, perhaps, the Volga, over which the ice, on account of the sluggishness of the current, is almost everywhere level, but where the presence of snow, however, does not admit of skating, I have seen in Russia no river whatever covered to any extent with a smooth surface of ice; indeed, many of them have a surface so uneven, that it would be impossible for any vehicle to pass over them.

The course of the Oka, however, is not of this character; its frozen surface is one of the least rugged. As for me, hitherto inexperienced in Northern locomotion, I should certainly not have supposed, on looking over the roughness of the route, that I was journeying over a frozen river, if my attention had not been attracted by a strange noise beneath, a noise too strange to be forgotten, and sufficient to dismiss from my mind any illusion that I was travelling over an ordinary road.

It was a hollow rumbling sound in a deep gulf below. To the excited fancy of the wayfarer, it seemed, at times, the echoed roar of some angry demon imprisoned in the depths of an icy cave; and the traveller, listening as he is whisked along, is affected by a terrifying sensation of sinking, produced by the alternate rising and falling of the sledge over the undulating surface—a movement from which he involuntarily recoils. Just as in a carriage, when the horses are rushing on with uncontrolled impetuosity, he instinctively throws himself backwards, as if to struggle against the force that would hurl him to destruction, or, standing on the ridge of a precipice, he impulsively recoils towards surer ground from the abyss yawning to devour him, so, the first time he travels over the frozen river, he shrinks from a movement, but from one against which it is in vain to struggle; for, in glancing over the fragile partition, he finds he is contending, not to attain solid ground, for there is no shore of safety near for retreat, but hopelessly against his own weight. He is irritated at the presence of others there, at their not becoming as light as air; he is angry with everybody and everything that is heavy, because what aggravates the danger by its weight, men or baggage, is exasperating, and, indeed, not without reason, for every ponderous atom, in his imagination, exaggerates the imminence of that desperate moment when, without the resource of a jutting branch or anything stable presented providentially to his grasp, this frail, frozen floor should break under the weight like a pane of glass, and plunge him into all the horrors of a glacial sepulture.

Scared with this appalling phantom that clung to me in my first sledging experience, it was a great relief to regain the solid ground with no roaring gulf beneath, and a still greater pleasure to arrive safe at Novgorod.

The city of Nijni-Novgorod is picturesquely constructed, and, at the same time, very interesting, on account of the liveliness of its bazaars.

The Volga where it receives the waters of

the Oka is, at least, four miles wide. A great hill, or rather a mountain, swells up along the right bank of this immense sheet of water, and Novgorod rises proudly on the summit of this mountain, watching on one side Asia and on the other Europe, ready to awaken the Russian empire to any danger that might menace it from one quarter or the other. Communicating freely with remote districts by aid of its railway and two fine waterways, protected against catastrophes of inundations by its elevated position, against the misfortune of poverty by its extensive commerce, and against the calamity of decadence by its important annual fair, Novgorod is one of the most agreeable cities in Russia to visit, because, contrary to what one generally meets with in this vast empire, everything here has an air of gaiety, of busy prosperity, and lively movement.

The streets of the bazaars especially present extraordinary animation. Even when it is not the season of the great fair, they are picturesque with the costumes, the most singular and dissimilar, of every Asiatic race, specimens of which the stranger encounters at every step. In this business quarter, the only one, perhaps, so constructed in Russia, the houses have several stories, and the shops rise one above the other, although they do not always belong to the same proprietor. Wooden balconies, ascended by means of exterior staircases, where one may circulate from one end of the street to the other, serve the public in going to make their purchases at the shops of the upper stories.

In the other parts of the city, the houses are elegant, and they are almost wholly built of stone, houses, in fact, which, in any city beyond Moscow, and still more beyond Kazan, would be considered even magnificent. Numerous comfortable hotels offer an asylum to the traveller, who sees around him here, as well as in the city, bustling though not extensive, conspicuous results of the activity of its inhabitants and the incessant movement of commerce.

From the foot of the column dedicated to Sviataslof Vsevolovitch, on the spot where he vanquished the Swedes and Poles, that rises on one of the highest summits of the great hill on which Novgorod is built, the stranger may contemplate a prospect that might serve as a type of a Russian landscape in winter. In the plain below sleeps the Volga, silent and still to the senses in its winter dress; for the frost, one of nature's forces, the most imposing from its effects, has already congealed the surface of its running stream into the solidity and quiescence of the plain. One sees on the left bank of this river, and to an enormous distance through the crepuscular gloom common to these latitudes in winter, a series of long, vast undulations, covered with boundless forests, leafless, dark and dreary. Here and there, however, the melancholy monotonous uniformity is broken by a few patches of pines, but elsewhere the white trunks of the birch start up like apparitions in this desolate expanse of savage nature.

This scene, characteristic of Russia in winter, is one of the most mournful and uninviting to behold, and the stranger who has once seen it wonders why any people, however wretched, do not shudder at the idea of establishing themselves in a land where nature is so cheerless and inhospitable.

CHAPTER IV.

FROM NIJNI-NOVGOROD TO KAZAN.

The Volga in winter—Varieties of podarojnaia—What is necessary for a long sledge journey—Departure from Nijni—Posting relays—A momentary thaw—The snow—Arrival at Kazan.

HARDLY had I arrived at Novgorod, when I wished to begin my journey in a sledge as soon as possible. Thus man is attracted towards unknown adventures, even should he feel he is doomed to become, in consequence of them, a sufferer.

I went at once to the governor of the province, in order that he might afford me every facility for obtaining horses at the several posting stages. To obtain relays, there are three kinds of recommendations, which are called in Russian *podarojnaia*.

The most valuable and important of the three is the *podarojnaia de courrier*, which can only be obtained for exceptional cases, for an envoy extraordinary of the Emperor for instance.

When a traveller arrives at a stage provided with this order, the posting master is obliged to furnish horses immediately, and if they are not there, to demand them elsewhere by requisition; he also commands the driver to gallop without intermission.

The Crown podarojnaia, although an order of the second rank, is, nevertheless, much appreciated. It is generally accorded to the functionaries who are returning to their posts, or to those who are travelling in the public service. It was with one of these orders that the governor of Nijni-Novgorod was pleased to furnish me. The posting masters should always reserve a *troïka* or *droïka* (a vehicle with three horses) in case a traveller should present himself furnished with a Crown podarojnaia. It is therefore a rare occurrence to the bearer of this important order when he presents himself at a posting stage not to be provided with horses immediately. The drivers, under this order, have copper badges attached to their caps and arms, which warn afar off other conductors coming in a contrary direction to clear the way immediately, under a penalty of severe chastisement in case of neglect; they also drive almost always at a gallop, like the drivers of the podarojnaia de courrier.

Between the Crown podarojnaia and the simple podarojnaia, there is a great difference. This is for the mass of ordinary travellers. It is necessary to pay at once, pretty dearly, to get it at all, and then the traveller is quite at the mercy of the postmasters, who will not give him horses unless they are disposed to do so.

The rule is that each relay should have six hours' rest between each course. It, therefore, often happens that the traveller finds at the stages no other relays than those taking their usual rest, excepting always the reserve for the Crown podarojnaia. I have frequently seen travellers who had been waiting, two or three days, until the posting master was disposed to accommodate them or had been tired out with having his guests on his hands.

Unfortunately, the contractors of relays find every advantage in prolonging such a delay. The guest does not pay for his lodging, which is gratuitous, but he always takes there some provisions, and the postmasters hope to receive in the end, when he is tired out with waiting, a liberal gratuity in addition, in order to furnish a troïka, even with horses fatigued from a recent course.

The organization of the posting between Nijni-Novgorod and Tumen does not at present belong to the Government. It is conceded temporarily to M. Michaelof, who is making a rapid fortune by letting his horses at a high rate.

Provided, as I have mentioned, with a recommendation from this fortunate contractor, and also with a Crown podarojnaia, for which I was indebted to the governor of Nijni, I thought I should be able to start the following morning.

But, alas! I had reckoned, this time again, without Siberian frosts.

To complete my preparations for a prolonged journey in a sledge, I was obliged the whole morning to run about from shop to shop. The number of objects to be bought was incalculable. Constantine had made out a list as long as an apothecary's bill. I did not get back to my hotel till one in the afternoon, worn out with fatigue, in a very bad humour, thirsty and dying with hunger, and, moreover, so knocked up, that I wished for nothing more than to go to bed at once and rest my weary limbs.

I was in this state, when Constantine said to me with all the coolness in the world : " Now, monsieur, we are quite ready; do you wish to start?" I was about to propose not to get into the sledge till the following day, or to wait at least a few hours, when I happened to cast my eyes over my acquisitions, standing in a great heap in the middle of the room.

The heap that had bewildered me, when I paid my visit to M. Pfaffius, was a mere hillock beside this mountain. There were here heaped up soft leather trunks filled with clothing, to be put at the bottom of the sledge to deaden the jerks, round valises, to serve as bolsters at night, *touloupes*, a *dacha* in sheepskin, cushions, mattresses, veal and mutton sausages, felt boots, felt rugs, bottles of brandy, ropes, a hammer, a liberal supply of tools for iron and wood work, eight pairs of large worsted stockings, belts, bags, a store of white bread, pillows, and I don't know what else. And then, my trunks being no longer of any use, all the clothing I had brought from France lay distributed everywhere in this little room, and for the first time found themselves in such strange company. Neither the most crammed railway cloak rooms, nor *chinoiserie* shops, nor back rooms of pawnshops, nothing, in fact, except perhaps the brain cases of certain inveterate political reformers or the witches' caldron in *Macbeth*, could give any idea of such a perplexing jumble.

This exhilarating spectacle at once restored my courage; I then had but one object in view—to get out of it as speedily as possible and start. I ordered horses on the instant.

While a servant had gone in search of the team, we, Constantine and myself, set to work to pack all the articles I have just enumerated into a sledge, which I had ordered from the manufactory of Romanof—the most celebrated of Russian coachbuilders. This sledge, especially, was wonderfully built. Lightness and strength, the two most important qualities of a good vehicle, were united in it to the highest point of excellence. The sledge being an open one, at least in front, we could enjoy, during the daytime, a view of the country;

whilst a fixed hood, which we closed in completely at night with tarred canvas, protected us pretty well against the wind and the snow. Two pieces of wood, fixed at a little height above the ground and disposed in a sloping position from the front to the back, prevented the sledge from overturning, at least in ordinary circumstances, and protected the body of the vehicle against obstacles and shocks—encounters that were met with, I believe, verily twenty or thirty times a day.

Just as you make your bed, you lie on it, says the proverb. And in Russia, just as one arranges his sledge, he bears up in proportion against the fatigue of the journey. Constantine had, in this art, real talent. He laid the mattresses in a slanting position, just nicely calculated; he adroitly smoothed over, in some way, every jutting angle or boss as often as one or the other arose from the settling of the contents during a long journey. As soon as a cavity had formed from the jolting, no matter where, he immediately filled up the vacant space with hay, and everything kept its place to the advantage of our ease. He transformed, in short, our sledge into a comfortable soft bed, which would have enabled us to support, without fatigue, the fifteen hundred leagues we had to traverse as far as Irkutsk, if circumstances, which I shall subsequently relate, had not occurred. When all these preparations had been made and the horses put to, I began to wrap myself in my travelling costume.

Those who have not visited Siberia have no idea of the excessive wrapping-up and muffling necessary to a traveller on a long journey in that climate.

To put on such a great number of garments is no light matter, and cannot be accomplished, the first time especially, without laughing outright a great deal and perspiring much more.

We first put on four pairs of worsted stockings and over them, like jack boots, a pair of felt stockings that covered our legs. We then wrapped ourselves in three garments of fur, one over the other. Then we covered our heads with an *astrakan* and a *bachelique*. When we had got into the sledge we wrapped our legs in a fur rug and then buried ourselves side by side in two more fur rugs.

These accoutrements, which would be excessive to protect one's self merely for a few hours against the cold, even the most intense, become light enough and barely sufficient when the traveller remains exposed to the air a long time, and especially to the fatigue of a sledge journey prolonged night and day, without stopping to sleep.

The only defect in the construction of Siberian sledges is the want of a seat for the *yemschik* or driver: this unhappy individual is obliged to sit on a wooden platform, that covers the travellers' legs, with his legs hanging either on the right or left side, and, consequently, has to drive from either side. When he has troublesome horses to manage he gets on his knees, or even stands up on the platform. This arrangement is all the more inconvenient, inasmuch as it requires unusual dexterity to drive and hold in the mettlesome little horses of Northern Asia. The moment they feel the harness on their backs, whether from natural ardour alone or from a want to get warm, there is no holding them; their impatience is unparalleled in horseflesh. They tremble with excitement, they paw and scrape the ground, nibble at the snow, or make a huge ball with it, and then scatter it in a cloud of fine particles. The drivers have a very difficult task to calm their impetuosity; they accomplish this in the most soothing manner, by means of a steady trill on their lips; they sustain this more intensely the moment they leap on the platform of the sledge, which is for them a very delicate gymnastic feat, demanding great agility. At this critical moment, the horses, feeling no further restraint, uncurbed, rampant, start off in a mad gallop, *le diable en queue*. If, on the other hand, the driver should lucklessly make an abortive attempt, he is hurled over the crosspieces like a tile by the passing gale, and the travellers go on without a whip, flying on the wings of the wind.

This was just the hairbreadth escape that happened to the first yemschik chance had thrown in our way. His horses, just as he seized the platform to leap on to it, started off at a furious pace. Like a brave fellow, he kept his grip on it like a bulldog, and, luckily, on the reins too, and was thus hauled over the snow at our side for some minutes. At the end of this critical interval he found some lucky projection beside the sledge, where he could support his knee, and at last, thanks to the herculean strength of his arms and the help we gave him, he succeeded in gaining his seat and then tenaciously clung to it to the end of the stage. Thus equipped, we left Nijni-Novgorod on the 17th of December at three o'clock in the afternoon.

This first day's journey in a sledge was delightful and exhilarating. We felt all the pleasure of the novelty of the locomotion without yet beginning to experience the least fatigue, and at every moment we met other travellers coming, twenty and even thirty leagues, to the city we had just quitted, on their business or pleasure.

However great the distance may be, it is never an obstacle to the Russians: they seem to make nothing of it, and never to calculate it. A lady at St. Petersburg said to me one day: "You should go and see the cascade of Tchernaiarietchka: I went there the other day, and I was charmed with it; I never dreamt there was anything so beautiful at our city gates." On making inquiries about it a few days later, and as to how I could get there, I found that it would take forty-eight hours by rail, and twelve by diligence. I daresay they will think of sending the poor seamen who are ordered to join their ships at Nicolaefsk to St. Petersburg gates; it is only three hundred leagues from the Russian capital. The reader will learn subsequently, if he is interested in continuing the journey with me, that the Siberians, of the fair sex even, are not at all dismayed at the prospect of undertaking journeys of fifteen hundred, nay, two thousand leagues in a sledge, with young children to boot, and these sometimes at the breast.

On account of the great novelty and variety of the spectacle, I found the trip delightful on leaving Novgorod. The time passed more rapidly than the banks of the river, over whose congealed surface our horses continued fleeing at a mad pace as if pursued by a phantom.

This imposing Volga is of a character truly quite exceptional. France, certainly, has no river worthy of so much admiration for its grandeur. During the summer it is enlivened with an incessant movement of steamers, and is of immense importance as a waterway; and during winter also it continues rendering great services to humanity, affording the means for the transport of the grain that it has fertilized with its beneficent waters. Nothing is grander than this glacial route of unusual width, and of a uniformity and smoothness which no road laid by the hand of man can approach; without a pebble or a rut, one glides over without a jolt. Nothing interests the traveller more, the first time, than to watch the shores passing before the eye like a panorama; to contemplate the mountains and valleys the frozen way spares him the trouble of traversing; to coast the islands without navigating; and to pass here and there some barque, or perhaps steamer, imprisoned in the ice.

In about three hours and a half after leaving Novgorod, we reached our first stage, it being then quite dark.

In all these posting stages, there is a room for the travellers; and this room, though heated at the proprietor's expense, becomes really a free home for the wanderer: he may eat, drink, and sleep there; do, in fact, whatever he likes; and what is still more singular, lodge there as long as he wishes, no one having a right to dislodge him.

Although this privilege is secured by contracts made between the posting masters and the Imperial administration, it would undoubtedly be quite consistent with the Russian character to accord it if it were not compulsory, the people being essentially hospitable.

This amiable quality results, perhaps, from the rigour of the climate; but I am rather disposed to believe—so general and spontaneous is it—that it is the consequence of a happy and generous disposition.

I shall have something more to say, by-and-by, on the merits of the Russian peasantry. I do not say that they have a monopoly of this benevolent spirit, for, indeed, it is common to all classes. The society of St. Petersburg cannot, certainly, be suspected to be wanting in kindness towards strangers; even the old Muscovite noble, notwithstanding his haughtiness, notwithstanding his hatred of new social institutions, notwithstanding his regret to see Moscow no longer the residence of the emperors, and, moreover, his antipathy for

European ideas and fashions, adopted in the new capital;—in spite of all that, the Muscovite lord has retained profoundly rooted in his nature the old traditions of respect towards him who is his guest, and he regards hospitality, not simply as a passive virtue, but seriously as an active duty.

At the Siberian posting stages, the stranger often finds pleasant company or something to amuse him in the travellers' room; it is rare to find it unoccupied; and when people are disposed to talk, subjects of conversation are not wanting. Those who are going in a contrary direction begin inquiring about everything that interests them on the way; about the state of the route; about the difficulties, more or less serious, that have been encountered in getting horses. Those who are taking the same way have generally already met at one or more stages, and now salute one another as old acquaintances. When the stage happens to be in a village, the principal persons of the neighbourhood generally come to pass away an hour or two very sociably with the travellers. They are very curious to know all about political matters from those who come from the West, and business affairs from those coming from the East. They all chat together in a manner perfectly free and easy, without the least exclusiveness on account of class, profession, or position. Their intercourse is always marked with the utmost good-nature and affability.

But at the stages that link Nijni to Kazan this kind of society is not always so agreeable.

The travellers around here are, in fact, a little too much *civilized* to be always quite so simple and warm-hearted. They are, perhaps, a little too well initiated in the new social principles of *égalité* and *fraternité* to believe that these amiable sentiments have so profoundly modified human nature as they find it in their surroundings. They look on the people accident throws in their way rather as competitors for accommodation, whose presence there may contribute to retard their journey, and would, if they had the *liberté*, such as their brethren and equals understand it (from the purely practical side of the formula), much rather smash their brethren's sledges, than give them a helping hand under difficulties.

I did not linger very long in these first stages, where, on account of the privileged recommendations I was favoured with for obtaining horses, I met only with unfriendly looks and gestures; therefore, in twelve hours from my departure, I had already accomplished more than a quarter of the distance that separated me from Kazan.

We continued travelling over the Volga. A little before daybreak I was surprised at the strange noise that was being produced by the horses' feet over the ice: it was no longer the dull, hollow sound that had terrified me at Nijni-Novgorod. It was to me one quite novel, and people generally, especially the most experienced,—a circumstance far from reassuring,—begin to get uneasy at it. This sound seemed to me the most fearful that one could hear on the ice; it was a splashing. I listened in terror; but as my companion had smiled at my first affright at Nijni, I did not venture, till after a long interval, to reveal it to him this time.

Through an excess of *amour-propre* which I probably now derived from intercourse with Russians, I was just going to allow him to fall off asleep, when I was splashed full in the face, and my terror, excited to its highest pitch, could no longer be smothered. I started up, leaping almost over Constantine, who, to use a Siberian saying, " was snoring enough to frighten the wolves." It was but a poor resource against actual danger. Whilst I was rousing him, my wits seemed to be going a-wool-gathering; what wonderful feat were they not going to perform in such a peril as this? My imagination in fact, stirred up, no doubt, by the poesy of the journey, brought to my mind Dame Fortune saving the life of a sleeping infant on the brink of a well. The complete absence of wheels, however, soon brought me round to sober reality, and I explained the situation to Constantine with a conciseness that might serve as a model to many an orator. He questioned the yemschik on the matter, who replied with complete indifference: " Yes, sir, it is thawing; but it is merely the snow melting: the ice is just as thick as ever."

The sky being very cloudy, the night was profoundly dark. Experience principally served to guide the driver in his course, and then the water—a fatal indication, indeed, of the way, when this way is over the bed of a frozen river! I crept back, without saying a word more, into the bottom of the sledge; but I must admit that it seemed to me that the ice successively yielded, cracked, and opened, and then, freezing over again with sufficient thickness, bore us up firmly. What does not the imagination shadow forth to an excited brain?

Gradually, but very gradually, the day came forth, or it would be more exact to say rather a kind of twilight, for a thick fog veiled nearly every object from our eyes. The summits of the hills that continuously command the right bank of the Volga marked a shadow on the horizon barely more sombre. Everything else appeared confounded in a general grey hue, and nothing, not even the shore, could be distinguished. Our ears soon began to catch the ominous sounds of a crackling under the horses' feet, thereby announcing that the thaw had begun its work, now, indeed, on the ice. Then we could just distinguish very portentous fissures, starting right and left under the passage of the sledge. The yemschik at last, discovering that the situation was becoming perilous, thought it now high time to take precautions. He therefore dashed on as if chased by a pack of famishing wolves as far as the first village, and here we were glad to set foot at last on *terra firma*.

The following night snow began to fall, to our great discomfiture; for no state of the atmosphere here is so disagreeable to travellers in a sledge only partially closed.

Fatigued by the exciting emotions of the preceding night, and especially by thirty-six hours' duration of a kind of locomotion to which I was not yet accustomed, I had fallen into a sound sleep. As it was not very cold, Constantine and I had never thought of lowering the canvas that partially closes in the front of the vehicle, and, moreover, we had neglected to take the precaution to cover our faces. But as the warmth of our breath dissolved the flakes that would otherwise have interrupted our respiration, we had scarcely noticed our situation. The snow, indeed, had penetrated and fallen thickly everywhere; our faces even were quite covered; it had insinuated itself in the openings of our *dachas*, and melting there, saturated our inner mantles: water was now running fast down our necks and sleeves; we were drenched: and it was likely to have been a very serious matter if the cold, which then commenced to make itself felt very acutely, had not roused us from our slumbers. But what a transition was that awakening! My mind, which seemed at first to be wandering far away from actual life, could in no way account for the situation; we opened our eyes, it is true, but were unable to distinguish anything; we felt a load pressing us down everywhere, and yet we were unable to grasp anything. I fancied myself one moment in a delirium and in the next the victim of a vivid nightmare; but the cold at last brought me to my senses. The first thing we did was to urge the yemschik to drive as fast as he could, that we might dry ourselves as soon as possible at the first stage. The wind now turned towards the north, the clouds had dispersed, and a piercing cold benumbed our limbs. Everything was frozen to our garments, which had become to the touch as rigid as tanned hides bristling "like quills upon the fretful porcupine."

Fortunately, in this plight, the distance that separated us from Kazan was not very great.

The surface of the Volga, on which we were enabled to continue our journey at daybreak, contributed very much to shorten the way, and on the 19th of December, about one in the afternoon, we drove into the ancient capital of the Tartars, after having accomplished what they consider in Siberia a short, easy journey.

CHAPTER V.

KAZAN—JOURNEY TO PERM.

The Virgin of Kazan—Russian manner of expressing disapproval—Dining with a grandee—His description of the enfranchisement of the serfs—The Tartars—Journey in a sledge—Caravan of exiles—The Votiaks—Aspect of European Russia.

THE city of Kazan is not situated on the banks of the Volga. It stands at the distance of at least half a mile from the left bank of this river.

The day after we arrived here, Constantine introduced me to one of his old college companions, a young man who had just finished his studies in medicine at the university of Kazan. Being desirous of seeing Kazan and its neighbourhood, and this young medical man knowing them well, I begged him to become my guide, which he most courteously consented to do.

We first went to the university, which is

celebrated; then to the cathedral, which interested me very much. Its style is different from the Byzantine—a style that obtrudes so often on the eye of the stranger in Russia that he at last gets tired of it; but this cathedral reminds one of certain portions of the ancient Kremlin, and is evidently a construction of a remote period. Its paintings are very crude, as in the early stages of the art, though well-executed specimens of the epoch. Another object that attracted my attention was the high altar in massive silver.

Then we went on a pilgrimage to the Virgin of Kazan, the patron saint of travellers. This virgin was formerly left hanging on a tree in the middle of the forest. There she performed wonderful miracles amid the awestruck peasantry, who made long pilgrimages to obtain pardon of their sins and find favour in her sight. One of the chief bishops of Kazan, touched at her exposure in so wild a spot, ordered her to be conducted to the cathedral, that she might be honoured in a sanctuary worthy of her merits. But on the day following the ceremony the lady excited the greatest wonder and admiration by returning herself to her accustomed place in the forest. It was in vain they led her back three times in a grand procession to the city; for the repeated miracle of her return just as often clearly indicated her will and pleasure. Since the lady would not go to a church, a church was obliged to come to the lady, and one accordingly came, or rather rose, on this privileged spot, and then followed in its wake a monastery which became, after that of Troïtsa, one of the richest in Russia. Then later habitations of the devoted began to cluster around, and now the Virgin of Kazan, whether she likes it or not, is shut up in a city.

This wonderful virgin, the reader will understand, is a little picture, pretty well executed in the Byzantine style and of great antiquity.

As I wished to see this treasure, we went there and sent to the abbess to obtain permission to visit it; but, to my disappointment and vexation, it was refused. This was the only occasion on which doors were closed against me whenever I presented myself, either in European Russia or Siberia, to gratify my curiosity in visiting any public building.

The young student who accompanied me

was disgusted at the scrupulosity or ill-nature of the abbess, and manifested his feelings in a way more significant than delicate—a way quite common with Russians—by spitting with great energy repeatedly on the ground. But in spite of this unseemly reception of the abbess's message, he was most respectful and courteous towards the nun who bore it, and we went away exchanging bows, as if she had conferred on us the highest favour.

This dainty habit of expressing disapproval or protestation by salivary effusion is so common and popular that it finds its way even into literature. It was here, just in this city, that I was present at a play wherein the author tried to represent as effectively as possible how far domestic quarrels might go in a household composed of members who were not very accommodating to one another. The representation was perfectly intelligible to me from beginning to end, notwithstanding my ignorance of the Russian language, simply because the best arguments employed by the leading characters in the play consisted principally in repetitions of this gesture, certainly far more expressive than delicate.

THE MOTHER-SUPERIOR OF KAZAN MONASTERY.

[*To face p.* 76.

And so far as regarded my young companion also, if anything would have withheld him from responding quite as demonstratively to the abbess herself on receiving her refusal, it would not have been any sentiment of reverence or scruples of piety, and for a very good reason: because the students of the university of Kazan pique themselves on being freethinkers.

But what is much more serious in the Russian territory is that they strain the theory of emancipation to embrace ideas of political liberty in its most liberal sense. The Government, however, knows how to suppress this excess of enthusiasm as soon as it manifests itself. At the time of the Polish insurrection, three students having a little too openly demonstrated their views, one was shot and the other two banished for life to the Siberian deserts.

The liberation of the serfs had naturally caused a great deal of bitter feeling towards the late Czar on the part of certain aristocratic landowners; and the Russian liberals have succeeded, in a great measure, in conciliating the latter by sympathizing with them in their imaginary wrong; thus it sometimes happens that nobles and liberals share the same hopes, and consequently draw closer to one another. With this spirit pervading these two classes, the reader will not be surprised to learn that I was introduced by a student of the university of Kazan to an important personage of the old Russian aristocracy.

He entertained me with an account of the enfranchisement of the serfs, and it was naturally from his own point of view; but since these views differ very widely among people with whom I have conversed on the subject, according to their interests or prejudices, I will give in his own words the opinion of this old Russian noble without making any comment on it. He thus began:

"Formerly all the Russian territory belonged to the nobles. The peasant, of course, was at the mercy of the lord on whose land he lived, and was obliged to give him a certain amount of work. The lord, however, never abused this privilege; on the contrary, he was in the habit of distributing every year among the peasantry a certain quantity of land to farm for their own benefit, as a recompense for their services. Under this arrangement, the peasant had an interest in working; he worked for his master, and the land consequently improved, and then he worked for himself, to obtain some comfort in his old age. The land under this system produced more, and the general prosperity could not fail to increase accordingly.

"But then the Czar, just like Louis XIV. in France, fearing the growing influence of the aristocracy, gave to the peasantry the lands they had hitherto merely farmed. The Emperor himself undertook to indemnify the lords, reserving to himself the right of receiving, in the form of a land tax, the established rents, which, in the absence of such a liberality, —a liberality more apparent than real—the peasant would have continued paying to his lord. Since that time, the lords, deprived of their authority, have almost all abandoned their lands; the peasantry discover that the profits of their lands are absorbed by the Imperial tax; and this tax, itself inequitably assessed, does not, without much difficulty, find its way into the coffers of the state. The consequence of this enfranchisement, accorded solely with the object of increasing the Czar's authority, is an injury in the first place to the serfs, then to the nobility, and finally to the state."

This noble, as it appears, would admit no advantage whatever. The most insignificant social changes, however just—and there are none now in Russia that are not—appeared to him in the light of iniquities.

In the presence of these retrograde views, the political creed of the most ardent French Legitimists would appear revolutionary.

I was very much entertained, nevertheless, the evening I passed with him, where the old Russian manners and habits were scrupulously observed. When we rose from the supper table each of the guests went up to the host and hostess to shake hands in token of gratitude, to which they replied in the prescribed form: "I beg you will excuse me for what God has this day given me to eat, when I have the honour to receive you." And to this they added such compliments as: "À votre santé"; "Les absents n'ont pas toujours tort."

These complimentary customs, however amiable they may seem externally, lose a great deal of their sincerity when the motive that gives rise to them becomes apparent; and this undoubtedly is vanity, and especially the vain desire of exhibiting a little magnificence and expense. The real meaning of these fine phrases is: "I pray you to take notice that I have just offered myself a bottle of champagne, and the satisfaction it gives me in making you a witness of this luxurious habit surpasses any other pleasure I could possibly get out of it."

The Tartar population that enlivens the streets of Kazan contributes very much to the picturesqueness of the city. Notwithstanding that they have been deprived of their territory ever since 1552, the Tartars can, with a very good grace, hold up their heads wherever they show themselves in Kazan, for they are not only the founders of the city, but they defended it with great bravery against their enemies, who captured it only after severe losses. After having made several bold sorties and repelled many desperate assaults, they courageously bore their sufferings from the want of water—a calamity the Russians inflicted on them by cutting off their communications with the Volga. When the last hope of victory died away the Tartar queen flung herself headlong from the top of the Sonnbec tower—a building which remains well preserved to the present day.

This interesting tower, from its combination of the minaret and the pagoda, reminds one of the people whose features are half Arab and half Mongol. It stands on a commanding eminence over the city, and forms certainly one of its most beautiful and attractive objects.

The Tartar harems are much less accessible than those of the Bosphorus or of Tunis, perhaps because Mahomedan fanaticism, in being here roused through impatience of Christian domination, has become all the more uncompromising. I therefore found it impossible to catch a glimpse of a single individual of these jealously guarded communities; and I was rather disappointed, because in judging from their lords, I had formed an idea that they must be very beautiful. The regularity and symmetry of features of the Arab race are associated in the Tartars with great muscular strength, and the dignified and haughty glance of a race impatient of conquest. This highly favoured physique is accompanied with moral attributes as elevated, and the Russians, however disdainfully they treat this people, have nevertheless adopted the proverb: "Honest and faithful as a Tartar."

Kazan is the last European city on the road to Siberia that still preserves a European aspect, in so far as many of its houses are built of stone, and are ranged in streets of definite form. I was, therefore, getting impatient to quit it, and to see something of an Asiatic character.

Constantine and I went together to purchase a supply of eatables for our journey. We laid in a supply of sausages, some caviare, cheese, not forgetting white bread, which, when soaked in tea, is the principal part of the subsistence on a journey in Siberia. To venture on a journey in these parts, one should be neither a *gourmet* nor a *gourmand*. I have often been astonished to find how very little is necessary to sustain the human body, and wonder why we Frenchmen at home take so much trouble to give our stomachs so little rest and so much unnecessary work.

We went through the operation, for the second time, of getting into our three heavy fur garments, and on the 22nd of December, at four in the afternoon, we were gliding along again cosily, side by side, over the frozen snowy dust of the road leading to Siberia.

In order to go at a brisk rate in a sledge, it is necessary that the snow over which it is moving be well beaten down. Private sledges are not numerous enough to prepare a way by crushing the snow, so this work is done by sledges carrying goods; and since these follow in a line in the wake of one another, the beaten part of the road, on which one is desirous of gliding, is of very limited width. The consequence of this narrowness of the chosen way is that two sledges never pass without clashing against each other; nor are the yemschiks very solicitous about avoiding a collision, since they know perfectly well their own necks are quite safe, the long projecting wooden guards, which I have already described, being amply sufficient to protect them from danger. The sledges thus guarded whisk rapidly along one against the other, sometimes striking one another with a shock in which horses and sledge are thrown down and shot off at a tangent across the road.

The worst kind of these collisions is the shock from two sledges of unequal size: the larger of the two, being generally too heavy to be simply hurled aside by its adversary, as is the case with the lighter vehicle, is taken underneath and lifted instead, and occasionally high enough to be almost overturned.

But it is never a complete overthrow: the sledge thus thrown off or lifted slides along on a single skate and on the end of the long wooden guard, and they do not stop for so trifling a matter. The yemschik, unable to keep himself on an inclined plane without holding, hangs on to the apron and maintains his place by the sheer strength of his arms; the horses still go on at a gallop, and the travellers proceed three or even five hundred yards in this half-tilted posture till some rut in the road brings the sledge down again on both skates.

Each part of the road to Siberia has its special advantages and disadvantages, but the incidents just mentioned are of common occurrence when the wanderer no longer travels over a frozen river. The most disagreeable effect of this constant jolting, to an inexperienced traveller, is the want of sleep. During the whole night after we left Kazan I never closed my eyes a moment, whilst Constantine gave evident proofs of the soundness of his slumber by a prolonged sonorous snoring, equally uninterrupted whether he fell on me or I fell on him, crushing him even with all my weight.

I was bemoaning sadly within myself a long, tedious night, passed without sleep, when we came up at daybreak with a caravan of exiles. These poor wretches, dragging their chains afoot, were wearily trudging along, with a long journey before them, to the far end of Eastern Siberia. I had not at that time more pity for assassins and thieves than I have now, and since the day I passed the Russian frontier, conspirators have appeared to me no better, perhaps even worse; still it touched me to the heart to see these unhappy creatures, with a wearisome journey of three thousand leagues before them, and their fate too—if they lived to reach the end of the dreary march—instead of there finding a home to cheer them, to find nothing but a gaol!

A few sledges were following this caravan, and when I inquired why they thus accompanied it, I was briefly informed: "For the invalids and princes." A phrase that had on reflection a great deal of meaning in it, and suggested very forcibly the formidable power of the Emperor in Russia, a sovereign power before which every subject, from the humblest serf to the highest prince of the realm, must bow down, with their differences almost lost in the equal degree of subjection.

The Emperor, in fact, may without trial condemn any subject to two years' imprisonment, and even, if he thinks proper to do so, banish him for life.

It occurred to me, as I was watching these poor exiles, that there might be one innocent, and this thought would have made me very uneasy if I had not by this time become too good a Russian subject to venture to entertain it very long.

It is not at all an uncommon occurrence in Siberia to meet travellers afoot. I have seen, it is true, but very few women that recalled to my memory " the Siberian girl " of Xavier de Maistre ; if I had, and our road had been in the same direction, I should have offered them perhaps a place in my sledge, just as the peasants of the Ural mountains compassionately helped the heroine, where she became so popular, to reach the end of her painful journey. But I have met men, very often in all kinds of weather and situations, trudging on foot, in spite of the snow and the intense cold, across a dreary extent of country where no human habitation could be seen, in order to reach some remote region with the hope of providing for a domestic want, to accomplish a pilgrimage, or to proceed to some destination under the coercion of the Government.

Amongst these was a young soldier on leave at home with his parents, and who had been ordered suddenly to join his regiment in garrison at Kazan. He was then in ill-health, but notwithstanding his feeble condition, he set off at once, and it might be said even with pleasure, because the will of the Emperor was in question. He was compelled to do so, they would tell me ; no doubt he was : but the sentiment of obedience and loyalty is so deeply implanted in the Russian peasant, that he will submit to suffering without a murmur the half of which he would not undergo for any other personage than his sovereign.

When he had nearly come to his journey's end, this brave young fellow, being no longer able to drag one foot after the other, and seized with giddiness and fainting, had wandered a few yards from the track beaten by the sledges, and there lay almost buried in the snow, the even surface of which had deceptively hidden a sudden fall in the ground. Just as I was passing by, a man of strange aspect had saved him from a terrible fate and was watching over him: this good Samaritan had a red beard and red hair under a thick shaggy fur cap; over his shoulder were slung a long bow and some arrows, and his feet were strapped on two long narrow planks of sufficient length to keep him whilst thus gliding over the snow from sinking into it, even at the spot where the young soldier was lying almost lost to sight in its ominous embrace.

As I had now gathered much information regarding the indigenous races, I recognized him almost at a glance to be a Votiak. With the aid of this good man, we helped the poor soldier on to a goods sledge, one of a file that fortunately happened to be passing at the moment, as if almost by a miracle. Having done this, we gave him some brandy to warm him, a little food, and then, being assured of his safety, we parted, each on our way.

I was much interested in examining this specimen of a race that has occupied the country, not only before the Russians, but before the Tartars. The Votiaks seem to have preserved all their ancient freedom, and they roam the intricate and boundless forests of Eastern Russia in pursuit of game, on which they subsist. I regretted almost the direction I had to take as I watched this Votiak disappearing gradually amid the trees like a spirit of the forest, careless of the rifts over which he passed without seeming to notice them, a mythological union of half beast and half man: externally, in colour and roughness of ways, a beast; and internally, in humanity and tenderheartedness, a man, as this act I have related proved him to be—a curious combination of savageness and sensibility. I would willingly have followed this man and have had the liberty to hunt, in his company, the deer, the wolf, and the bear, to study his simple manners and lead his strange life; but when I could not make without fatigue a simple excursion in a sledge, I felt on comparison humiliated at the thought of having so little power of endurance.

In 1774 the Votiaks were fifty-five thousand in number, and since this period no census has been taken. Many have been converted to Christianity, though a large number remain idolaters, and still practise the superstitious ceremonies of their worship in the depths of their forests.

Tents pitched at certain distances from each other, generally in some picturesque spot, covered with groups of pine and birch, serve them as a sanctuary; these tents have but one opening, and that always facing the south. They are entirely void of furniture or ornament.*

The Votiaks have three principal divinities: a Master and Supreme Lord of everything, called *Inmar*; a god that protects the land and

---

* Müller.

the harvests; and a third god that has dominion over the waters. Inmar dwells in the sun, which is an object of their highest veneration.

The principal fête of the year is in the month of August, and then the grand priest known as *Toua* proceeds to one of the sanctuaries. I have just mentioned, and there sacrifices, in due order, one after the other, a duck, a goose, a bull, and a horse. The horse should be chestnut, though in cases of necessity it may be of any other colour, except black. Afterwards the faithful have a repast on the flesh of these animals; then the Toua collects the blood and the fat, and, putting them into the stomachs, he burns them with a portion of the bones; the heads are hung up on a neighbouring pine, and the skins sold for the benefit of the high-priest.*

Before burying their dead the Votiaks wash them carefully and clothe them in rich ornaments. When they are about to close the grave they throw in a few pieces of silver, and say: "This ground is thine." Finally, when a member of the family is dangerously ill, the

---
* Pallas.

parents are accustomed to sacrifice a black sheep.* As these practices are always carried out in secret, it was not without much difficulty that Pallas and Müller were able to penetrate the mysteries I have just mentioned.

It is the custom in Russia, whenever a new emperor mounts the throne, to oblige the Votiaks to take a fresh oath of fidelity. The ceremony is curious. They stretch a bear's skin on the ground, and then lay on it an axe, a knife, and a bit of bread. Every Votiak cuts off a morsel of this bread, and, before eating it, recites this formula: "If I should not remain ever faithful to my sovereign during my life, or should I rebel against him with my free will and knowledge; if I neglect to perform the duties that are due to him, or if I offend him in any manner whatever—may a bear like this tear me to pieces in the heart of the forest, this bread choke me at once, this knife pierce my body, and this axe cut off my hand." There is not an instance, says Gmelin, of a Votiak having violated his oath, although they have been so often persecuted on the ground of their religion.

* Müller.

The road leading from Kazan to Perm passes through immense forests of evergreen trees. My journey through this region was attended with a degree of cold rather severe. The thermometer varied from twenty to thirty degrees below zero (Centigrade). At this temperature, a temperature not at all unusual in Siberia, it rarely happens that the least breeze comes to disturb the tranquillity of the atmosphere. All the trees of the forest were therefore almost perfectly at rest: the only movement perceptible from time to time was a branch bending down slowly to relieve itself from a too heavy burden of snow.

This complete silence—this all-pervading stillness of nature, in which she seems to repose from the terrible manifestations of her power, as in the tempest and in the billows of the ocean—is not without grandeur, and to the thoughtful, perhaps, if less imposing, is more solemn than her other phases. On the one side she presents to us vicissitude and transitoriness, and on the other unchangeableness and duration; the agitation and the turmoil of the one may, indeed, remind us more vividly of life, but the quiescence and sepulchral muteness of the other draw our thoughts nearer to eternity.

The aspect of Asiatic Russia produces on the mind an impression not dissimilar from that derived from contemplating the ocean, or the African desert, and this is immensity—mournful immensity.

To be lost amid this inhospitable, boundless space is not to pine away simply from hunger and thirst, as on the sands of the desert, with some prospect, however remote, of relief; here one dies pierced with cold to the marrow, lingering without hope; for what hope could exist to escape from a region interminable to the desponding eye, whose glacial temperature without movement means inevitable death?

With the muteness and unchanging aspect of these limitless wilds is associated another of a fantastic character, doubtless one of the causes of the all-pervading superstition of this country. In the depth of these forests, which may be called virgin forests—not that they are untrodden, for they are inhabited—the snow falls very unequally. Here and there enormous cedars preserve beneath their branches large bare spaces; and farther on the avalanches from weaker branches accumulate into high pyramids. On one side the wind rounds off the angularity, and on the other it is pierced by protruding branches of vigorous shrubs. It follows that the snow, thus heaped up in these spots, takes many irregular forms, which, to the excited imagination, may easily become terrifying, especially at approaching night, when these white phantoms stand forth from the mysterious obscurity under the spreading cedars.

When we dismounted at the end of our stage, there was a little adventure that made me blush, I must admit, for my French gallantry. We met here two women, who had been waiting the whole day long, till the posting master was pleased to give them horses to continue their journey. This autocrat had at last relented just before we came up; the horses were put in their sledge, and they were going to start at once, when Constantine presented our Crown podarojnaia order. "That is my last troïka," exclaimed the master of the relays; "I shall be obliged, I am sorry to say, to my great regret, to keep you waiting here——"

"Take the horses out of that sledge," said Constantine authoritatively, perfectly indifferent to the distressing embarrassment into which he had thrown these two poor travellers.

I did not clearly understand the affair at first, but I doubt whether, after having examined these two personages, my gallantry would have overruled my selfishness, for their departure or detention depended on the one or the other. If at night all cats are grey, in Siberia all women swaddled for a journey are uniformly unattractive; and the face, besides, is disfigured with a look of uncleanliness from intense and prolonged cold.

I do not know what Don Quixote would have done in the presence of these two Dulcineas: as it was quite impossible for me to follow them, the only alternative was to precede them.

The reader will soon learn what followed from this incident. I am ashamed to say I had the cowardice to approve, at least by my silence, Constantine's decision; and we continued our journey, without any other adventure, as far as Perm, where we arrived on the 26th of December at day-break.

CHAPTER VI.

PERM—THE ROAD TO CATHERINEBURG.

Hotel accommodation in Siberia—A councillor—Opinions and examples of Russian administration—National music—The passion for aggrandizement of territory—Entry into Asia.

Though Perm is still within the limits of Europe, it has quite the aspect of a Siberian city: the houses are constructed of wood, without upper stories, and disposed without regularity with regard to one another. Its position reminds one a little of that of Nijni-Novgorod. Overlooking the Kama from the summit of a hill, Perm commands beyond also, from the same eminence, an immense plain covered with forests.

I put up at the Hôtel de la Poste. The reader would smile, no doubt, if he could only see the building to which I give the name of *hôtel*. And yet the poverty of our language obliges me to use this term: I could not give the name of *auberge* or *gargote* to the most important resting place the traveller could find in a city—a city which is the capital of a province as large as France.

In the way of familiar terms, the Russian language has a richness almost disheartening to those who have had the courage to commence its study. Constantine would frequently attempt to gratify his curiosity by putting questions to me like these: "What do you call in French, monsieur, a field of corn whose ears are just beginning to show?" "What do you call in your language a book that has its leaves cut by the reader as he proceeds with the reading?" Sometimes I replied: "We have no special term corresponding to the meaning of this periphrasis"; but more frequently I said I didn't know; preferring that he should have a less favourable opinion of my knowledge than of the comprehensiveness of our language.

The walls of my room, like all those in Siberia, were whitewashed. The furniture consisted of a few chairs and a sofa; but no toilet table nor washstand, nor even a bed. This, in Siberia, is the traveller's room, and indeed, one of the most luxurious; for the sofa, here quite an *objet de luxe*, is often wanting. Nobody, moreover, in this land of primitive manners, knows the refreshing comfort of reposing on a bed. At Kiachta, where I accepted the hospitality of a rich merchant, he found it quite sufficient for his night's slumber to roll himself up in a blanket, and thus stretch himself on two chairs standing front to front.

The substitute for a washstand and its accessories is, to the stranger, even less satisfactory than the makeshift for a bed. In every hotel, this consists of a little reservoir of water, furnished at the bottom with a minute copper tube, and fixed against the wall in the passage. The traveller, desirous of performing his usual ablutions, lifts this tube, and a tiny jet of water spurts forth and trickles over his hands, which he endeavours to appropriate and utilize as well as he can, though he allows it to "slip through his fingers." This cleansing operation, however, is apparently deemed by every Siberian of either sex, if not as effective, certainly quite as serviceable, as the more elaborate process of a Turkish bath.

I rarely experienced in the whole course

of my travels so much disappointment as at Perm, where, after a long and fatiguing sledge journey, I had looked forward to the refreshing comfort of a thorough ablution, and found nothing more than this trickling stream to stand under. Knowing well it was perfectly useless to go elsewhere in search of any superior accommodation, I determined to enter my protest against it at once, and went out to buy a big copper basin, which I procured, had brought into my room, and insisted on having filled with water. My ablutions then became, more than once, the subject of very lively altercations between the proprietors of the hotel and Constantine. The latter, fortunately, fully understanding the importance I attached to them, took upon him my defence so warmly, that he invariably came off victorious, but not without strenuous efforts, and not without much reproach for my *want of* cleanliness, as manifested by the splashing all around.

There is also another very great inconvenience for the traveller, and that is, there are no means of ventilating the chamber: he is shut in there with every chink closely puttied, and the temperature raised to twenty-eight, thirty, and even thirty-five degrees centigrade of heat,—that is to say, the summer temperature of Bombay. And since the winter cold of Central Siberia is seldom less than thirty degrees centigrade, one has to submit, on going out of doors, to a difference of sixty or seventy degrees.

When they had brought everything out of my sledge into my room,—for when these objects, however diverse they may be, are no longer in movement they should always be before the traveller's eyes,—and I had almost retired for the night, Constantine led into my room a gentleman who was introduced to me as a member of the general council of Perm.

A councillor, whatever may be his origin, his rights, or his functions, seems to be a sign of liberal institutions. This dignitary, with his ideas savouring a little of decentralisation, and an ambition to augment his prerogatives, is not generally met with, except in democratic lands. Therefore, I must admit, I was not a little surprised to find, breathing in Russian atmosphere, a man marked with the title of 'councillor.' I found him very communicative and courteous, knowing thoroughly our history and our institutions, and expressing himself easily in French. He held besides the office of engineer of mines. I therefore felt I could enter into many subjects with him, and I received some encouragement to do so from the courtesy of his manners and his desire to be communicative. Perhaps, under the colour of holding similar views, he might have allied himself with the old noble I met at Kazan against the Emperor, reserving the disguised power to get rid of the aristocracy when they had fully served his purpose.

When I complimented him on the dignity of his office, the exercise of which then drew him to Perm—" I can do very well without this honour," he replied, " for our provincial assemblies are far from enjoying the prerogatives of yours. The Emperor, in creating them, would fain make believe in his liberalism, but in reality, he has given them but illusory rights. In the first place, the members of the council are nominated by important proprietors in the province of Perm, who have received from the Czar the faculty to send to the sessions one or several representatives. The president of the council is nominated by the

Government. It is in no case whatever permitted to discuss politics. The Governor-General of Perm may, if so disposed, disregard entirely the wishes or votes of the council. The council may, it is true, appeal to the Senate of St. Petersburg, but the response is invariable: it emanates directly from the cabinet of the Emperor, and pronounces the dissolution of the council. Our votes, therefore, are very far from having the force of law. Three times have we demanded some repair of the road from Perm to Catherineburg: you will soon see in what state it still is for your journey."

Among the interesting opinions with which this agreeable and well-informed man entertained me, I will mention one regarding the finances of the empire. I expressed my astonishment at not seeing in Russia, a country supposed to be rich, more coin in circulation. "The Government," he said, "is wrong in not seeking its principal revenue in agriculture, and in the metallic resources in which the country abounds. It has been dazzled by the auriferous riches of the Trans-Baikal district, and hopes with these to maintain its financial

PERM—THE ROAD TO CATHERINEBURG.

position. A decree punishes, with the severest penalties, proprietors of gold mines who neglect to send to St. Petersburg all the precious metal they extract from the earth. The Emperor thus monopolizes, at its source, all the Russian gold, and then reimburses his subjects with bank-notes only. This state of things can only get worse, unless immediate and important reform be duly made in the administration and in the distribution of the tax. The budget, in fact, amounts to four or five hundred millions of roubles, whilst the State draws from the mines no more than seventy-five to eighty millions of roubles. To what rate of depreciation will not Russian paper fall, if they continue issuing such a quantity?"

This interesting mining engineer then turned from finance to the more comprehensive subject of politics in general, and added: "It is impossible for a single man to know all that takes place over such an immense territory. But if the Emperor could indeed be enlightened through the interpolations of a wise and intelligent opposition, he would still take good care not to introduce this element into the Constitution. To give you an instance of the ignorance of the high administration of the empire, I will only tell you that I regularly receive every year four thousand roubles, officially as engineer, for superintending the working of a Government manufactory that has been closed for five years!"

I could not help smiling at this candid avowal; and on learning this significant fact it seemed to me conclusive and peremptory.

I thanked my visitor for his agreeable society, and thought that this Russian proverb might justly be applied to him: "No one lets a bird of the Government escape without plucking out some feathers." I begged him to introduce me in the evening to a sitting of the Council General, and then went with Constantine to visit an important cannon foundry situated at about three miles from Perm.

The director of this foundry pretends that the cannon turned out here are superior to anything that has been hitherto made in Prussia.

This sitting of the Council General was void of interest, and soon ended from default of speakers. The members, having replied to their names, left at once to be present at a concert given by a company of travelling musicians under the direction of Monsieur Slavenski.

The Russian people, essentially musical, sing on all occasions. After a marriage ceremony the guests mount into eight or ten sledges and then make an excursion, following one after the other in line, singing all the time. They do the same at funerals and baptisms; sometimes—provided the season is not too severe—for no other reason than because it is winter and there is no work to do. These songs, which were executed by a company of forty *artistes*, who travel over the country to give their popular airs, constituted the entire entertainment: their voices united an exuberant richness to a remarkable simplicity of harmony.

The nearer one approaches an object he is intent on, the more impatient he becomes; I was longing, therefore, to tread at last on Siberian ground. As the distance was not very great that separated me from Catherineburg, I imagined I should get over it very speedily. But, alas! the Councillor was quite right. The road was, indeed, in a deplorable state. I do not know, indeed, how they could give the name of *road* to a long course of land whose surface was not level for a single yard, and where wide pits succeeded each other without interruption—not simple ruts, but pits three, four, nay, five feet deep! The yemschik has to calculate very nicely the fall of the sledge into these pits, that the horses' legs be not broken by the shock of the vehicle shooting forward against them; then he has to climb up the other side of the ditch, but not without great efforts, and no sooner does he get out of it than he has to prepare to dive into another.

The reader may easily conceive what the result of such a locomotion must be to a poor traveller: he is doubly wearied on account of the creeping pace accompanying the usual fatigue. It took me twenty-four hours to get over twenty-eight English miles! I was exasperated. My hope was to get a glimpse at the chain of the Ural Mountains, but a boisterous wind swept up the snow and whirled it round and round in moving columns reaching to the sky; beyond a few hundred yards nothing was visible.

To pass away the tedious hours I began questioning Constantine. "What is there in summer under this snow?" "Grass." "Of what use is it?" "None at all." "Who takes it?" "Nobody." "Who cuts these woods?" "No one." "Do all these lands belong to any one?" "Not always." "This land then is not capable of producing anything?" "On the contrary; it would be very productive if they cultivated it." "But then, why has your Emperor such a passion for conquest, when he can get so much out of his own land? Why does he go in search of gold in the Trans-Baikal, in the valley of the Issoury, and will soon perhaps in the Corea, as it is said among you, when he has at home more abundant and surer sources of riches? Why does he lead his armies into the burning deserts of Tartary, that were formerly independent? Why does he waste so much money in the conquest of Khiva when he could make far more on his own lands?"

When I waited for a reply to these questions, Constantine, who clung like a burr to the glory of his Emperor—and I congratulate him for his spirit—gave me one disdainfully: "I can easily understand, that the French, whose country is less extensive than our government of Perm, should be jealous of the immensity of our territory. You see, monsieur, that we are marching to the conquest of Asia entirely, which is the cradle of our race, and to Constantinople also, where our religion originated."

My companion was much offended; it was easy to perceive that; and I held my tongue to give him time to recover his equanimity. An hour after this conversation, I wished to see if he continued to have a grudge against me; "How I long to come to the end!" I exclaimed, "this long route tires me out." "Ah! Indeed, monsieur," he exclaimed, bridling up, "how grand Russia is! There is not another empire in the whole world of such vast extent!" "You are mistaken," I replied, duly estimating the lands uncultivated and absolutely useless, we had just traversed. "And which, if you please?" "The empire of the seas!" I replied gravely. His flattened nostrils then distended and quivered with indignation, and I patiently waited to be greeted with some emphatic Russian execration.

In spite of his *amour-propre*, Constantine

was, nevertheless, of a congenial humour,—towards me at least. Sometimes he excited in me a feeling almost of pity, which I could hardly conceal. Just while we were passing the Ural—that almost imperceptible elevation that is called mountain because it is in Russia, but which would be a mere hill in the Vosges, a mere hillock amid the Alps, a ridge in the Himalayas,—just here, we came on a village of wooden houses, like all Russian villages, but perched against a slope that gave it a picturesque air. A little further down stood a house of less wood construction than the others, and surrounded with a few trees. On this spot Constantine's eyes were riveted in a kind of reverie. "What a charming abode! Those people should indeed be happy!" he exclaimed. This remark moved me a little with commiseration, and I wondered what enthusiasm he would feel if he could only see our smiling Pyrenees or our Norman valleys, beaming with joy on a sunny May day.

Two days after our departure from Perm, on the 30th of December, about nine in the morning, we passed the boundary that marks the separation of Europe from Asia. It is a construction of stone, neither very high nor very fine, but which strikes the traveller on account of its simplicity and isolation.

Providence has decidedly withheld from this portion of the Russian Empire the imposing marks of its European limits. The quarters of the world generally (their states also, not unusually) have their boundaries defined by grand and prominent frontiers, such as the sea, high mountains, the desert, or some noble river. But here the border of the Ural is so little elevated, so unworthy of its *rôle* of boundary, that man has thought it his duty to interpose with his pigmy work, and say: *It is here!*

And here it is at last! We will enter with a beating heart, and advance as far as possible into the strange lands of ancient Asia—the dream of every traveller. We will endeavour to reach, as soon as we can, the shores of Lake Baikal, Mongolia, and the frontiers of China; for I fear my readers are tiring from the monotony of my narrative, as I have myself suffered since I left Perm from the monotony of this long route.

CHAPTER VII.

OUR PARTY ON THE ROAD TO TUMEN.

Trade and manufactures at Catherineburg—Carolling cherubs—Christmas at Kamechlof—Grand gala at a posting stage—Tumen—Its situation—Its gipsies—Fruit preserved in ice.

AFTER we had been journeying nine or ten hours in Asia, we arrived at Catherineburg. This city should serve as an example to many other Russian cities. Its inhabitants are very industrious, and know how to turn the resources of their land to account. They have iron foundries and many other metal works. They sculpture artistically coloured and transparent stones that are found in the Ural in great abundance, converting them into objects of very good taste for domestic ornamentation.

The manager of the establishment where these stones are so artistically chiselled, showed me a chimney-piece of inestimable value that had just received its last touches, and was to be sent away to the Emperor. I asked him who was the owner of the establishment. He replied, "L'état." "And who will pay for such a marvel of art?" "L'état"—and he added: "L'état payera, l'Empereur recevra." There are not many sovereigns, perhaps, who have a better right than the Emperor of Russia to say: "L'état c'est moi."

When I returned to my inn, I heard that Monsieur Pfaffius had just arrived at Catherineburg, and that he wished to see me. I was all the more pleased because it was something unexpected, and I consequently lost no time in paying him a visit.

And, at the house pointed out to me, I was delighted to find again the courteous and distinguished man I had left at St Petersburg. "Do you intend starting soon?" he inquired at once. "As soon as possible." "Shall we travel together, then?" "With all my heart." "Then that is settled."

During the conversation two ladies made their appearance in the room of the Commissary of Kiachta: one of them was about thirty, tall and as beautiful as an antique statue; the other was less in stature and much younger.

The beautiful, luxuriant, fair hair of the latter fell perfectly free and charmingly, methought, over her shoulders. Her youthful countenance beamed with freshness and vivacity.

"I am going to introduce you, if you will allow me," said Monsieur Pfaffius, "to Mrs. Grant and Miss Campbell. These ladies are also going to Kiachta, and I have no doubt you will be highly delighted, as I shall be, with their agreeable society."

On talking a few moments with these fair travellers, I learnt that Mrs. Grant was not English, but Russian, and had married Mr. Grant, an Englishman, at Kiachta; that her husband had been obliged to return to England for two or three years, she having accompanied him thither, and that now she was just returning to Kiachta, her native place, to meet her husband, who was expected there, taking Miss Campbell with her as a companion.

The latter, a young English lady, a little adventurous, like a great many of her countrywomen, had left her native land just as readily and just as merrily as she would have remained there, and now seemed to take pleasure in this wandering life, though she could foresee neither the end nor the consequences of it; and from day to day, penetrated still deeper into Asia, happy in running about everywhere, merely to see everything and pick up every scrap of information. "Have you been fatigued with the road?" I asked them, fully expecting to hear bitter complaints of it. "Not in the least, monsieur," replied Miss Campbell, with an air that seemed to say she was hurt at the suspicion of having suffered from such a trifle as the jolting. "Do you go by way of Omsk to Kiachta?" "That would be going out of our way to no purpose: we go straight to Tomsk." "You will travel quickly then?" "As fast as we can." "For my part," I remarked, "I prefer, on the contrary, going on slowly." On this observation her eyes seemed to sparkle with some lively thought. "Indeed, we should not have supposed so." "Well, and for what reason?" "They say that you are exceedingly clever in procuring horses everywhere."

This observation made me open my eyes with astonishment, and I added: "Even at the expense of ladies?" "Quite possible." "Then you know one who has had the misfortune to be a sufferer from my impatience, at a certain stage?" "It is not unlikely." I could never have believed it if it had not been positively affirmed. I could not believe that the elegant toilettes then before my eyes could in any way ever have adorned two such figures so incapable of embellishment as those that appeared to me at the stage between Kazan and Perm. For they were quite hooded and overloaded with rough and draggled fur; so much like bales of raw hides, so little like human beings, that one would never have suspected that beauty lay there so many skins deep. The reader will readily understand how ill-adapted is the rigorous climate of Siberia to setting off the charms of female beauty.

I warmly pleaded to be pardoned for my conduct, and on behalf of Constantine, who was the guiltier of the two, and the following day we were all gliding rapidly along in three sledges, one after the other, on the road to Tumen; happy in the opportunity of chatting together at every stage, smiling at the embarrassments of the post-masters, which Monsieur Pffiufas coolly disregarded, and facing cheerfully the snow and the cold (those two enemies with which travellers in Siberia are doomed to struggle), but without venturing on the slightest murmur.

Of course the reader is well aware that Russia has not accepted the reform brought to the calendar by Pope Gregory XIII.; therefore when we arrived in the little town of Camechlof, on the 6th of January, at break of day, it was actually then only Christmas-day in Russia, and we were no sooner quietly seated at table, taking our tea, as is customary with Russian travellers at every stage, than five or six little children entered our room, singing Christmas carols.

I have rarely seen a more touching and adorable *tableau* than this little group of fair heads, celebrating, with the warbling pure voice of early childhood, the most poetic episode of sacred history. Is there really any day more appropriate for singing? Indeed, I have always thought that if God should, for an instant, lift the veil from the supernal world on Christmas Day, we should see passing, to and fro, groups of innocents, around whom was resounding sweet music, breathing peace and joy to man below. The little children, who thus agreeably surprised us at so early an hour at Camechlof, suggested to my imagination a flock wandering from this celestial host.

This vision, brief like their visit, had hardly vanished when we saw appearing from the other side—the mundane this time—a young couple, accompanied by a nurse, carrying a very young infant. "Ivan Michaelovitch," exclaimed Constantine. "Madame Nemptchinof," cried Mrs. Grant, and then followed hand-shaking and embracing; we were again among acquaintances.

This Madame Nemptchinof was the wife of a tea merchant of Kiachta, who, notwithstanding her advanced interesting situation, had been to see one of her daughters at a boarding school in Moscow; her son had accompanied her, and the little being that had come into the world during the journey was now on its way to Kiachta.

In our country, undoubtedly, few women would have been equal to the task of undertaking such a journey, especially under such circumstances; in Russia, however, such an enterprise is not at all rare.

Then, before we had finished our tea, another

group of children entered, singing the same song, but these would speedily have dispelled any lingering vision of cherubs had any now remained, for these earth-born, unlicked cubs were clearly unhallowed and unlovely.

Having now sufficiently rested, we resumed our journey.

The horse, placed in the centre before the Siberian troïka, has its collar always surmounted by a bow, which serves as a stay or spring, to keep the shafts apart, and these are, at the same time, kept in their places together by a stretched cord. The collar, sustained by the bow above and resting on this cord, no longer weighs on the neck of the horse, and thereby diminishes its fatigue. This system of harnessing is really quite ingenious. Five or six bells are generally suspended from the bow, and the lively ringing of these relieves a little the monotony of the journey.

Our departure from Camechlof, with the bells of our caravan of four sledges in movement, was rather a noisy one. M. Pfaffius and his servant led the way; then followed, in a second sledge, Mrs. Grant and Miss Campbell; I occupied with Constantine the third, and Madame Nemptchinof and her *smalah* brought up the rear of the caravan in an enormous closed sledge drawn by four horses.

This part of the journey, if not the most interesting, was at least the most agreeable.

We were a party of seven, and a very convivial party too, that sat down to dinner in the evening. The bill of fare contributed largely to our merriment. Each of us produced our reserves, and it was a charming picnic, that furnished interesting incidents in abundance. We brought forward frozen bread, frozen caviare, frozen preserved fruits, and sausages, so rigid, that they resisted any attempt to yield, even against the knee, whatever force was employed.

Let one picture to himself seven famishing guests sitting round a table of thirty dishes any one of which would inevitably break his teeth if he had not the patience to wait for the effects of a little warmth. But gradually this element did its work; and in proportion as each aliment gave way before it, a smile of satisfaction beamed on every countenance, and, when the point of the knife succeeded at last in penetrating any part, shouts of triumph announced a victory at hand.

Subjects of conversation were not wanting, and, as I was French, and the Russians spoke French well, to the great advantage of foreigners not knowing the Russian language, French was the sole language used at table this evening.

The youthful Nemptchinof, who had not wandered much nor very far from Kiachta, was the least conversant with French; knowing Chinese and Mongolian well, he thought, perhaps, this acquisition well compensated for his ignorance of the Western languages. In order to express contentment, satisfaction, approbation, pleasure, he used but one word: *très gai*, and he pronounced it only with great difficulty; his accent made the expression still more odd. "Si vous voulez bien m'apprendre l'Anglais," said he to Miss Campbell, "je serai *très gai*." This young lady, knowing French very well, seemed to watch every opportunity that offered her amusement by rallying him on his phrases.

When dinner was over, the incessant *badinage* between the young English lady and her new Russian acquaintance, that had entertained us so much with an occasional corruscation like a fresh bottle of champagne, had subsided into more serious and probably more genial intercourse between the young couple—a *tête-à-tête*, suggestive of the smoothness and tenderness of Glinka's music. This change led me to speculate on the possible issue of an apparently interesting flirtation, to which the *badinage* had so effectively, though probably undesignedly, prepared the way.

Whether I was justified or not in my conjectures, Mrs. Grant took another view of the matter, and, on mounting into the sledge, whispered to me: "I am quite certain that your M. Constantine is in love with my young English companion, and therefore you will never prevail upon him to go by way of Omsk. I see clearly, as a consequence, that we shall all form one party as far as Irkutsk." "Constantine in love!" I exclaimed with a smile of incredulity; "that would seem to me very droll, too droll to be probable. I am disappointed that I shall be deprived of the pleasure of your company *en route*, for I have decided on going by way of Omsk, and Constantine is so useful to me that I cannot,

I am sorry to say, dispense with his valuable services and agreeable society." Constantine, as I gauged the nature of his sentiments, was far more likely to derive gratification in contemplating the influence he might exercise over some fair victim to love for him, if he, in his self-conceit, imagined it to exist, than in indulging in any vague similar emotion in his own heart. Mrs. Grant looked disappointed at my decision. "You will not on that account," I added, "be deprived of the enjoyment of a romantic incident; for, if I am not mistaken in trusting my eyes, the young Ivan, no longer *très gai*, is a little smitten with the graces of your fair young companion, and he has been, I think, so far favoured as to rouse the green-eyed monster. *Nous verrons.*"

The following day we arrived in Tumen. This city, like almost every other of the empire, commands a river from an eminence on its banks, and this river at Tumen is the Tura.

Its only striking feature is that it is built at the confluence of the Tura with another little river, which is considered here as a mere rivulet, one whose existence even is ignored by geographers, but which nevertheless is as wide as the Seine at Paris, and of sufficient force to have scooped out a profound gorge in the Tumen hill to discharge itself in the Tura.

A bridge has been constructed over this river, but it is at the bottom of the ravine. No care has been taken to diminish the steepness of the opposite banks, so that, to ascend the last, the traveller is obliged to descend the first with great rapidity and maintain the impulse over the bridge and for some distance beyond.

The sledges accomplish this feat at full gallop. As to wayfarers afoot, they descend the slope generally otherwise than on their feet and much faster than they like. The cattle, generally so slow, roll down in a few seconds, as if at the sport of Russian mountains. Everything there goes down at a giddy pace. The city offers little to interest the stranger, but it has all the aspect of the East; bazaars in the open air, in spite of the rigour of the climate, call back to the memory those of Syria and Africa.

In the *cafés*, the women deck themselves

out, at certain hours, in silks, without divesting themselves of their dirty petticoats, and make it their business to sing and dance for the entertainment of the guests.

In Africa, they are pleased with the bellowing of the Arab *almees*, through love for the picturesque, and because there is nothing else to listen to; but in Russia, the country of sweet and mystic melodies, I cannot understand how these repulsive gipsies are encouraged to raise their voices. Those who have eulogised the gipsies of St. Petersburg and Moscow are not altogether wrong in their appreciation; there they are civilised, educated a little, and, in some way, denationalised in character. But here, at Tumen, they are in their native element. I had the unlucky curiosity to venture into one of these *cafés*, and lost no time in escaping again, to join with pleasure my travelling companions.

At the end of our evening meal, we had some excellent fruits preserved in ice. This method of preserving fruit is quite special to Siberia. So soon as the severe cold sets in, these fruits are exposed in the open air, if possible to the north, where there is no sun to reach them; they freeze completely in this way, and are thus preserved, like meat and all other fresh aliments, in Siberia.

These fruits retain their flavour, notwithstanding their change from a state of rigid congelation. When they are served, they are as hard as wood, and if they fall to the ground, they sound like a stone.

The heat gradually softens their texture, and then they reassume their primitive form. I tasted a pear at Tumen that had become over-ripe, and then in which any further change had been completely arrested so far as flavour was concerned. This method of preserving aliments seems to be simple, economical, and thoroughly successful.

In summer, Tumen is a great place of call for steamers coming from Tomsk by the Tom, from the Obi, the Tobol, and the Tura. This city is therefore a considerable mart for merchandise,* its only claim, apparently, to notice; for it has neither manufactures to interest the curious in the useful arts, nor beauty of situation to attract the lover of nature.

* See note 2 at end of book.

CHAPTER VIII.

A PERILOUS NIGHT ADVENTURE ON THE STEPPE OF OMSK.

An ostentatious Siberian custom—The steppe—The cemeteries—Omsk—Its situation—Its society—The emancipation of the serfs related by a citizen—M. Kroupinikof—Visit to an encampment of Kirghiz—Masquerade at Omsk.

WE left Tumen about eight o'clock in the morning. Constantine, thoroughly familiar with Siberian customs, had put into the sledge several bottles of champagne, to provide for what was about to take place. The precaution was good, but the supply, alas! insufficient.

To open a bottle of champagne is in Siberia the greatest luxury that can be paraded before admiring eyes. This is the consequence of its high price and the caprice of fashion. In America, it is said that "the keeping of the proprieties is as indispensable as clean linen"*;

---

* Emerson.

here, perhaps, if doing *the right thing to do* be considered as one of them, the clean linen would have to give way to the proprieties. A dinner, a fête, an anniversary, or any like ceremony in Siberia without champagne, would be marked as being wanting in its most necessary element; and it is certainly not here that common-sense is so robust as to disregard the whimsical consensus of opinion that holds the civilized world in subjection *à la mode*, from Indus to the Pole.

About six hours after we had left Tumen, we arrived at a place where we had to take different roads. M. Pfaffius, Mrs. Grant, and Madame Nemptchinof, were going to take the road to Tomsk, whilst I had to turn a little more to the south. In order to defeat this project, Mrs. Grant had recourse to a little manœuvre, which very nearly turned Constantine's head. With a view to dissuading the latter from yielding to my plan, Mrs. Grant had taken her place in the closed sledge of Madame Nemptchinof; then she had arranged to bring Ivan and her young companion together, by making them mount side by side. Constantine, who was apparently smitten with the charms of the young English lady, seeing her *en tête-à-tête* with Ivan, seized a bottle of champagne, and cutting the wire, directed the cork at his rival's head, which Miss Campbell carefully shielded with her great fur glove; then the fire commenced on all sides, whilst I wondered what unseasonable and scandalous bacchanals were about to be inaugurated with so much uncorked wine. Happily, however, we tasted but a very moderate quantity. Then all my companions, in conformity with an ostentatious custom in Siberia, dismounted from their vehicles, each of them holding two bottles, and, advancing before my horses a few paces, poured the precious beverage on the snowy ground, just at the spot the skates of my sledge were destined to pass over. I scrupulously performed the same ceremony, a ceremony too solemn to be profaned with a laugh, which I could hardly repress, and then I took leave of this very agreeable caravan, but not without the prospect of meeting again, either at Tomsk, Irkutsk, or Kiachta.

As we resumed our way, but now in different directions, I heard a few more detonations of corks; and when the sound of the bells had died away and all had vanished from sight, Constantine looked at me most piteously. The *tête-à-tête* had evidently left some rankling effect in his breast that would have resisted any attempt at consolation had I ventured on so delicate a task; for, as far as I could see, he had received no encouragement whatever from Miss Campbell, and as, in this instance, the wounds of self-esteem and slighted love could not be salved with this same remedy, having no other to offer, I left the malady to cure itself.

What struck me all at once on this route was its absolute solitude. The carrying sledges bringing tea and other merchandise from China and the products of the Trans-Baikal to Nijni-Novgorod avoid passing by Omsk; it would be going out of the way to no purpose. It is therefore a rare occurrence to fall in with a sledge in this district. The snow, besides, is scarcely sufficiently beaten down to admit of an easy march. Here, in the absence of such movement, one is oppressed with an impression of wild waste, cheerless immensity, mournful silence. Gradually, vegetation diminishes, becomes more scattered and stinted, then disappears altogether, and the traveller enters at last on the great steppes.

But how changed during summer! Then the steppe is an immense prairie, whose rich, curly grass soothes the eye with its refreshing tint, and protects the body from jolting with its luxuriant bed.

And in winter, it is a vast plain rendered level and white by the snow with which it is covered. The French language, unfortunately, is here again insufficient to explain in a word the character of its outline. We call La Beauce a flat country; now the steppe in its snowy dress is not like La Beauce; neither is it level like the Mediterranean in calm weather, nor like the bed of a river. The surface of the steppe is strictly horizontal throughout. But Providence—as if to compensate in some measure to the eye of the artist for the absence of interesting scenery—has diffused, it is true, over this bare country, some of the finest effects of light with which any land is beautified and resplendent. And yet, in spite of this attraction, however varying and diversified, its joyless aspect preys on the mind of the traveller who enters on such a desert.

We had passed Ischim at nine in the morning; about five in the evening, we had again changed horses, when it was quite dark, and wearied with fatigue, I had fallen asleep. Suddenly I was awoke with a start by a fearful shock that had as suddenly roused Constantine. Our yemschik had gone astray in this frightful wilderness. The absence of the moon and the veiling of the stars with heavy snow clouds were together the cause of this misadventure. His fear of being underrated, and perhaps of animadversion, had hindered him from avowing immediately his awkwardness and blundering, and for three hours at least, he had been wandering about, where chance led him, with the hope of finding his way again—a hope poor indeed when he had lost all idea of direction and every vestige of landmark. The fall into a pit, concealed by the snow, which we had just experienced, obliged him now to avow his blunder.

Constantine and I unrolled ourselves from our blankets, got down, and set to work, with lantern in hand, to find the road. On looking round, we contemplated the spectacle of our sledge and horses almost buried in the snow, and it was one of dire significance. Of the sledge the only part visible was the hood, and of the horses little more than their shoulders and heads.

Sinking ourselves up to the waist, and consequently unable to move one foot before the other without great effort, having to battle besides against the violent cutting wind loaded with the snow it had swept up in its passage and hurled in our faces, we struggled thus desperately to see a few paces, as much as we could hope to see before us, but to no purpose, and were forced to return to our sledge in despair, to breathe again and recover a little more strength.

After an hour of this painful work, we were no more enlightened as to the way we should take than at first, and, moreover, we were exhausted. Over the land there was not a vestige of anything but the snow to be seen; for at a short distance all around there was nothing but darkness, impenetrable; not a star in the sky was visible, not a sound in the air audible, to induce us to risk the chance of

PERILOUS ADVENTURE ON THE STEPPE OF OMSK. [To face p. 131.

attempting one direction in preference to another. The situation was portentously critical, and, unless we would resign ourselves then to our fate, it was necessary to make a supreme effort. In this dilemma we consulted together as to what expedient we should next try. This decided on, the yemschik unharnessed one of the horses with the object of riding as quickly as possible in search of some village, and began, with a lantern in one hand, leading the horse with the other, to discover afoot some trace of the way from which he had strayed.

We watched him struggling with the elements till the last beam of light died away; then Constantine and I, thrown back on ourselves in the darkness—a night with no day near at hand, and a solitude without refuge or clear prospect of retreat—had little to contemplate but our dismay. We thought of our poor horses exposed without movement, of our inability to relieve them from the cold, and, seeing how utterly helpless we were, we wrapped ourselves in our furs and blankets and re-entered our shelter. There we made some effort to cheer each other. We saw passing, in imagination, caravans of Kirghiz, from whom we were, in reality, not distant, and we fancied ourselves led prisoners into the heart of Tartary, in some wild lawless territory not yet brought under subjection. We saw also—but this time it was not a vision—five or six packs of wolves prowling around our poor beasts, watching for a meal if they should be dying or dead, but, happily, these prowlers scampered away at the sound of my revolver. The first shot was not without a moment of terror, for I was not at all assured that the result would not be disastrous. Having my rifle packed up in my trunk through not having foreseen what was likely to come to pass, I found myself absolutely defenceless, in case they should be emboldened, in the lonely position we were, to join in a united attack. Retreat we had none, except behind the canvas; we might close in front; but how long would this resist their assault, met with the shot of a single revolver? Their disappearance therefore was hailed with joy.

Many tedious hours thus passed away, and, since our thoughts were occupied in waiting for the return of our man, who might bring us the relief we had not yet despaired of, every hour passed seemed in the aggregate as many nights in succession. He had long been absent, when I began to be tormented with a suspicion of his fidelity. If we ever stirred from the spot and should be fortunate enough to reach the first village, might he not there expect a severe chastisement for the serious consequences of his culpable neglect, involving perhaps the loss of the horses, from which he might think to escape with impunity by leaving us to our fate? Then we thought of the small store of provisions we had brought with us; and, determined not to surrender ourselves yet to our prospective fate of desertion and protracted hunger and cold, I proposed to Constantine to descend and follow on foot the footsteps of the yemschik, with the hope of extricating ourselves from our perilous position.

We had got out, and were on the point of putting our project into execution, when we perceived, to our horror, that no track could be found. The blast had been strong enough to sweep the snow across the path he had taken; no depression, however slight, was visible;

every vestige of a footprint had been effaced. To wander from where we were, we should be speedily lost; to remain on the spot, our fate seemed not less inevitable, but as we had some provisions and shelter, it would be prolonged, and the return of day might bring us rescue. " Let us wait daybreak," said Constantine; " then perhaps we may catch a glimpse of our man in the distance, if he is still alive; for at this moment, if he has not succeeded, he must have given up further searching."

We had been an hour, I thought, so well as I could conjecture time, sitting side by side in the vehicle, when I fancied my ears caught the sound of cries in the distance. But it was so feeble, that I trembled lest my excited imagination should have deceived me. I replied, however, though my voice was too weak, and Constantine refused to join his to mine. I thought he had resigned himself to his fate; but it was fear, overpowering fear that closed his throat. He yielded at last to my entreaties, and then voices in response, the last glimmer of hope, seemed really approaching.

After a little while, we attempted to shout more intelligibly a few words, and then came replies. At last, to our infinite joy, we saw our liberators. They were coming in great number and with many horses, to rescue us from our impending fate.

No mariner lingering on a wreck and watching for rescue, in any sign of movement on a lonely shore, could have hailed deliverers with more exultation. Our spirits mounted now in proportion to their recent depression. We joked pretty freely on the stupidity of our yemschik, whom his comrades now turned into ridicule. The two poor beasts, that remained harnessed to the sledge, paid dearly for this adventure. When they attempted to drag them out of the hollow, they were rigid and benumbed with the cold; they could not follow us a single pace, and Constantine understood at once that these men had decided on putting an end to their suffering.

Daylight had just appeared, when we made our entry into the village. All the inhabitants having heard of the great peril we had encountered, ran out to see us pass, and bowed and made the sign of the cross to the great St. Sergius and the Virgin of Kazan in expression of their gratitude for our deliverance.

Our journey continued this day without any particular incident; the reflection on that of the preceding night, and the congratulation on our narrow escape from such peril, were sufficient to engross our thoughts. The aspect of this great desert, covering the vestiges of many an untold catastrophe with its snowy shroud, made me tremble at the remembrance of it; and I have often thought since that if our yemschik had not come to our succour in time, the only abode he would have had to conduct us to would have been a cemetery. In the steppe, the resting places of the dead are the only spots planted with trees, and, on that account, are seen at a great distance. They bring to these melancholy spots birch trees from Krasnoiarsk, at a great expense, and these little groups of white trunks, glittering in the sunbeams, become so many landmarks for the lonely wanderer. They give also to this desolate spot, from one point of view, notwithstanding the mournful association from another, an aspect of calm joyfulness, when the solemnity of the scene draws the thoughts nearer to hope and resurrection, rather than to despair and definitive annihilation. When the sky is clear and the cold intense, these cemeteries on the steppes are radiant with reflected beams, even where everything is luminous in the immensity around.

The following morning when I awoke at daybreak, I found we were stopping on the way. I opened the canvas curtain that closed in the front of the sledge, to ascertain if we were still on the road, and finding that we were, I could not help laughing at the situation we were in. The scenery had not changed; it was still the steppe, and nothing but the steppe around in view; but our driver was in a profound slumber, with his head resting on our provisions; the horses also, feeling themselves allowed to have their own way, were standing stock-still, and probably were slumbering also; but as to Constantine there was no doubt, for his snoring, loud enough "to frighten the wolves," proclaimed his happy condition, and considering the exhausting effect of the emotions he must have experienced, I was at first loth to rouse him. Still this indulgence could not go on very long with the prospect of a journey of eighteen hundred leagues before us, and having contemplated a few moments the drollery of this quiescent attitude—a drollery all the more irresistible from contrast with the seriousness of the situation—I resolved to wake him and accordingly did so as gently as possible. Now fully roused from his drowsiness, he regarded the driver a moment with irritation, and then, instead of employing the bland proceeding I had adopted towards him, commenced pommelling the yemschik's head with his fist, the only efficacious method, he suggested, for a skull so thick. The horses now, in their turn, were quickly set going with means still more energetic and as we whisked briskly along in the fresh morning air, I admired with rapture those sublime changes of light that invariably accompany the rising of the sun in a cloudless sky in these latitudes, and their reflection in paler tints successively passing over the surface of the snow.

At last, after this eventful course, we arrived at Omsk, in a cutting atmosphere of forty-five degrees,* an intensity of cold that scarcely diminished during the remainder of my sojourn in Siberia.

---

* Nearly 50° of Fahrenheit's scale below the lowest temperature indicated thereon, = 82° below freezing point.

Many geographers erroneously represent Tobolsk to be the capital of Siberia, but the honour belongs to Irkutsk. Tobolsk is not even the seat of a Government, for Omsk is the capital of Western Siberia.

I needed but a very short stay at Omsk to congratulate myself on having chosen my route by this city. This fortified place, for such it is, is situated on the top of a little hill, on the borders of the Irtish. The view, therefore, is commanding over this river; then beyond, over its opposite bank, which is marked by a mound, the steppe stretches away in front and on the right and left till lost to sight in the horizon. The steppe, viewed from this point, has not the same uniformity to the eye which I before mentioned. The snow takes here and there tints so distinct and dissimilar, and these are ever varying with such inimitable beauty and artistic combination, that the steppe seen from Omsk is lovelier, more diversified, and more imposing even than the sea. A Frenchman, whom I have already mentioned, and in whose company I have spent hours in contemplating this magnificent spectacle without ever tiring of it, told me that, during summer, the steppe was still more interesting. The grass, he said, takes changing hues so deep as to be almost black; then it seems that instead of a boundless green sward, there is a vast gulf of immeasurable depth yawning before the spectator; and then, perhaps, an hour afterwards, according to the position of the sun and the state of the firmament, an illimitable field of brilliant verdure rises under the eye, and replaces, as if by enchantment, the mysterious gloom of the bottomless abyss by the inspiring gaiety of a vernal landscape.

The steppe, to the inhabitants of Omsk, is as the desert to the wandering Bedouin, the sea to the navigator, the Alps to the Swiss. They search in its changing aspects for prognostics of the weather, and these determine their daily movements. At Omsk, the people have a strong attachment to the steppe; it furnishes abundant pasture to the flocks and herds, and an exciting hunting ground to these ardent lovers of the chase, who find here no lack of wild animals. The public fêtes take place here, and the promenade is in view of the steppe. To go on the steppe, or merely to see it, constitutes, in fact, the chief occupation of life for the inhabitants of Omsk, and, indeed, when one has once seen the steppe, it is not difficult to conceive this passionate attachment; as for myself, who had very narrowly escaped leaving my bones to bleach there on its snowy bed, and on that account, perhaps, should have been repelled from it rather than attracted to it, I was probably more enthusiastic over its charms than anybody, and it was with regret and tender melancholy that I was obliged to withdraw from the contemplation of a spectacle so truly magnificent and sublime.

Society in Siberian cities is composed of functionaries, who are deemed the aristocracy, and traders and miners. At Omsk only is there found a third element, a real middle class of retired citizens, that is to say, men who, having made their fortunes, devote their time to study or amusement.

The first of these citizens to whom I was introduced having spoken very favourably of the decree of the emancipation of the serfs, I mentioned to him the conversation I had with the old aristocrat of Kazan. "This gentleman has not told you," he said, "all the vexatious proceedings that the serfs were constantly obliged to submit to by their lords, and the extortions of which they were the victims. He has not told you that the serfs never had the right to quit the land of their lord, how many cudgellings they may have been made to undergo, and how often the lords gambled away between one another, on the throw of a die, a property consisting of five or six families. He has not said a word about the manœuvre of the lords, who, being obliged every year to abandon to the service of the Emperor a certain number of their vassals, choose, as might be expected, the least vigorous, who, notwithstanding the feeble state of their health, become soldiers for life. Certainly," he continued, "we do not yet enjoy complete liberty; we cannot quit Russian territory before having complied with the requirements of the military law; we can change neither religion nor country; but after all, every one is treated alike, and the sovereignty of the Emperor is not to be compared with the vexatious seigniory of the lords."

It will require, certainly, great address for the Czar to introduce, without violent transition or revolution, the necessary liberal reforms. It is to be hoped he may succeed, thanks to the fetishism that surrounds his person. He puts, perhaps, a little too much confidence in the ever-increasing power of the trading class, the possessors of the great wealth of the country, who are still devoted to the Emperor, on account of their hatred to the aristocracy, but who might well turn against their benefactor so soon as they found themselves in a position sufficiently strong.

Another citizen of Omsk entertained me with his views on another subject, not less interesting. It was M. Kroupinikoff, who had been fifteen years among the Kirghiz, as Government official, charged with a difficult duty.

The Kirghiz, whose territory is subjected to the Czar, have, nevertheless, remained in their wild state, and with a longing to recover sooner or later their lost national independence. In order to prevent them from uniting anywhere in great masses, the Government has assigned to each tribe a zone, and they are interdicted from going beyond this limit under penalty of death.

It was M. Kroupinikoff's duty to take care that every Kirghiz kept within the bounds of his respective territory.

To accomplish this difficult and dangerous task, he had but an insufficient escort. "To give you an instance," he said, "I was attacked and made a prisoner by these wild people, and I don't know what would have happened if I had not fortunately made my escape, and, indeed, without horse and almost without anything to eat. This enterprise, probably, is much more hazardous for me than another to sojourn among the Kirghiz, whose character on the whole is not ferocious. What they detested in me was the functionary, and not the man.

"For a period of fourteen days and fourteen nights, I was exposed to the rigorous cold on the steppe, wandering on foot, amid deep snow. I was suffering from hunger, and yet hardly dared to touch a morsel of the food I had succeeded in bringing with me, for fear the last crumb should disappear long before I should be able to drag myself as far as Omsk. But I arrived in a state painful even to remember; for it was in this adventure that I was seized with the malady with which, you see, I am now tormented, without a hope of ever being cured." This poor man, indeed, had a nervous trembling from head to foot, that did not allow him a moment's repose, the bare contemplation of which was sufficient at the first glance to make one shudder.

"If you like, monsieur," he politely offered, "I will take you to see a Kirghiz encampment I know, not very far from here; I shall be most happy to have a little excursion in your company; that will recall my old occupations." I accepted his proposal gladly, and early the following morning we left in a sledge, and took our way towards the south.

The Kirghiz anciently formed a part of the great Mohammedan family, and roved along the flowery banks of the Tigris and the Euphrates. It is not exactly known at what epoch, and in what disaster, they were defeated by the Turks, and subsequently driven from their old haunts into the great Tartar steppe. They tried many times to reconquer their ancient land, but only in vain. One expedition of the Kirghiz is mentioned, that penetrated, in 1738, as far as Tashkend.

Müller gives us an account of some of the institutions of these people during the period preceding their final submission to the Russians. When war was declared, the chief named those who were to enlist, and assigned them the quota of arms and horses they were to furnish to the army.

In administering justice, judgments were given by an assembly of elders. He who was found guilty of murder first suffered the penalties pronounced by the tribunal, and was then delivered over to the relatives of his victim, who were at liberty either to kill him, or to keep him as a slave. In the latter event, the assassin had to furnish to his masters one hundred horses and two camels, with liberty to substitute five sheep for every horse.

If the victim of an assassination were a woman or child, the relatives of these had no right to demand the life of the murderer, and the fine was reduced to one half. The crime of rape was punished in the same manner as the murder of women or children.

The Kirghiz still have among them a great number of diviners, * in whose revelations they

---

* *Pallas.*

have more or less faith according to the method these magicians employ in predicting.

Some divine with books without having recourse to the stars. Others employ the shoulder blade of a sheep. It is absolutely necessary that this bone be denuded of flesh with a knife, and that human teeth have not gnawed it, otherwise it would have no virtue. When one of these magicians is consulted, he puts the shouder blade on the fire, and makes his predictions according to the fissures produced by the heat. These diviners pretend with their science to determine how far distant an absent person may be.

The Kirghiz call the third class of magicians *bukscha*. To obtain a prediction from them, they exact a horse, a sheep, or a goat. The magician begins the ceremony by chanting and beating on a drum furnished with rings; and whilst thus occupied, he goes through a succession of leaps and contortions of the body for half an hour. When this part of the ceremony has ended, he has a sheep brought to him, and killing it, receives the blood in a vessel, expressly made for this purpose; he then keeps the skin for himself, and distributes the flesh among the spectators, who eat it. He afterwards takes the bones, and, dyeing them red or blue, throws them towards the west. Then he scatters the blood in the same direction, begins again his contortions, and, after an interval, gives his response to the question proposed to him. A fourth class of diviners are called *kamtscha*. They augur from the colour of the flame that rises from butter or fat thrown into the fire. The latter class of diviners is not much esteemed.

I had been about two hours on our excursion in conversation with M. Kroupinikoff, when I perceived three tents made of pointed stakes, pitched side by side, and covered with felt. As we had been some time announced, the head of the family received us before his encampment. This man was tall, and of a haughty look, and his dress, composed mostly of trophies of the chase, was really very picturesque. His head was covered with a hood of red wool, surmounted with a wolf's head stuffed, the ears of which, being turned forwards, seemed as if they were his own. His shoulders were covered with a red shirt and a wolf's skin. From his waist hung a pouch, similar to a Highlander's, but made of the skin of the white deer of the desert. His legs were swathed in skins of different colours; his sandals were of plaited straw, his feet disappearing under leather gaiters, that expanded below like Mexican trousers. In imitation of the ancient savages, this man bore at the same time his weapon of war and of the chase. He had a bow over his shoulder, arrows suspended from a shoulder belt, an enormous club hanging from his waist, and a falcon perched on his hand. This club served him to strike down the wolves as soon as he ran them down with his fleet courser. Near him stood a hare-hound of a breed, it appears, found only among these people. They are hairless all over the body, excepting on the ears, where the hair is of unusual length. On seeing this one, I fancied it had been shaved by the Kirghiz, who are very much attached to these dogs, but M. Kroupinikoff assured me that this was their natural state. These animals, they say, are swifter and more intelligent than Scotch or Syrian hounds. Excepting the peculiarity of the long hair on the ears, which detracts from their beauty, they are extremely graceful animals.

The Kirghiz being Mohammedans, the women of this tribe hid themselves from our eyes in their tents. M. Kroupinikoff being unwilling to displease the chief by asking to be admitted into the tent, preferred asking him to show me how he hunted the wolf with the club.

He was in his saddle in an instant, and executed before us a manœuvre with a dexterity that would have been envied by Arabs if they could have seen him. Off he went, cutting through the air like a dart, hiding himself from view by leaning down close beside the shoulder of his courser, and low enough to strike the snow with his tomahawk. And the next moment, hanging on by some part of the harness, he appeared completely close under his steed.

This wild, wolf-eared figure, arrayed in red; this sinewy, sinuous hunter of the desert, guiding his courser, like the bound of a tiger on some imaginary prey, was altogether a striking spectacle, and one quite as interesting as it was startling and fantastic. We bid adieu to this son of Genghis Khan, and returned to Omsk, with this vision ever present to my imagination, like a vivid dream.

I was amused with a diversion quite peculiar to this city, that takes place during the three first days of the year. It consists in going to pay a visit to one's friends disguised in costume and masked, in a way so effectually, that it is impossible to be recognized. To give more animation occasionally to the amusement, families mutually exchange houses, disguising themselves also, and then the visitors and the visited find themselves equally mystified. These merry *réunions* are generally accompanied with dancing and refreshments. The society of Omsk is too limited to afford facilities for any intrigue, and too strict even that such, if any, should be attended with any serious consequence; but for all that, there are few cities in the world, perhaps, where during these three days so much boisterous mirth may be heard as in this privileged spot on the Tartar steppe.

CHAPTER IX.

THE COLD ON THE WAY TO TOMSK.

The intense cold—Its inconveniences—The fine effects of light at a very low temperature—The baptismal fête of Christ on the Obi—Tomsk—Its commerce—An evening on the banks of the Tom.

I LEFT Omsk on the 17th of January at one in the afternoon. This day was intensely cold; the thermometer indicated almost fifty degrees! I could hardly open my *bachelique* when I wished to do so, in order to admire the fine effects of light that invariably accompany so low a temperature.

The snow, through some optical effect I am unable to explain, presented, from certain points of view, reflections so dark as to be almost black; and then, in contrast to these, innumerable little crystals, reflecting the sun's rays, sparkled with such resplendence, that one might fancy he was admiring particles of diamonds scattered over a rich velvet cloth.

After a few hours of this journeying, we came to a part of the steppe called the long grass, on account of an abundance of it in these parts reaching a great height.

When I saw it, it was quite covered with a hoar frost. Towards evening, when the sun was disappearing in the horizon, the mass received the expiring rays and became dazzling white. The snow at the same time, disposed to take its hue from the sky, presented a dark blue tint. This fine spectacle, unfortunately, was of short duration. The sun had now gone down, and a feeble, mystic twilight began spreading over this immense plain, which presently became illumined by the aurora borealis, suffusing the whole with its rosy hue.

It would be impossible to depict in words the diverse and ever-varying tints I have witnessed, from time to time, beautifying Siberian landscapes. When the cold is very intense, the play of light that enters on the scene is far too subtle for art to give any conception of it. It is during some of these beautiful transformations I have mentioned that the light vapour in the air freezes; at these times, I have seen shoals of fine crystals, almost imperceptible, swimming in the air, glittering in the sunbeams, and casting their rainbows superimposed on the horizon. As we see these colours in France, generally in a more sombre sky, they are dull in comparison with the lively, fascinating, and mystic hues presented here on an azure of infinite purity.

A cold so rigorous is not without serious inconvenience to poor human beings who venture to brave it. The part of the face around the nose and mouth disappears completely, in a few moments, under a thick icy coating, formed from the moisture of the breath; and as it is necessary to remove this glacial crust from time to time, the operation occasions much suffering.

To prepare at night for sleep, the Siberian wanderers are accustomed to moisten their *bacheliques*, which speedily freeze and stiffen, and thus present a solid partition or case, at a few inches from the face. The respiration then congeals against the inner surface of this improvised wall. But in spite of these precautions, when I awoke in the morning, I found my eyelids completely sealed up with little icicles around the lashes, which I was obliged to dissolve between my warm fingers before I could open my eyes to the daylight.

Another strange effect of cold so intense may be seen on entering a village, at an early hour, when the inhabitants are just lighting their fires. The hot smoky air rising from the chimneys ascends straight up to a certain point, where, becoming rapidly cooled and condensed and meeting with a stratum of equal density, it commences spreading out horizontally, on every side, like a kind of ceiling or canopy, and this, increasing in thickness, obstructs radiation, and thus forms a protecting cloud for the whole village.

Between Kolivan and Diorosno, two little towns, standing face to face on opposite hills, the telegraph wires extending to Kiachta are encased in a cable underground, an expedient adopted to avoid repeated destructions of the communication by floods which occurred when formerly placed on poles.

The Obi freezes in the same manner as the Oka; the protuberances are so exaggerated in magnitude, that it is difficult to realize that they cover the bosom of a river; they form, in fact, hills and valleys, obliging the traveller to ascend and descend.

We arrived at Diorosno at eight in the morning, on the anniversary of the baptism of Christ. A hole, about a yard in diameter, had been made through a thick flooring of ice; and, through this aperture, the Obi might be seen flowing rapidly towards the north, as if seeming to make sport of the cold trying to arrest its course on the surface. The clergy of the village, followed by a crowd of devotees, came in great pomp to this hole to bless the water of this river. When the ceremony ended, all the inhabitants drew near with their buckets, vases, and vessels of all kinds, to fill them and then carry away to their dwellings the water that had just been blessed. When they had all taken what they desired, three or four fanatics divested themselves of their clothing in the twinkling of an eye, plunged into the freezing water, and dressing themselves again as hurriedly, hastily ran home to warm themselves at their fires. These people consider it a miracle if one escapes without perishing from the consequences of an act of such rashness. I think that the short duration of the bath and the reaction subsequently produced by the violent run are the chief safeguards against danger.

After having passed the Obi, we entered on a country of most singular aspect; it was still flat, but inclined, an inclined plane, in fact, that rose gradually, seemingly without end, to the horizon. I think that the magnitude of the rivers in Siberia arises, in the first place, from the vastness of their basins, and then from these prolonged inclined planes, that facilitate so much the descent of accumulating waters. Whatever it may be produced by, this strange sloping land gives rise to wonder, and at first brings on giddiness, especially when one is gliding downwards. Although the slope is not very steep, the sensation of slipping down gently into some distant, unknown abyss is unpleasantly suggestive of danger. As the ground sinks under you, the world might easily be imagined to have broken loose from its moorings, and to be floating away to some inconceivable destination. One is instinctively urged to put out his hand to seize something, but since there is nothing but the bare ground in view, he is thrown back on himself more completely, and this singular impression becomes all the more vivid and painful.

We had now been three days journeying from Omsk, when, about five in the morning, we were roused by some violent jerking from the rugged ice of the Tom, which announced our approach, accomplished not without difficulty, to the city of Tomsk. It is always a great relief in Siberia, after a long journey, to have a resting place in view, and then to arrive there. I made up my mind to stay a while in this city, where the inn, by comparison, appeared relatively comfortable.

The chamber they gave me contained nothing more than is usual elsewhere, but considered here completely furnished; still the room was lighted by four great windows, and the floor was well swept. Finding it therefore rather inviting, I opened all my trunks, and begged Constantine to keep me company for a little time in this important centre of Siberian commerce.

The city is divided into two parts, the lower city lying in the valley of the Tom, and the upper perched on a hill, running along the right bank of this river. The first is the business quarter; there are found the bazaars and warehouses. The other, on the contrary, is composed of elegant dwellings, at least elegant for the country, occupied by those who have either acquired large fortunes, or are on the way to this enviable object.

In order to have a good idea of the nature of the commerce of Tomsk and its importance, it is necessary to have been an eye witness of that disposition of the inhabitants of Western Siberia for a *far niente* existence on the one hand, and on the other, to know that absorbing passion with which the Eastern Siberians devote themselves to gold-hunting and the working of gold mines.

At Irkutsk, the centre of this second part of Siberia, the land is fertile, and yet not a grain of wheat is put into it; the city is at the confluence of three rivers, but, for all that, not a fish is taken from them. Although there are in the neighbourhood iron mines, and china clay of excellent quality for the manufacture of porcelain, all these raw materials are neglected, and the material for building is brought from the Ural, and domestic utensils from Moscow and even St. Petersburg.

The inhabitants of Tomsk make profit out of the indolence of the Western Siberians and the gold fever of the Eastern, and become corn merchants, forage providers, butchers, and—what is surprising—the fishmongers for nearly the whole of Siberia. The enormous distance between Tomsk and other important cities, of which I have spoken, might throw doubt on the soundness of such a view; but this commerce is rendered quite possible from the curious effects of extreme cold on aliments.

One day, on dining on a plump fowl that had been placed before me, I asked, from curiosity, how long it had been since the bird was killed; they replied, in order to diminish the natural repugnance of a Frenchman for anything not fresh, "Two months only; not more." For beef, no precautions are required to preserve it; it takes care of itself. Nearly all the butchers kill, for a stock of fresh provisions, at the commencement of the cold, a quantity sufficient for the winter. There is no fear of any fresh aliment changing under such a temperature. It is the same with the fish, which become so solid and stiff, that they are set up on their tails against the walls of the

[To face p. 164.

MARKET-PLACE AT TOMSK.

markets, be the tail ever so long and the fish ever so heavy.

The climate of Siberia has also very marked effect on the germination and growth of grain: the sowing is done in May only, and in July the corn is ripe for harvesting.

It is quite clear, besides, that the spring here in Siberia makes its effects felt much more rapidly than in England or France. If one watches the trees, their leaves and twigs, he will perceive very sensible differences in the development from day to day. This arises in part from the increased vigour of a sap long dormant under the snow, but more particularly from the great length of the days, and consequent increase of sunshine, whereby vegetation enjoys not only considerably more heat and longer periods of diurnal activity, but from the shortness of the nights, suffers a proportionately less share of refrigeration and retardation of its development.*

The inhabitants of Tomsk being always occupied, and principally in the cultivation of the soil, have, on this account, preserved,

---

* See note 3.

more scrupulously than elsewhere, the ancient Siberian customs. I will mention only a few of them. In every house and even every room, one or several lamps may be seen burning before some picture, some object of piety, according to the day or religious solemnity. When a visitor presents himself he bows two or three times, at the same time making the sign of the cross before the picture; then, but not before, he salutes his host in a manner according to his occupation at the moment. If he is eating, they say: "Tea and sugar," which signifies: "I hope you will be able to put sugar in your tea." This luxury here is not given to everybody. On leaving the room, they say: "Rest in peace!" When the inhabitants of Tomsk enter a shop, they make use of an expression of this meaning: "I wish you may make a bargain with me quite to your own advantage."

Great quantities of merchandise are brought from China and the Trans-Baikal and discharged at Tomsk during the summer, to be conveyed hence by steamboats to Tumen, and this additional traffic adds considerably to the wealth of the former city.

Tomsk is, it appears, one of the coldest spots in all Siberia. During certain winters, the thermometer has been known to descend to fifty-five degrees and remain for some time at this temperature, and one is known even so low as fifty-eight degrees!

When I was here, the temperature, on the contrary, was less rigorous than during my sojourn at Omsk. It snowed heavily for some days, and that induced me to confine myself to my room, which I in no way regretted, with the discomfort of so many long days and nights, just passed in the open air, still fresh in my memory.

One night only, urged by some motive for exercise, and perhaps adventure, I went out alone afoot, and took my way, musing, along the banks of the river. The night was very dark, and heavy clouds veiled the stars; but the ground was lighted up with the snow fallen during the day. The frozen surface of the Tom was nowhere even, and I was able to account for the joltings we had experienced in the sledge on crossing this river. Blocks of ice were rising one above the other, sometimes to a great height, presenting their edges upwards, and the aspect of having struggled with tremendous force to escape from the crushing embrace of the solid mass on which they rested. It might be said to have been the result of a terrific combat between two great forces of nature—between the river and the frost—the one visible and vanquished, and the other invisible and victorious. Now, however, this struggle was suspended till the time would come for the victory to be reversed, and meanwhile all was motionless and silent.

I stood regarding it with awe for some time, like the pale visage of death on whose features the convulsions of agony told some dreadful tale. The night was too dark to distinguish the other bank of this great river; and what was before me, in its chilling inhospitable state—total estrangement from the world in this white solitude as far as the eye could reach through the gloom—made me shudder in my loneliness. It was the first time I felt myself so entirely abandoned, so utterly cut off from the world, exiled from my country and home and all that was dear to me. To think of taking to the sledge again, and continuing my journey through this chilling air and darkness, made me shrink with repugnance and fear. To struggle against such a force as had stopped this gigantic river in its course seemed to me foolhardiness. It was indeed a true picture of the extreme North I had come so far as Siberia to see; and although I had gratified my longing as a tourist to see wonders, I wended my way home overwhelmed with this aspect of nature, and it required all the brilliant sunshine of the morrow to brighten my mind with more cheerful thoughts, and give me some courage to resume my journey.

One thing I noticed peculiar to Tomsk was the great number of Corean servants, male and female, that are there met with. I asked the governor the reason of this, and he informed me that many natives of this land took refuge among the Russians to escape from the severe laws in force there. "They know well enough that they will be well received among us, for we have already a protectorate over their country."

This announcement of a protectorate afforded me some matter for reflection. The Corea, it is known, is only tributary to China. The sovereign of this territory is opposed to Europeans, who are not only not allowed to establish themselves there in any way, but are often persecuted by this tyrant with extreme cruelty. The conquest of the Corea by the Russians—a conquest quite imminent according to the views of the governor of Tomsk—might, if accomplished, occasion important modifications in our trading depôts of the extreme East. It would be an important step towards the complete conversion of China and Japan to modern ideas.

CHAPTER X.

THE GOVERNMENT OF YENISSEISK AND KRASNOIARSK.

Wretched aspect of the villages of this province—The country at last becomes hilly—The night watchers at Krasnoiarsk—M. Lovatine's three collections—A Polish exile's ball.

I TOOK my departure from Tomsk on the 26th of January. The appearance of the road at first did not differ materially from the one I had recently passed over.

In the villages, however, there was a great difference. Certain details showed the absence of civilization and industry of any kind. The poor inhabitants, instead of admitting light into their dwellings through glass, which would be too costly for them, plug the holes with the skins of their sheep. One may easily imagine how little light can penetrate through these small apertures, and how gloomy the existence of these poor creatures must be during a long winter's darkness.

These dwellings are raised without any prepared foundation, and are composed of posts or beams bound firmly together. When a thaw takes place, the result is a subsidence, and these hovels, instead of falling down altogether, being secured laterally, simply lean in a mass on one side. In this position they generally remain; for their inhabitants give themselves no trouble to set them upright again. The consequence is that the flooring inside is frequently so inclined, that it is quite an effort to climb across it. This accident, so very common in this part of Siberia, gives a miserably dilapidated look to the villages; the roofs seem ready to fall over each other, or fall away in another direction; the upper story in some is brought down on end almost to the ground, and in others the ground floor is thrown up on an inclined plane to the height of first stories. On beholding this disorder, the spectator would suppose the village had been scourged with a hurricane or an earthquake.

The day after our departure from Tomsk, we entered into a vast birch forest—so vast, that it covers all the central region of Siberia. These trees, which in our country never come to any great size, and which we lookupon as some of the most attractive ornaments of our woods, acquire here enormous proportions, but at the same time, I must say, to the detriment of their gracefulness and beauty. In growing old, the bark of their trunks loses its bright pale colour, which we are accustomed to admire, and looks dirty beside the snow; and then, when they advance to decrepitude, it becomes quite black. The most noticeable peculiarity of these forests is that they have never been cut and turned to account. Such an enormous mass of trees allowed to perish is a thing unheard of in France. Here and there may be seen huge trunks, lying on the ground, or leaning against others, ready to fall, or broken off half-way, attesting the violence of some passing cyclone or the destructive power of lightning. Enormous birds of a black or deep blue colour, known generally by the name of cock of the wood, roost on the branches of these venerable trees, and then may be seen huge owls, all white, turning lazily their flat faces towards the passing traveller, regarding him without moving, with the utmost indifference. Here, perhaps, more than elsewhere, is the domain of the strange and fantastic, and it requires little effort of the imagination to people it with all the fanciful and grotesque creations of mediæval poesy.

We continued a long time travelling on through this primeval forest, whose mournful silence and savage grandeur disposed me to muse rather than to talk. My companion also seemed to have his thoughts engrossed with something weighty; he was thinking of the future—of his parents and friends he was shortly about to join, and, what I suspected, of Miss Campbell, who had preceded us on this road. Mine, on the contrary, were rather of the present and the past ; I thought of the long distance I had already glided over in my sledge; then my soul wandered from the dark, mysterious forest to the unveiled, prosaic steppe, and finally went astray in bewilderment at the immensity of this trackless space.

The surface, over which we were now moving, was becoming gently undulated, then little hillocks succeeded, and at last the monotonous flatness disappeared.

This reminded me very forcibly how indifferent we become in time to the endlessly repeated or continued scenes of everyday life, however congenial they may be, and how readily we wake up to even a bare consciousness of them after a merely moderate interval of their interruption.

Since leaving the Ural, I had been travelling from six to seven hundred leagues over a country absolutely flat, presenting some interesting features, it is true, and not least the marvellous effects of light; but for all that, it was void of variety and life; and this novel contrast revealed how dear to me were the animated and changing scenes to which I had been habituated, and how little, from too much familiarity with them, was I then able to appreciate them.

During the two days preceding my arrival at Krasnoiarsk, I passed several hills, sometimes abrupt and sometimes gently sloping, and then again others rising to a peak high over valleys, that appeared to me very deep. My eye was at last interested in some change, and could be attracted on the right by reflections of sunbeams from the snow mantling striking diverse objects, or repose on the left in the impenetrable shadows. In short, the monotony had ceased, and to the fatigues of the journey had succeeded the excitement of locomotion, the variety and life of picturesque nature. At the view of this change, I vividly felt how lonely and joyless had been the dead, changeless plain I had left behind me. I thought of the poor inhabitants of Omsk, who look over the steppe so often with longing eyes. It is not from a love for this immense plain, it struck me at the time, but from some vague instinctive hope, of which they are barely conscious, though sensible, to see beyond in the horizon the dawn of something brighter than this endless uniformity, and perhaps in such a hope they find their happiness.

On approaching Krasnoiarsk, the hills rise higher and higher, and become at last, around the city, imposing mountains. We made our entry into this capital of the province of Yenisseisk on the 29th of January at three in the afternoon.

As the day was closing in, I went out at once, and was able to contemplate and admire the picturesque position of Krasnoiarsk. It is built on the banks of the Yenissei, which meanders between two very high mountains, whose precipitous sides give more striking depth to the valley they overhang. It is in a hollow at the foot of one of these towering cliffs that the city is built.

My first impression of Krasnoiarsk was therefore favourable. It seemed to me that the inhabitants of this city, having such a fine view of nature before their eyes, ought to be gayer and more inventive than those I had just left behind me, and my expectation in this was not at all deceived. The society of Krasnoiarsk, from another cause, however, might have been thought to be sedate and little disposed to hospitality, since it is composed of Polish exiles having little reason for mirth, and some gold-seekers, to whom anything else than heavy glittering nuggets seemed unworthy to occupy their thoughts.

I did not look up my letters of recommendation to make use of them till the following day. During the night, a singular and continuous noise hindered me from sleeping; it was the harsh clank produced by the violent shock of two pieces of metal. The sounds were repeated at quick intervals, and seemed to move from one part of the house to the other. Conjectures as to the cause of this strange noise increased the excitement of my mind, and contributed to keep me awake. The explanation came in due course. It appears that the Siberians here have borrowed from the Chinese this strange custom of warning thieves by this ceaseless jangling noise, that the inmates are on the alert within, and that any attempt at a burglary would be discovered and frustrated. Lucky thieves who thus know which house to avoid and which to pillage! Happy families who have their ears charmed and their slumbers lulled with such music!

The first visit I made at Krasnoiarsk was to a *savant*, M. Lovatine, who has three remarkable collections: first, a collection of objects in stone—prehistoric stone implements of the aboriginal inhabitants of Siberia, which are quite similar to others I have seen in other countries of Europe and in other parts of the world. M. Lovatine seemed quite devoted to this study, and I could well understand the pleasure it gave him without being able to enter into it myself. Next, there was a numismatic collection, on which he gave me some interesting explanations. I will mention, among others, a medal struck under Peter the Great, the possession of which at that time exempted compliance with the general regulation prescribed by this great reformer to his subjects under which they were obliged to divest themselves of their beards. Those who wished to indulge in the luxury of this hirsute appendage were made to pay very dearly for it; for the Emperor was not indulgent towards those who did not approve his orders: and thus a tax on a luxury was obtained. The form of this medal is rather singular, having a piece nipped out on one side like a barber's shaving dish. The third collection was geological, to which Siberia, with its abundance and variety of minerals, could contribute largely. In connection with this M. Lovatine had some political theories, the principal of which was that the further south people lived, the more turbulent and the more difficult to govern they were, and that Southern lands were better fitted to despots.

The Siberians dance a great deal; balls are frequent and very elegant, but they rarely take place in private houses. In every city there are generally two clubs, the club of the *noblesse* and the club of the *bourgeoisie*, to either of which one is invited to come and pass the evening, according to his position, the *noblesse* being composed of the Government functionaries and the other of traders.

The day after my arrival at Krasnoiarsk, I was invited to a ball at the club of the *noblesse*. The functionaries not being numerous in this city, they had invited a few of the commercial class, and particularly some Polish exiles. A ball of convicts seemed to be something incongruous, but it would be an error to suppose that the Poles exiled in Siberia are at present all ill-treated, and that they while away their time in weeping for their beloved country. When I come to Irkutsk, I shall have occasion to speak more fully of the fate of the Polish exiles in Siberia. But now, here in Krasnoiarsk, nearly all were members of good society. Their political opinions, like those of all Poles I have met, are, it is true, extremely advanced. They had not only taken part in their war of independence, but had been nearly all implicated in insurrections beyond the borders of their country; they admired our violent French demagogues, and found excuses for our Commune; but in spite of these preposterous opinions, which ignorance of contemporary history and distance from the scene of action may have rendered excusable, I found at Krasnoiarsk a society of enlightened Poles and perfectly well-bred men. As they formed the majority, the ball was quite *à la mode polonaise*, and it is a kind of dancing, in my opinion, that ought to survive for ever their lost nationality. One never steps as in an ordinary walk. To proceed from one side to another, it is necessary to adopt the step called *la polonaise*, rather difficult to master, it is true, but which is, undoubtedly, very graceful. The consequence is that in these dances, and especially the *cotillon*, there is a liveliness that is never seen in our salons, considered the gayest in the world. As another proof of the knowledge which the Russians and Poles have of our language, I will merely observe that here, in this city lost in the depth of Siberia, when the ball was over and we sat down to supper, a very numerous party spoke no other language than French.

It is here at Krasnoiarsk that one begins to

become acquainted with a few gold-seekers. I was first received at the house of M. Rodosvenny, who, although enormously rich, is here considered simply in pretty comfortable circumstances, on account of his neighbour M. Kousnietzof, whose mines are considerably richer. After I had seen at Irkutsk and at Kiachta the houses of Nemptchinof, Bazanof, and Trapeznikof, the luxury of M. Kousnietzof did not appear to me more extraordinary; but knowing the cost of living to a simple traveller in Siberia, and having gleaned some information as to the cost of an elegant house in stone and ironwork, materials that have chiefly to be brought all the way from the Ural, I was lost in wonder at this palace of M. Kousnietzof, quite as extensive as our grand Parisian mansions and almost as luxuriously appointed.

To mention two or three luxurious follies in which these great proprietors of gold mines in Eastern Siberia indulge, I will refer to the cigar ash receptacle— where the smokers in the salon drop the ends of their cigarettes, according to the Russian custom, after a meal—composed of a pure nugget of gold, worth sixteen hundred pounds sterling, and just in the rough state in which it had been found in the mine. The Czar has permitted, in an exceptional case, M. Kousnietzof to retain possession of this nugget in his house, on account of the rarity of such a godsend. The proprietor of this treasure did not omit to inform me that having had this precious receptacle for thirty years, he had lost not merely the sixteen hundred pounds sterling, but also the interest, two thousand four hundred pounds, and, consequently, this luxury had cost him four thousand pounds. Having gratified my curiosity by weighing in my hands again and again this enormous nugget, I took leave of this opulent family.

The next day, we found ourselves again seated in the sledge with a journey of two hundred and fifty leagues to accomplish without a break, at the end of which we hoped to find ourselves in Irkutsk, the capital of Siberia.

CHAPTER XI.

KRASNOIARSK TO IRKUTSK.

Social position and education of the country people and citizens—Uselessness of Siberian forests—Journey to Irkutsk—A pack of wolves—Cleanliness of the villages—Congelation of the Angara—The government of Irkutsk—The college—The prison—The fire brigade.

WE started along the banks of the Yenissei, and, on our way, observed some idlers amusing themselves by line-fishing. Their process is rather ingenious: they break a hole through the thickness of the ice, and down this aperture they drop one end of their line, the other end being attached to a little apparatus gliding on two skates like a sledge. The fish, on taking a bite, sets this little vehicle in movement, and thereby announces its simplicity. The remainder of the performance does not differ from that practised everywhere, and in the end, as in many other ingenious contrivances, cunning fattens on credulity.

A short time afterwards Krasnoiarsk disappeared from our view, and then we found ourselves again amid the most complete solitude. The bosom of the Yenissei was really a fine sight; it occupied the whole valley, which, notwithstanding its width, appeared very narrow and profound, on account of the imposing height and steep sides of the mountains forming precipitous cliffs along the shores. In presence of this grand scenery, it was amusing to hear the tinkling of our puny bells, agitated beyond measure to announce our important passage over the rough ice; it was a contrast of the ridiculous and the sublime. We went on in this way till we reached the end of the ravine, cut by an abrupt turn of the mountain, when we left the river and continued our course eastward.

During two days again, the country presented nothing to interest the traveller.

On wending our way through these pine forests, extending from Krasnoiarsk to Irkutsk, the trees of which are gigantic in height and circumference, I supposed that they would furnish to the Russian Government, whose property they are, considerable sums; but I was mistaken. The Government allows the peasantry to cut timber for their own use, but forbids the felling as a commercial undertaking, and particularly the exportation of this wood, even for its own account and profit. But the reason for this strict regulation is a mystery. The Mongols, for want of timber, make use of dried camel dung as a combustible, as the Egyptians do in Egypt. The Chinese and the Japanese have barely fuel enough to warm themselves; the Russian Government therefore might find a large source of wealth in these forests, as well as in the coal beds of the island of Tarakai. There may be valid reasons for neglecting them, but of what nature they are I have no conception.

One night, when the moon was pouring down a flood of silvery light over the snow-capped trees, we caught sight of a pack of enormous wolves, about two hundred yards ahead of our sledge. "Wolves!" cried out our yemschik. "Wolves!" I repeated, getting out my revolver and laying it down in readiness, whilst I hastened to charge my rifle, which, since the perilous escape near Omsk, I had taken good care to have at hand, and not stowed away in some inaccessible baggage. I had everything ready, and was waiting for a serious attack. Being the best armed, I knelt down beside the yemschik, with my revolver, rifle, and a formidable big knife. The driver and Constantine both smiled at me, and wondered what feat of prowess I was about to perform; and their smiles, evidently, proved their experience. As soon as the wolves heard us, they all stopped, turned round attentively to face us, then watching us a few moments without moving, and finding we were drawing nearer and nearer, turned and trotted along the road before us in the same direction like a pack of tired hounds after a good day's run.

All praise be due to the lively imaginations of poets and artists, to whom I was indebted for a thrilling emotion! I waited with panting breath for the realization of a long-cherished exciting dream, and to become an actual participator in those soul-stirring adventures I had pored over many a time with fascinating delight in the *Magasin Pittoresque*, the *Habitation au Desert*, and many similar books, with all their fantastic illustrations; and now, instead of a thrilling scene of real life, I had to content myself with a spectacle provokingly prosaic; for there was nothing more to interest me than the tame march of fifteen fine wolves, fleeing calmly at our approach, at a respectful distance before us.* It seems that the depth of the snow in the forest impeded their free course; and the poor beasts, consequently, preferred taking their way over a road well beaten down, even by their enemies. We kept each other company, in this way, for a mile or more, when the approach to a village, with which probably they were well acquainted, though not to the extent of the door latches, induced them to turn off, and plunge into the depth of the forest. Doubtlessly, discretion more than fear was the motive for this movement in avoiding conflict with a force directed by the superior intelligence of man. What better proof could there be of their sagacity and just appreciation of valour?

The villages and adjacent properties of the inhabitants are all enclosed together. The Emperor accords to each village a certain portion of land, which is generally equally

---

* See note 4.

distributed among the male inhabitants. In the forest beyond the enclosure, they have the privilege of pasturing their flocks, but are not permitted to till the land. This apparent liberality has not much significance, on account of the immense extent of territory to the small number of inhabitants; the little plots, in comparison with the non-utilized soil, are mere minnows to a whale.

But this act of graciousness, on the part of the sovereign towards his subjects, is not admitted by the Baron de Haxtäusen, who maintains that the system had its origin in the natural development of the mode of life of the Russian people. "The Russian people," he observes, "were nomadic, and among the nomads, there is no defined individual property—the land was utilized in common, for the benefit of the whole tribe. Then gradually these nomadic hordes, established in Russia, ceased their wandering life, and became fixed in permanent dwellings, and it was at this time that the pasturages became constant, instead of temporary, as they had formerly been. Then agriculture advanced, in combination with the pastoral occupation and breeding of cattle, the ordinary life of the nomad. But the old element of nomadic life was too deeply implanted in the existence and character of the people: it was a part of their nature, and could not be eradicated. Pasturage was carried on in common, and agriculture likewise was carried on in common; all the members of the tribe or of the community laboured together, and the harvests were gathered by their united work, and then distributed in equal parts to every member entitled to share. In Servia, Bosnia, and Sclavonia, villages may be seen having the same principle in practice. In Russia they have improved this organization without, however, attacking the principle. They have divided and distributed the land in equal parts between all the members of the commune, not in perpetuity, still for a period of many years."

The same author shows all the advantages of such an organization: " It develops in the people the desire to remain in the country; it fortifies the sentiments of homogeneity, community, fraternity, and justice, and love of the country and attachment to a place. It strengthens the ties of family life, and in

Russian villages, contrary to what is seen elsewhere in Europe, a great number of children are a source of riches."

I have just mentioned that the Siberian peasants have the right of felling timber in the forests for their own use. Since they obtain their fuel gratuitously, they maintain in their houses an extremely high temperature. In elegant houses, constructed of stone, neither stoves nor open fires are there seen; the heating apparatus is between the two surfaces of the walls. The heat is transmitted by contact with the surface, and uniformly from the ceiling to the floor. This process has not the disadvantages of our system of closed stoves, and does not affect the head with carbonic gases diffused in the room. In the peasants' dwellings the wooden walls do not admit of the same arrangement. In the centre of the habitation is raised a construction of stone or baked clay, and this, heated at the centre, throws off the heat from the surface.

The women seldom leave their houses; therefore they are loosely clad in no other garment than a kind of dressing gown, like the fellah women of Lower Egypt. This scanty clothing seems strangely inconsistent with the snow on the ground out of doors. So soon as the outer door is opened, the hot air in the interior, charged with vapour, becomes suddenly condensed, and forms a cloud around the entering visitor for a few moments so dense as to prevent his recognition. He makes his appearance, as in the stories of "The Thousand and One Nights," wrapped in a cloud that has accompanied his passage, and which is dispersed so soon as its mission is accomplished. At one of the stages where I stopped, between Krasnoiarsk and Irkutsk, the heat was so great in the travellers' room, that in spite of the season, a butterfly, some flies and mosquitoes were fluttering and buzzing around in full vigour.

I was informed that in this part of Siberia the mosquitoes form very formidable enemies to battle with. Constantine told me that during summer here one is obliged to put his head into a sack, and in spite of this precaution, is often a victim to these terrible insects. Madame de Bourboulon, who had passed there in the month of July, mentions these pests, and that travellers, and even horses, have perished from the effects of their stings.

After having been on the road eight days and eight nights, we penetrated at last into the valley of the Angara. This river proceeds from Lake Baikal, passes on to Irkutsk, and finally loses itself in the Yenissei. As the difference of level between Irkutsk and Lake Baikal is considerable, though the distance is only fifteen leagues, the current of the Angara is extremely rapid. The frost, consequently, does not succeed till very late and after great efforts in arresting its lively course. Nowhere else in Siberia does this struggle between a running stream and hibernal congelation—the arrest of motion and the transmutation of force—produce effects so remarkable. In order to become master of its adversary, the frost attacks the running water at first from below, beginning at the banks. It is in the bottom of the Angara and contiguous to its shores where the first solidifications appear. Whilst these are spreading, little blocks of ice form and float over the surface, and then these two opponents gathering force, seek to join their efforts in a simultaneous and combined attack.

The river threatened to be stopped in its course struggles desperately. Pursued and being closed in, it rushes frantically onwards, and if it could thus break loose and carry its floating enemy with it, it would perhaps gain the victory. But these restless foes, increasing in size and number, maintain their hold and menace further retreat. The Angara has then recourse to a supreme effort. It changes suddenly its ordinary course, and leaping in torrents over the barriers, spreads out over the valley, scattering its force in every direction, as if routed by its implacable enemy. It is then that the victory is decided. The waters that have overflowed are speedily overcome so soon as they relax in their retreat, and are transfixed and congealed in an instant; and those also, retreating along the course of the river, weakened in body and velocity, yield too in their turn to a terrific conflict of eight or ten days' duration, and there, at last, repose under a white shroud, vanquished and still, leaving monuments of might that strike the eye with astonishment.

These mountains of ice are heaped up on this river to a great height. They rise irregularly, sustaining huge, jagged blocks awry on their mass of contortions, presenting the most singular and grotesque spectacle of unaccountable disarray. The whole width of the valley, on account of the inundation, was filled with this startling convulsion of nature. When my eye first rested on this wondrous sight, the sun was shining through one of these blocks, pitched on one of the highest pinnacles, and produced a natural pharos of dazzling splendour; here its rays, refracted from innumerable icicles, coloured the valley with rainbows, or there fell on minute crystals of ice, formed from the watery vapour floating in the air, and with these depicted two luminous columns, that rose and melted away in the depth of the sky. It called up in my fancy that sun palace sung by Ovid, sustained by shining columns. Had the poet, when he described these marvels, already known the bitterness of exile in hyperborean lands? had he, like me, contemplated this strange phenomenon in the same latitudes?

My arrival at Irkutsk was accompanied by these grand fairy scenes of light, so startling in their novelty and splendour.

This city is built at the confluence of three rivers, the Angara, the Irkut, and the Küda. Instead of being perched on a commanding hill, like most other Siberian cities, it is, on the contrary, placed in the centre of a circus, formed between the mountains, that opens only on the side formed by the course of the Angara. Irkutsk is inhabited by the representatives of a great variety of races, who there retain not only their physical type, but their costumes and manners; the aspect of the streets is therefore extremely picturesque. At every moment you pass on the way Buriats, Tungus, Samoyeds, and then Chinese and Mongols, and Mantchous and even some Kirghiz, who have been permitted by the Government of Omsk to quit their districts. But I will first present to my readers the Russian society of Irkutsk and the Polish exiles.

The Russian society here may be classed under three categories: the functionaries, the gold-seekers, and the clergy.

At the head of the first is the governor-general; he represents directly the Emperor in the whole of Eastern Siberia; he has, moreover, full power, and his acts are controlled by the Emperor alone. This appellation might lead one to suppose that this supreme dignity must be enjoyed by a military man ; but this is not the case. In Russia, in every department of the civil administration, there are grades, corresponding to those in the army, having the same designations. At the time of my sojourn at Irkutsk the governor-general was M. Silegnikof. I presented to him my recommendations from St. Petersburg, and he received me with all the usual hospitality of a Russian functionary and the courtesy of a great lord of this country. He appointed a young man attached to his office to accompany me wherever I wished to go or to be admitted.

Immediately after the governor-general in the hierarchy comes the military governor, who is not only commander of the troops, but in a certain way Minister of War of Eastern Siberia.

The first establishment in Irkutsk I visited was the Lyceum. There is only one thing to remark there, especially when free instruction is the order of the day. There are no professions in Russia free and independent. Not only are engineers, as in France, Government officials, but also the lawyers and doctors. The Government gives them appointments according to their rank, just the same as to other servants of the Crown. People that are rich, it is true, are accustomed to pay for the services they receive, but a poor patient may call in any medical man he pleases, without being under any obligation to give him the smallest recompense. The Government, contrary to the general opinion, is desirous of extending instruction; fearing, however, the consequences of an education absolutely gratuitous, it enters into an engagement with its young subjects desirous of instruction, by virtue of which it gives at first to the student the necessary instruction, and this accomplished, the latter, in return, is bound to give to the State five years of gratuitous services in the profession he has chosen. If the young man, however, does not succeed in passing his examination, he is obliged to enter the army to acquit himself of the debt of five years' service. As this gives undoubted facilities in the choice and adoption of a career, it seems to me a very ingenious organization.

Then I visited the prison, but it was a sight

to make me shudder. To be bound not only to Irkutsk, but to a prison in Irkutsk, is something terrible. When I had contemplated the features of these assassins and robbers, faces no longer human, where, instead of intelligence and sensibility, nothing but rage and thirst for blood is seen depicted, my commiseration speedily vanished. I lamented only one thing here, and more than elsewhere, and that is the pernicious Siberian habit of keeping the windows always closed; certain chambers of this prison were tenanted by seventy or eighty prisoners without having ever been ventilated!

Before leaving this lugubrious sight, my guide took me to the chamber of political prisoners. There were about fifteen men there, nearly all very young, thrown together without any consideration, and probably for long periods. Let us drop a veil over such unhappy beings. Be it far from me to hurl any reproach at the Czar; for, considering the enormous responsibility that rests on him, he must necessarily be driven sometimes to cruel decisions, if there be no other means of securing the tranquillity and welfare of his people; but for all that, I tremble on thinking of the victims of these arbitrary judgments, of these young spirits, similar to those misguided lights led astray by guilty revolutionists in France, and who so innocently imagine that true liberty is to be found elsewhere than in respect for law and order. If justice could be ubiquitous and reach every culprit, I know which class of offenders would predominate in the prison of Irkutsk and in our *bagnes* also.

The wives of these prisoners are allowed to follow their husbands into Siberia; they are even maintained at the expense of the State, but, at the same time, are subject to a severe regulation, that obliges them, in the first place, to renounce all rights proceeding from their birth or social position. And in the next place, they can neither send nor receive letters nor money but through the hands of the authorities. Besides, they see their husbands only at fixed times and places. If the husband is exiled for life, the wife can under no pretext return to Europe. The local administration has the right to exact from them the most humble services, such as the scouring of floors, and similar work.

On leaving here, I went to see the barracks

of the firemen. This corps, second in utility only to the police in every country, is of the first importance in Siberia, where the towns are built of wood. An observatory surmounts each of the four barracks of firemen at Irkutsk, and a watcher is constantly there to give the first alarm of danger. My guide begged the commanding officer to give me an example of the turn-out. He at once pulled a bell, and ordered the hoisting of certain colours at the top of the observatory. In two minutes, neither more nor less, sixteen horses were found harnessed to an engine and accessories, and appeared in the court where I stood; and five minutes afterwards, three other engines arrived from the other establishments. The rapidity with which fire spreads in wooden buildings requires the promptest resources, and these are furnished by sixty-four horses bringing four engines fully equipped to the spot in five minutes.

CHAPTER XII.

IRKUTSK.

The gold miners—Their luxury; their wealth; their wives—A few words about the clergy, and the code of religion—The Polish exiles—Travelling maniacs—A dinner en famille.

I HAVE spoken of the gold-seekers of Eastern Siberia, and given an instance of their prodigality in the wonderful cigar ash receptacle of M. Kousnietzof. The miners of Irkutsk are still more extravagant in their fancies, favoured by their greater wealth.

But it is not every gold-seeker that makes his fortune; many even ruin themselves when they have insufficient capital for the preliminary outlay and this is not rewarded with immediate success. It is rare in Siberia to search for gold in a comminuted and commingled state, and I doubt if the Siberians would trouble themselves about so hungry a pursuit, at least to their eyes, accustomed to see it in a less occult form, and their hands to test its weight more sensibly. What they here call a gold mine is a place where great glittering nuggets of pure gold are found here and there in the sand, and where they may be extracted without having recourse to expensive machinery and chemical manipulation. The greatest accumulations of ingots, though not at the surface, are generally at about two or three yards below, and where they may be won by open workings.

The machines, the most commonly used for separating the gold from the sand, consist of large inclined cylinders, into which the auriferous sand is thrown and there submitted to the action of a stream of water. The sand, comparatively light, is soon carried off by the force of the water, whilst the heavy gold falls to the bottom of the apparatus. The smaller particles of gold, too light to resist the force of the water, and that are consequently carried away with the sand, become the property of the labourers.

The most prolific mine in all Siberia yields *annually* one million two hundred thousand pounds sterling ! It is the property of three proprietors only, MM. Bazanof, Nemptchinof, and Trapeznikof. The latter, who is a young man, displays beyond the others the extravagancies of a millionaire that would seem senselessly lavish in Europe, but which in this country of exaggerated profusion do not appear to exceed the bounds of reason. Finding, one day, the road too muddy for the wheels of his carriage, and being desirous of taking the air, he had carpets laid down the whole length of his drive. When he came back, he had the satisfaction of regarding his carriage and horses perfectly free from the serious disfigurement of a spot of mud!

This example of luxury unhappily is imitated in a feebler degree, though perhaps not with a feebler spirit, by the labourers, the effects of which are the more frequently felt when they come home in autumn to their wives, who have barely a crust left, and not a kopeck to receive from the pretty round sum earned by their devoted partners during their summer's work at the mines. M. Silegnikof, the governor-general, has tried to remedy this evil. An official nominated by him makes it his duty to hold in deposit the sums gained by these workers in the mine, and to restore these savings to them on their arrival at the village. The first year this functionary received in deposit from the miners of a single commune fifteen thousand roubles. But since this organization had not been generally accepted by those for whose benefit it was designed, and had been resorted to, it was supposed, by a small number only, it may be calculated that the depositors had gained thirty-five or forty thousand roubles, from £3,500 to £4,000. If these thoughtless miners would amend and acquire habits of economy, they could easily become rich ; but these poor deluded creatures imagine that the mines are inexhaustible, and it is by no means clear to the engineer that the Government is not equally credulous.

To show to what extent gold is squandered at Irkutsk, even among the humbler classes, I will give an instance. On arriving at this city, I found I could not open one of my trunks, in consequence of having lost the key during my journey, and sent for a locksmith, thinking I should have to pay about twenty-five or thirty kopecks, such as I should pay in

Paris. This locksmith said to my messenger: "How much will your master give me for this job?" "Two or three roubles, I suppose." "Then I am not going to bother myself for such a trifle." I was therefore obliged to break open my trunk.

Perhaps it may be asked why these lucky mine proprietors do not go to St. Petersburg and Paris, to get something more tempting for the big nuggets they have found, and how they manage to gratify their exaggerated wants in the cheerless depths of Siberia. They prefer, no doubt, to be seen and known by every inhabitant of Irkutsk and Kiachta, than to pass unnoticed in the immense crowds on the banks of the Neva, in Hyde Park, or in the Bois de Boulogne. I have already given an idea of the cost of the merest trifle in this land of gold mines, void of all industry. In spite of the exorbitant price of everything, indeed, perhaps for that very reason, these nabobs indulge their fancies in building immense palaces in stone, and in filling their apartments and conservatories with orange trees, banana trees, and all kinds of tropical plants, which have been dragged half across the globe at an enormous cost to furnish insipid fruit or sickly flowers and some visible sign of wealth.

They must have grand pianos from Erard's, or the best makers of St. Petersburg. They give magnificent dinners of a hundred *couverts*, where sterlets, brought alive from the Volga, are served in the most *recherché* style beside the choicest wines France can produce. They mantle themselves in sable, beaver, and furs of blue fox, or even blue fox feet, a luxury that involves the purchase of four or five hundred of these animals; they shackle their fingers with heaps of rings. In short, their living, their clothing, their display in general, are in complete and constant opposition to this precept of Montesquieu, which they all certainly ignore: "En fait d'apparat, il faut toujours rester au-dessous de ce qu'on peut." And then their wives, whose lot, doubtlessly, the reader will be curious to know. It is very simple, at least from the husbands' point of view, for they are necessarily neglected. Being absorbed with this passion for aggrandizing their fortune, the pressing need of satisfying ridiculous vanities, of what importance is a wife beside a nugget? what are the soft whispers of love beside the delicious music of the gold in the cylinder? During the summer all the lords are at the mines, and their ladies are left to themselves at Irkutsk. During winter the former are still absorbed in their business, and when they are not these votaries to feverish pastimes are at the gaming table, watching the fall of the dice, and their wives are still forgotten at home. There is one thing very curious, and which in this instance, though subordinate to a dominant passion, proves, perhaps, the strong spirit of contradiction in woman. The ladies of Irkutsk manifest in no way a taste for the costly vanities of their husbands. They are ambitious of assimilating themselves to the ladies of St. Petersburg; they learn foreign languages, translate Jules Verne or Paul Féval into Russian, and imagine themselves to be endowed with high mental qualities. But the instances are rare where these gifts and accomplishments exist in reality and not simply subjectively in the imagination. These need too active an alimentation to develop and fructify in so petty a colony as Irkutsk. Mischievous intrigues and *cancans* form the staple of all the gossiping that usurps the place of conversation. It would not be too severe to apply to the society of this city the judgment of Madame de Maintenon on the society of Versailles : " Nous menons ici une vie singulière. Nous voudrions avoir de l'esprit, de la galanterie, de l'invention, et tout cela nous manque entièrement. On joue, on bâille, on ramasse quelques misères, les uns des autres, on se hait, on s'envie, on se caresse, on se déchire."

The gold mine proprietors at Irkutsk and— to finish with these instances of the flaunting of stupendous riches—the tea merchants of Kiachta, gratify their passion for exciting envy and wonder, in a way by no means displeasing to themselves nor to the recipients of their roubles, by considerable donations to the churches.

At Irkutsk, the convent of St. Innocent is the principal object of their attention. It is quite *haut ton* among these millionaires never to set out on a journey before having made a gift to the monastery. Therefore, in a few years, a stupendous church rose over the tomb of the old Siberian metropolitan, where immense wealth is now heaped together. The rivalry between this convent of St. Innocent and the cathedral of the village of Kiachta is not at all inactive, and is certainly to the advantage of both.

At the time of my visit, the latter bore the palm. It is singular to find, in the midst of a group of houses which in France would be considered a mere hamlet, a church where the altar is of massive silver and gold, and where the *iconostasis*, hiding the sanctuary from the eyes of the congregation, is sustained by fourteen columns in rock crystal. These columns, each three feet high, are formed with three blocks of crystal a foot high and a foot in diameter, and are very remarkable.

I will not enter on the subject of the orthodox religion, inasmuch as it is not a question exclusively Siberian. Certain writers in France have given a deplorable aspect to the manners of the Russian clergy. I am far from assuming that the conduct of all the Greek popes is irreproachable, for I have myself seen several of them tippling and committing even greater faults, but it would be rash to deduce from so limited a number of isolated facts general conclusions. In what hierarchy shall we not find lamentable exceptions? The Russian clergy are distinctly divided into two classes: the secular priests, who may marry, but to whom are closed the high ecclesiastical honours; and the regular priests, who live at first in the convents, to rise afterwards to bishops, archimandrites, and metropolitans. The first live retired in their villages, bringing up their children in their homes in the fear of God and with a taste for the ministry. The second are restrained in their youth by a severe rule, and later by the respect for their high dignity.

The most striking feature at the first view of the orthodox religion is its organization as a political power. In this empire of supreme despotism, the Church stands out, *imperium in imperio*, an actual republic. This republic, it is true, is subject to the authority of the Emperor. It is his will and pleasure to ratify or not the decisions arrived at, but all the questions are nevertheless discussed by a synod, held at St. Petersburg, composed of all the metropolitans. What could be more ingenious than this system of complete dependence, enjoying the appearance of liberty? It would be interesting to conjecture what would have been the state of Europe if the Catholic Church had been thus subjected either to the emperors of Germany or to the kings of France. Frederick Barbarossa would probably have made himself master of the world; he would, in any case, have driven the infidels, not only out of Europe, but from Western Asia. It is also equally probable that, without the authority and wise foresight of the popes, the great revolution of the Crusades would never have occurred, and that Europe, then subject to civil authorities more bellicose than warlike, more chivalrous than politic, would have been swamped with the flood of Islamism, against which the popes alone were able to raise a barrier.

If the Russians, in adopting the religion of the Greek Church, had not inherited its inconsiderate hatred of the Roman, they would certainly recognise this great work of the popes. Unfortunately, human motives of action absolutely prevent every Russian from embracing the Catholic or any other religion. Intolerant laws punish with the severest penalties the converted, and especially those who attempt to convert others.*

The Czar, invested in the eyes of his people with an imposing sacred character, profits by the inviolability it confers to dominate over the revolution whilst accomplishing the reforms he deems efficient. Liberty of conscience is therefore a long way from the advent of its enjoyment in Russia. May the Emperor, in preserving the respect of the masses, suffer no derogation in the eyes of his enlightened subjects, who are already, as I have seen everywhere, breaking loose from all ties of religious faith, and who may well one day claim by force, and before all other rights, the liberty to embrace a new faith.

This religious intolerance is painful to all, and especially to the peoples recently subjected to the authority of the Czar, to the Polish exiles for example, who, although sincerely Catholic, are compelled to bring up their children in the orthodox faith. Alas! since the insurrection this grievance is only a part of the sufferings these poor wretches have had to endure.

* See note 5.

They have, at first, been led on foot, with their hands bound behind their backs, to the spot of exile that has been assigned to them in Eastern Siberia: some to Irkutsk, and these were the most favoured; others to Yakutsk, or the island of Tarakai, known to the Russians by the name of Saghalien, or to Kamtchatka. Many perished on the way, as may easily be supposed, and those who were strong enough to brave exhausting fatigues were, on their arrival, thrown into the gaol, to keep company with thieves and assassins.

It is singular to remark a circumstance that clearly shows the fetishism with which the Emperor's person is surrounded; these assassins at the gaol look down on their comrades from Poland with the utmost disdain, and often refrain from speaking to them, under the pretext that the crime of the Poles was rebellion against the Czar. The Russian assassins have therefore, it seems, a kind of conscience when it involves a question of conspiracy.

The Polish exiles I saw here were submitted, for five years, to the same treatment as the other convicts. They were numbered in red on the back, and for a mere trifle were punished with the strait-jacket, or twenty strokes with the rod. During five years, they passed the winter in this prison I have mentioned, sixty or eighty thrown together into this horrible chamber without air and almost without light, and the summer in working at the mines with an hour's rest during the day and a nourishment barely sufficient.

Their lot, happily, is now much better: except the liberty of going beyond the limits of a certain assigned district, they enjoy the same advantages as other Russian subjects. They constitute, besides, at Irkutsk, it must be admitted, the most intelligent part of the population; and receiving no assistance from the Government, they gain not only their living, but sometimes even a fortune. They are medical practitioners, professors, musicians, or theatrical performers. Some even, who in Poland formed a part of the aristocracy, have taken to opening shops, where they sell all kinds of objects from Moscow, St. Petersburg, or Warsaw, articles which, brought from such a distance, fetch a high price and reward their sellers with a considerable income. One among these enjoying the title of count, and for this reason unwilling to follow from the beginning the general example, was, at the time of my visit, reduced to the humble occupation of cabdriver.

Among the exiles I saw at Irkutsk, I will mention, in particular, M. Schlenker, because I met at his house certain persons already introduced to the reader. This gentleman was occupied during the day in selling linen, cloth, *pâtés de foies gras*, wines, in short the usual wares of a bazaar, and in the evening, after the hours of business, forgot all his affairs to become in his *salon* a perfect man of the world, such as he had formerly been in Poland. He took in the *Revue des Deux Mondes*, many French and Russian periodicals, played the piano, and had ingratiated himself with the military governor, with whom he often went hunting; he was, in fact, a man very well informed, and, having seen and read a great deal, could speak in the most interesting manner on many subjects.

To remember the date of any occurrence, it was calculated from the year of his condemnation to hard labour. Nothing seemed so odd and sad at the same time as to hear this distinguished man say calmly: "I am sure that such a thing took place at such a time, because I know it was so many months after I was thrown into gaol."

And yet, fully alive to all these severities, I must abstain from recriminating too readily: in the first place, because I learnt on my arrival in China that fresh liberties had been accorded to the Poles in Siberia; and next, because chastisements undoubtedly severe have probably preserved Russia from great evils and the necessity of making the punishment still heavier if a more lenient one had been found insufficient. We must not be blind to the fact that the Poles are not always patriots, and when they demand liberty, it is not always on the side of law and order. How many Poles were there not mixed up in our Commune of 1871, and how many other lawless adventurers shut themselves up in Carthagena with the last Spanish insurgents! Russia, that has these smouldering embers of insurrection on its hearth, has been more fortunate than France in preventing them from bursting into a consuming conflagration. But I cannot help pitying their sufferings, and especially the sufferings of those who, with all their faults, possessed in the highest degree the noblest of God's gifts—an intelligent head obeying the dictates of a tender heart.

Having been invited to dine one day at M. Schlenker's, I met there, to my great delight, the whole of the little caravan with whom I had made my entry into Siberia. Mrs. Grant, Miss Campbell, M. Pfaffius, Madame Nemptchinof and her son Ivan Michaelovitch, had just arrived at Irkutsk, and were about to start again for Kiachta. Constantine was also among the guests, as well as a young Russian, M. Isembech, an intimate friend of M. Schlenker, who was a complete personification of those travellers in perpetual movement of whom I have spoken.

"You are going to Japan," he remarked, "and I hope to have the pleasure of meeting you again there, for I am going there shortly." "Come with me," I said; "the pleasure of the trip will be doubled." "That will be impossible: I must go to-morrow to the Amoor river, and shall not have returned before a fortnight." "I intend to remain longer than that here, and shall have no trouble in waiting for you." "But before going to Japan, I must go to St. Petersburg for a fortnight." "Then we shall see each other no more." "Why not?" "How long then do you take to go to St. Petersburg?" "Twenty-three days and twenty-three nights." "And you do not stop on the way?" "Four hours at Omsk only, in order to transact some business with the governor-general. In two months to the day, I shall be here again; it will be the time of the breaking up of the Amoor, and then it will take hardly a month to get to Japan; I shall therefore want three months to accomplish the whole, and will meet you on the 25th of June at the Hôtel d'Orient in Yokohama."

This hardy mercurial traveller had little else than his winged feet, for the whole of his luggage consisted of some linen and a black dress coat.

The black coat, in fact, is here, even in the morning, the costume *de rigueur:* from ten in the morning to noon, the residents pay and receive visits; at half-past two they dine, always in formal dress; in the evening, at the theatre and supper, the same coat, and one is obliged to retain the whole day this inconvenient garment.

Our party at M. Schlenker's passed off most gaily. We recalled the incidents of our journey between Kamechlof and Tumen, the fear we indulged in on parting, the tender reminiscences that followed; and when dinner was over, our agreeable host sat down at the piano to accompany the sweet voice of Miss Campbell. Thus ended a delightful evening.

What delicious enjoyments are obtained through a few days passed thus, in the interval of a long arduous journey! One muses over the adventures of the road already passed, and speculates over those that may come; the novelty of the scene and situation, the society and topics of conversation, the fresh direction to one's habitual current of thought, the total change, in short, of one's surroundings, brings an exhilaration that nothing else can supply. Every incident during these days seemed to gleam serenely in a sunshine of poesy. And yet, when sensation becomes thus more keenly alive to the enjoyment of congenial society, we see in the persons around us but the brightest sides of their character, and the hour when the disillusion comes we have already parted each on our way. How many perfections of this kind have I not met with on my route which, unhappily, I have never had the chance to live with more than one short day!

> " S'il est des jours amers, il en est de si doux !
> Hélas ! quel miel jamais n'a laissé de dégoûts ? "

CHAPTER XIII.

ATTEMPT AT ESCAPE BY A POLISH EXILE.

Why the Polish exiles cannot escape—Narrative of a attempt by M. Bohdanovitch—Encounter with a bear—Sanitary arrangements in Siberia—Wolf hunts—A blue fox—Different values of furs—A few words on the passion for displaying riches.

AFTER the description I have just given of the mode of life of M. Schlenker, the question may occur to the reader why the Poles banished in Siberia do not avail themselves of the quasi-liberty they enjoy at present to effect their escape. They could not, it is true, return to their own country, but no doubt they would like to live in some other land of their free choice, where the climate would be less rigorous than that of Siberia; such a favour, however, would not be accorded.

But Siberia is barely inhabited, except in the neighbourhood of the great highway that leads from the Ural to the banks of the Amoor and to its mouth. All the rest of this vast territory, known under the same denomination, —excepting, perhaps, that also along the banks of the rivers,—is nothing but an immense wild tract of steppes and forests.

The frontier, moreover, that separates the Russian empire from the Chinese, is formed of a chain of mountains very elevated and by no means easily accessible. And even if the poor fugitive should succeed in reaching the frontier, he would find himself afterwards in the great desert of Gobi, without shelter, without provisions, and even without a passport, necessary for admission into China proper; he would then have to dread being placed under restraint there, infinitely more terrible than exile in Siberia or, what is more likely, extradition, followed by a fresh incarceration, and then perpetual exile to Kamtchatka or the island of Tarakai.

On arriving at Irkutsk, I was indisposed, in consequence of the fatigue from so long a journey in a sledge. During these long, gloomy days,—for nothing is more depressing and painful than illness far away from home and in loneliness,—I frequently had a visit from a Polish exile, who, having formerly lived in France, was delighted to come and chat away an hour about the places where he had passed his youth, and the happy days he had known during his eventful and troublous life. His name was Bohdanovitch. Our long conversations were a great solace, and an effective means of dispelling *ennui*. Among all those of his nation exiled in Siberia, he was the only one who seemed doomed to suffer perpetually from the bare exile itself. He spoke of the prison with the utmost indifference; he repeated many times that he would willingly give all his fortune to see France again, especially Poitou, where he had lived a long while, and whence he had set out to join in the Polish insurrection to please his father, who urged it against his son's will.

As soon as he was free in Irkutsk, such a man could not resist the temptation to regain France. He gave me an interesting narrative of this attempt, which I will reproduce in his own words:

"Two of my countrymen and myself had resolved, in the month of April, 1871, to reach China through the forests. We succeeded in procuring rifles, though it was forbidden by

BURIAT MAN AND WOMAN. (p. 246.)

[To face p. 224.

the regulations to carry arms.* We obtained also some enormous knives, and having everything in readiness, we attempted, at the end of May, to put our project into execution. At this time of the year, unfortunately, the thaw that has set in is still too recent, and the land consequently too swampy, to enable any one to accomplish forced marches. We were therefore compelled to return to Irkutsk, hiding our rifles under our clothes, fearing every moment to be suspected and searched.

"Our absence did not escape observation, but, since our project of fleeing from exile was not for a moment suspected, one so rash being here regarded as impracticable, we were simply reprimanded. After this time a numerous patrol was moving all over the country, and so discouraged us, that we thought many times of abandoning the enterprise. Our courage, however, in the end prevailed over our apprehensions, and during one fine night in June, we slipped out of the town unobserved.

"All the provisions we had with us were contained in wallets, which we had to throw over our shoulders; for the thick, obstructed

* See note 6.

woods of Siberia, untrodden by the foot of man, are not, except by wild beasts easy to penetrate. We easily crossed the Angara, making the ferrymen believe we had come from Yakutsk, and were on a pilgrimage to the convent of St. Innocent.* Hardly had we landed on the opposite bank when we left the road and plunged into the depth of the forest and, as soon as we thought ourselves sufficiently advanced to be safe from any possible pursuit, we made a halt, to pour out our pent-up feelings on the exciting and momentous event. Tears of joy were trickling down our cheeks; we believed ourselves free at last!

"Never shall I forget," he here passionately exclaimed with all the bitterness of the recollection, "this moment of enthusiastic joy, which, alas! was followed by such bitter grief! We made vows to each other of mutual aid and protection till death, and continued our forced march towards the south.

"During the first few days, we were in high spirits, and leapt with joy. When night came, we regretted a little, it is true, not being able to find some shelter, even if it were only

---

* See note 7.

under a tent, to repose from the fatigues of the day. Our meal, however, composed of provisions still fresh, restored our strength, and cheered us with the hope of overcoming all difficulties in soon reaching the frontiers of China. How many enchanting dreams had we then, how many alluring projects of the future, which, alas! for my two poor companions, were to change into a painful and premature death, and for me into a banishment which I now believe to be perpetual!

"When the first few bright days had passed, we were assailed with a heavy and continuous rain. Our clothing was very soon wet through, impeding thereby our march; and the fire, which we could only succeed in lighting every evening after repeated failures, was far too feeble to dry them. Sleeping thus, wrapped in our wet clothing and without shelter, we found on awaking, in the morning, our limbs so benumbed with the cold as to seriously impede our movements. In this state, fever was not long in making its appearance, to threaten the remnant of our strength and render us incapable perhaps of further movement; and to aggravate the whole, our stock of provisions was sensibly diminishing. To eke out this scanty supply as well as possible, we had recourse several times to hunting, but this had the disadvantage of retarding our march.

"And then the animals did not often show themselves in these regions, except the cock of the woods, which could only be brought down on taking the greatest precautions. As soon as the hunter perceives one of these birds, he immediately stops short, and remains completely motionless till the moment it begins to crow. As soon as it commences to make its note heard, its senses of hearing and seeing, which are very quick and acute, are, in a certain way, diverted and, as it were, bewildered. This is the moment to advance. But if the hunter, in his progress, should make the least movement the instant the crowing has ended, he is unerringly discovered, and then loses all the expected fruit of his patience. We were able to get near a very great number of cocks, and, luckily, had a good shot sometimes; but it was necessary to sacrifice many precious hours merely for a single bird.

"Near the banks of a little river, which we were obliged to cross by swimming—an incident that very much increased our fevers—we fell in with a few hares, half yellow and half white, a colour determined by the season.* But all these resources in no way compensated for the fatigue we had to endure in marching, the weakness from the fever, and the discomfort from the rain; and when we arrived at the foot of the chain of mountains that marked the limits of Siberia, our limbs began to fail so much that we could hardly manage to drag ourselves along. We had brought with us a large quantity of brandy, and a little of this stimulated us to further exertion, but the stock of it was diminishing rapidly, and when we had arrived about half-way over the chain of mountains, where all vegetation but grass disappeared, and with bare inhospitable rocks before us, the remainder of this and our other provisions was exhausted.

"My two unhappy companions, feeling themselves unable to proceed any further, were obliged to lie down to rest before making any renewed attempt, but alas! it was the final one, for they rose no more! I watched two days over their cruel sufferings, striving

---

* See note 8.

to soothe them and to allay their agony, and at last heard their dying murmurs and consoled them with my tears. With my enfeebled arms, I buried them in the best way I could, and I made two rough crosses, which I planted over their graves. Then, when this tragic end of my comrades was consummated, and feeling all the horror of my loneliness and the impossibility of continuing to live beyond the forest without provisions, I took the resolution to retrace my steps, and to attempt to get back to Irkutsk, in spite of the dungeon cell, in spite of the renewed sufferings, that would infallibly await me there.

"But before quitting this fatal spot," exclaimed this poor fellow with a shudder of abhorrence, "I heaped maledictions on the crests of those mountains that rose before me to dispute my way like a battalion of Russian gendarmes, and there shut out from my longing eyes the sight of some other land that was to give me life and liberty."

"But this empire," I replied, "is not so hard, since it has not punished you for your rebellion."

"That is true," he said; "they have not

only pardoned me on account of the sufferings I had endured, but they have even given me more liberty, knowing full well," he added sorrowfully, "that I should never renew so rash an attempt."

I then asked him what miraculous intervention enabled him to get back alive.

"I was indebted for that to my robust constitution. I managed to live upon roots, and gum from the trees, and that little red fruit with which the Siberians make a sort of wine.* I was so weak that I could march only very slowly, but the rain having ceased, I began to gain a little more strength, notwithstanding the miserable nourishment I was forced to subsist on. When I arrived as far as the little river I mentioned, I took it into my head to construct a small raft, that I might float down the current, and thereby diminish my fatigues. I succeeded, after a great deal of trouble, and when I ventured on this contrivance, I believed I was saved.

"But a few days after I had been borne along in this fragile craft, seeing a favourable spot to obtain a fresh supply of roots and fruit, I attached my float to the shore, and went in

---

* See note 9.

search of them. I had not gone far before I found myself in presence of an enormous bear of appalling ferocity. My rifle was on the raft, and I had only my big knife at my girdle, and although I had heard of the artifice practised by the Siberians in slaying this ferocious beast, I shrank at first from exposing myself to such a danger. I tried to flee, but it was useless; I began climbing up a tree, but the bear followed me everywhere. At last, seeing no escape and no means of avoiding a struggle, I summed up all my courage as a last expedient, and stood facing the beast, waiting the onslaught with a firm foot, determined to sell my life as dearly as possible. The formidable brute came up with a slouching gait, and rose on his hind quarters to seize me with his forepaws; just at this critical moment, according to the Siberian mode of attack, I leapt suddenly into his forepaws, as one human being would into the enthusiastic embrace of another and, raising instantly my right hand, plunged my knife into his back to the right of the backbone and to the depth of the heart. My grim antagonist fell dead on the spot, and with a few scratches on my shoulders I escaped.

"I then retraced my steps, dragging my prey after me, and re-embarked in my craft with a good stock of provisions. At last, I delivered myself up at Irkutsk to the Russian authorities, who pardoned me, as you are aware, thinking probably I had been sufficiently punished, and convinced, as they doubtlessly were, of my intention to live henceforth peaceably in this city in expectation of my ultimate liberty."

It may be seen from this touching narrative how difficult it would be for exiles to escape. Should even the greatest precautions and the most ample stock of provisions allow them to remain concealed a long time in the forests, the abundance of snow in winter would drive them out on to the beaten road, the only practicable way, and consequently into the hands of the authorities. An evasion, therefore, similar to the one just related to me, should, in order to succeed, be accomplished in three months, and that would be quite impossible.

During my stay at Irkutsk, M. Silegnikof, the governor-general, was recalled to St. Petersburg. Several people, whose acquaintance I had made, left also and preceded him on the road in order to warn the authorities of all the villages they passed to level the snow on the way, so as to spare this old gentleman the fatigue of so long a journey. When these had left, M. Bohdanovitch was my most constant companion.

In Siberia, during winter, none of our methods of cleaning the streets or removing sewage can be employed. Refuse of every description is collected by carts, and deposited over the bed of the river. So long as the frost lasts, no inconvenience is felt from this accumulation: but, when a thaw begins, it is quite otherwise; then the air is pervaded with a noxious odour, and the water, for a week afterwards, is not potable. The Siberian towns are, therefore, very unhealthy at the breaking up of the frost.

During my sojourn at Irkutsk, a quantity of enormous birds constantly alighted on the fetid ice of the Angara, and M. Bohdanovitch and I went into the country, to get a shot at them on their way to this repulsive spot, where they were accustomed to feed.

Then we made excursions together in the

neighbourhood of Irkutsk, and visited some country houses, the residences of some of the millionaires I have mentioned, and particularly that of M. Trapeznikof. When a district is covered with forests and watered with three. rivers, it is easy to create charming residences. Our French taste, with such elements, would have worked marvels. Although the architect of M. Trapeznikof has not made the most of every natural advantage, it is, nevertheless, remarkable: lakes and cascades, mounds and slopes, are there in abundance, and these, though fashioned by the hand of man, form in the centre of a fine forest, a charming seat.

As soon as the new governor-general, M. Solachnikof, made his appearance, I was invited to join him in a wolf hunt in the neighbourhood of the Siberian capital.

These animals are allured, a day or two previously, by the carcases of horses or oxen; then, when they are well assembled at their repast, people come in large numbers, and gradually enclose them by forming a circle. It was very exciting sport to bring down this kind of game, so soon as they slipped through the circle of hunters. I have never seen in any menagerie wolves to be compared with these Siberian beasts; they are of formidable height and size. But when they are dead, it is almost impossible to approach them, on account of their odour and the swarm of repulsive parasites escaping from their fur.

We were returning very lazily on our hunters, that had taken us, by the road to Lake Baikal, to the rendezvous in the forest, when a little animal, to which my attention was directed by one of my fellow-huntsmen calling out: "*A blue fox!*" could be seen darting away among the trees. "A blue fox!" they all echoed, to warn the party of huntsmen at a little distance behind. A shot was heard; the animal limped, and then took its course. "Hit!" exclaimed the governor-general, giving directions at the same time to the Buriats, who, being equipped with long snow skates, could run the animal down. It was soon bagged; and the next day I received, as a present, the carefully prepared skin of this little quadruped, that had occasioned more excitement than a pack of wolves.

As I have already mentioned, a man is

appreciated in Russia according to the fur he is wrapped in. The most highly esteemed is doutblessly the fur of the blue fox, still only that portion of it that covers the paws. They do not here even wear any other part of the skin of this animal; but these furs, without these choice bits, are exported to France and England, to the great joy of the ladies of these countries, who, if their husbands are disposed to be obliging, esteem themselves very elegantly attired in them, though in Russia, and particularly at Irkutsk, their wearers would be regarded by connoisseurs as eccentric and ridiculous. And the relative value here will show the difference of appreciation, for the whole fur, except that of the four paws, fetches no more than the latter; that is to say, from two pounds fifteen shillings to three pounds five-shillings. But the difference in appreciation in Russia is much more remarkable if it be borne in mind that certain cloaks of blue fox, so highly esteemed throughout this empire, composed entirely of the fur of the paws, are estimated at from one thousand four hundred to one thousand six hundred pounds sterling the cloak, the whole of which could be swallowed up by a few moths and their progeny in the course of a few weeks!

The next highly esteemed fur in importance is the beaver; consequently very few cloaks are seen of these skins.

And then comes the sable, which is frequently employed for mantles, at least for the cuffs and collars. These luxurious-looking furs are lined inside sometimes with commoner ones; I have even seen at St. Petersburg some that were not lined at all.

The jenotte is in the fourth rank. This is very much appreciated by travellers, because it is considered elegant, though the value may vary considerably according to the length and thickness of the hair. I have seen jenotte cloaks so low as ten pounds, and others estimated at about fifty pounds. As the difference of value cannot be appreciated at a distance, a man is considered elegantly clad in this fur even when the real value is very little.

The marten is generally placed in the fifth rank. This is the fur of an animal quite different from the sable, though it is frequently erroneously designated in France as *martre zibeline*. The fur of the sable is dark-coloured, very thick, and a little rough to the touch; that of the marten, on the contrary, is light yellow, and feels like a silky down.

Finally, the fur the least esteemed, and consequently the least worn by the *beau monde*, is the Astrakan. In certain cities, such as Moscow and Irkutsk, where the fashion is scrupulously respected, it would be even considered very venturesome to appear in public clad in this fur. The Astrakan cap, especially, is regarded with the utmost disdain; and if certain Russians have adopted among them, as a principle of conduct,—and I have heard it from their own mouths,—never to stoop to salute persons *on foot* in the streets, they would recoil, no doubt, with repugnance from the idea of being acquainted with any one so low as to wear Astrakan.

Other furs, such as sheepskin, bear, and elk, are used by the untitled and obscure million. But, since they are the warmest, the rich do not disdain to wrap themselves up in them when travelling, thinking at the same time to give these cloaks a more elegant appearance by setting them off with collars of beaver, fox or jenotte.

The extraordinary price of fur from the paws of the blue fox is apparently no criterion of its value in the eyes of the *beau monde*, but rather the result of a conventional caprice of millionaires, who find in this object a convenient badge and mode of displaying their riches; for none, perhaps, but the very opulent and the prodigal, would be disposed to pay so dearly for no other object than to shine as a star of fashion. And this presumption appears to be well supported by the fact that the Russians keep this special luxury for themselves, and very naturally, because the English and French would not appreciate it as a sign of wealth, and, consequently, would pay no higher for it than the price it would command merely as an article quite *à la mode*.*

But this foible for parading riches is by no means limited to the expedient of wearing this exquisite fur. Pearls, for instance, have long been a favourite medium, and this the Muscovites seem to have derived from the Romans. Two hundred years ago, "the Russian grandees," says Lord Macaulay, "came to court dropping pearls and vermin."

---

* See note 10.

There is, however, no reason to suppose that "dropping pearls"—with or without their concomitants at court—was a mode of parade ever held to be *haut ton;* for a continuous dropping of "unwinnowed" pearls would have involved a burden as intolerable as the Muscovite chasuble. But if this particular art of display did not bloom into a fashion, it was at least a device full of meaning and "movement." For was not an abundance of riches not only dropping, but "running over," suggestive of super abundance—a sign of something *de trop?*

The spectator gazes in wonder, no doubt, at the many bushels of precious pearls garnered under glass cases at the monastery of Troïtsa; but the spectacle after all is a mere Dutch picture of still-life in comparison with this nacreous shower—this *tableau vivant* at court, as full of life and flowing riches as the golden drops falling animated at the feet of Danae.

This epigram of Lord Macaulay's is so amusingly droll that the reader will excuse one more digression. Pascal has said: "Si le nez de Cléopâtre eût été plus court, toute la face de la terre aurait changé."

Now, might not the portentous difference in

the history of the world, implied in the release of Antony, have been as readily brought about by the Egyptian siren if, instead of dissolving and drinking her precious pearls to detain her lover, she had dropped them at his feet *rigoureusement à la russe?*

A nose "plus court" might not have changed in either sense " toute la *face* de la terre," for,

> Mark Antony led astray by the nose *so long*,
> His head, when *by another turned*,
> Would still have gone wrong;
> For Egypt's queen—in spite of a nose too short by far—
> Might then, by his own have led him,
> "As asses are." *
> If women always *will* lead the World by the nose,
> It goes better than pulled by the ears,
> They suppose.
> But ears less long it needed; not a nose so small,
> To have otherwise changed the *face*
> Of the world at all.

But as history records no precedent that would deprive the Russian grandees of the honour of having been the originators of the "courtly" mode, Cleopatra obviously could not have imitated it in all its integrity. The Muscovite nabobs, however, like Sir Thomas

---

* " And will as tenderly be led by th' nose
　　As asses are——"　　　　　　*Othello.*

Gresham, might imitate Cleopatra. The rich citizen of London, to rival the Spanish ambassador in a magnificent dinner, is said to have pulverized a pearl of the value of fifteen thousand pounds, and then drunk it in a toast to his sovereign. And these nabobs, since they are decidedly of opinion that prodigality is the most intelligible mode of displaying riches, might win more applause by likewise drinking their pearls in bumpers to their czar, or, perhaps, in throwing away their pearls and drinking their wine, by changing the Siberian custom of flinging champagne on the road before horses to actually casting their pearls before swine.

CHAPTER XIV.

IRKUTSK TO LAKE BAIKAL.

The natives—The Olkhonese—Shamanism—The Buriats—The Tungus—The Samoyeds—The Carnival at Irkutsk—Pablo—Adieu to Constantine—Another perilous night on the ice of Lake Baikal.

AMONG other races, natives of the island of Olkhon are occasionally met with in the streets of Irkutsk. The shores of Lake Baikal, before the Russian conquest, had served, from the most remote times, as a place of banishment for the Chinese. They called this country, in their figurative language, the land of long nights. Some of the descendants of these exiles still exist in these parts, and inhabit a little island on the western shore of Lake Baikal, called Olkhon. Many of these islanders still adhere to the ancient Shamanic religion, from which sprang later, they say, the widely spread worship of Buddha. Not much is known of this religion of Shamanism beyond the fact that they worship a supreme being, who resides in the sun.

Müller, in his important work on Siberia, refers to the superstitions of these people, and gives some account of their ceremonies.

"The Shamanists," he says, "fear especially ghosts, and the resentments of the dead, to whom, when alive, they had done some injury. To charm away the evil that these may visit on them, they leap on certain days over burning faggots.

"They believe in sorcerers who predict the future for them.

"On fête days, they assemble round one of their priests, who beats on a drum and recites prayers, whilst an acolyte sprinkles the faithful with milk and alcohol."

One of these old Olkhonese, one day, related to me a legend, concerning the sect inhabiting the Trans-Baikal. In order to understand this legend, it is necessary to know that there is a great difference of level between Irkutsk and Lake Baikal, and that all the waters of this lake are held in check at the highest by an enormous rock, at the opening of the Angara. If this rock, they say, were to break away, all the water in the lake would rush down in a single wave, annihilate Irkutsk and, carrying everything before it with frightful rapidity, would form a vast sea filling the valley of the Angara. The Shamanists believe that the souls of the departed are transported on to this rock after death. The top of this rock where they sojourn is so narrow and precipitous that they are seized with giddiness, and being close to the turmoil and rush of the flood into the Angara, they are so bewildered with it, that they can hardly keep their footing. If they succeed in doing so, it is because they have been good and have the grace of God; if, on the contrary, their life has been wicked, they are drawn in and lost in the rushing waters. The roar produced by the impetuosity of these waters of the Angara, is, according to these people, nothing more than the united lamentations of the souls who fear losing their balance. It is true, that at this spot, the mountains give a striking echo from the uproar of the fall. I do not suppose I should be suspected by my readers of belief in the supernatural, and yet, I could easily fancy, in this imposing concert of nature, that I was sometimes listening to human voices from the Shamanic rock.

But the Buriats, a people who originate from the neighbourhood of Nertschinsk, to the west of Irkutsk and Lake Baikal, and the Tungus, who pretend to be even better horsemen than the Kirghiz or the Mongols, are the most numerous of these divers races seen at Irkutsk. These two races have become so Russianized in their habits, and almost in their costumes, that it is unnecessary to say much about them. Neither the nose, nor the cheek-bones, nor the forehead is prominent: one can then easily realize to himself the appearance of the profile of a Buriat. The women redeem the plainness of their faces by a figure generally very fine, and an extraordinary smoothness of skin, which has become proverbial in Siberia. Now and then some Samoyeds are seen, a race formerly nomadic, but who begin, I am informed, to people Yakutsk, just as the Buriats and the Tungus have established themselves at Irkutsk and around there. The clothing of these people of the extreme north, is made of the skin of the reindeer, ornamented with little bits of cloth, generally of bright red. I have seen several of them clad in seal skins, and skins of other amphibious animals: but these it seems, are the poorest, for this kind of fur is cheap and not warm.

There is no race more degraded in the characteristic of regarding the women as inferior beings, and among no other, are they treated so harshly as among the Samoyeds. "They are annoyed and oppressed," says Pallas, "even in their own tents. The men put a pole behind the fire-place, facing the entrance, and the women are not allowed to stride over this. This stolid, idiotic race of beings believe that if the wife should unluckily pass within, the night will not end without a wolf coming and devouring one of their reindeer. To be in a delicate state, euphemised as 'interesting,' is considered degrading. During this period, women dare not eat fresh meat; they are obliged to be satisfied with less palatable food. They are particularly ill-treated at the period of their *accouchement*. They are obliged to make their confession in the presence of the husband and the midwife: to declare whether they have been unfaithful to their lords, and if so, to name the paramour. They

SAMOYED PEASANTS.

take good care not to deny the imputation, fearing, that in doing so, they would have to endure cruel sufferings at the critical moment: on the contrary, if they are guilty, they avow their peccadillo with perfect frankness. Their confession, however, is attended with no inconvenience. The husband merely goes in search of the accused, and exacts from him some slight compensation."

The revelry of the carnival at Irkutsk is quite different from that in France: it consists principally in continuous promenades in large open sledges, around which are suspended numerous bells: the harness also is covered with bells wherever they can be attached. But this is not sufficient; enthusiasts violently agitate others in their hands to produce a more effective resonance; and, by way of accompaniment, that nothing may be missing, children and the lower classes, who, in ordinary times, slide rapidly on their skates over a little wooden causeway, covered along the houses with frost-hardened, well-beaten snow, flit past in greater numbers at these rejoicings, in which bells again are not wanting to complete the stirring hurly-burly.

My windows unhappily were towards the principal street, where this abominable jingling was ever present. Never did I feel so much the want of a little quietness, as during these ten days of carnival, than which nothing better could be contrived *à porter le diable en terre.*

Never did I salute with more pleasure the arrival of Lent.

During the first three days of this period of penitence, a singular custom permits the coachmen attached to the house where you are staying to pay you a visit and demand a present. I, being a foreigner, was unduly honoured in seeing defile before me, in the rear of the drivers of the establishment, all the *isvostchiks* or cabmen that had profited by my fares during my sojourn.

In order to escape from these importunities, I went to the convent of St. Innocent, where I witnessed the solemn ceremonies at the commencement of Lent.

During this period, the saint is the object of the highest veneration. His tomb is not only opened, like that of Saint Sergius, but his body, unlike that of the patron of Troitza, is not covered with any shroud. The body is wonderfully preserved, except in the colour of the skin, which is quite black. A pious legend informs the inhabitants of Irkutsk, that this colour arises from the sins of the faithful, that have quitted their souls the instant they kissed this precious relic. I have often witnessed the enthusiasm with which the devotees of Eastern Siberia embrace the venerated remains, and the contentment they feel, in removing with their nail or a pen-knife, a splinter of the coffin, the remainder of which will soon in this way inevitably disappear.

It may be noticed also, in many other practices, how very sincere and profound is the piety of the Siberian peasant.

I have observed, many times, with what scrupulousness, these simple folks keep the fasts that are prescribed. It occurred to me sometimes, on days marked for penitence—and there are many—on arriving at a posting stage, to ask, from curiosity, if I might be provided with some food. "It is Lent, Monsieur," they invariably replied, "We can take nothing but tea to-day: we have no bread even, to offer you." It seems strange that a Government which has known how to employ so well a religion as a political power, should not modify a regulation so enervating to a poor population needing more food and vigour.

Before leaving Irkutsk, I visited the museum to see the collection of fossil mastodons, remains that abound in certain strata in Siberia: and now after having been hunting with the Governor General several times, and enjoyed myself here for six weeks, I thought it time to resume my journey.

M. Pfaffius had promised to inform me, from Kiachta, when a caravan of Russian tea-merchants would form there, in order to proceed to the south of China.

"Try to find an interpreter," he told me, "in order that you may never be at a loss to understand these tea-merchants, and they will undertake all the necessary arrangements for your journey among the Mongols and the Chinese." But I had no choice to make, for only one man presented himself to accompany me from Irkutsk in the capacity of interpreter. He was honest to the backbone, I admit, but his history must have been curious. He claimed to be a French subject, but he was born in Constantinople, and had never seen France. He was known by the Spanish name of Pablo, and his passport was written in Greek.

He pretended he could speak all the languages of the Levant, Russian even, as well as Italian and French; but to make myself intelligible I was frequently obliged in speaking French to interlard my phrases copiously with Italian, Russian and even German words. He had, however, the faculty of making himself so well understood to everybody, by aiding his jargon with signs, that I considered myself very fortunate in my acquisition. This genius of elucidating the signification of his words by gesture, was evidently derived from his former profession, which was that of a player of pantomime in a circus.

Although this Pablo was now in my service, and was ready to do anything I required, Constantine wished to help me, for the last time, in my preparation for departure. Though our characters were opposed in many features, one does not separate with indifference from a travelling companion, who has been by your side day and night in a journey of fifteen hundred leagues, and especially when the parting is to be for ever. My young fellow traveller moved me by the uneasiness he manifested on my intended passage over the Lake Baikal. He begged me again and again, for three days, not to expose myself to this danger, but to turn the lake on the south; and, as a proof of the interest he took in my safety, in order to dissuade me from my purpose, he brought to me, when I was about to start, the chief of police, who assured me that the Government had taken no precautions this year for the safe passage of the lake along the ordinary track.

On receiving this intimation I yielded, and, alas! I had much cause to regret my determination, or rather, having modified it, as the reader will learn; for prudence, under these circumstances, did not secure safety. Pablo was overjoyed at my decision. His exaggerated fear of the dangers, and his solicitude for his personal comfort, had inspired me from the first with uneasiness regarding our future relations.

I set out from Irkutsk on the 20th of March, at one in the morning. Constantine came into the sledge, between Pablo and me, and kept me company as far as the opposite bank of the Angara. This short trip was a kind of *résumé* of the three months we had just passed together, and, when we warmly pressed our hands for the last time, we were equally deeply moved by the parting. He had before him the prospect of an indefinitely prolonged sojourn at Irkutsk; and I, a turning point in my adventures; for the phases of my journey, without him, were about to change completely.

When Constantine was gone, I was not much disposed to begin a conversation with Pablo. I could see no utility in this man, except the prospective one in a future still very uncertain, and, as I then knew Russian well enough to accomplish alone a journey in Siberia, his presence for the moment was anything but agreeable.

The country we were passing through was very picturesque. Mountain after mountain covered with pine trees, producing in the dark a singular and striking effect with their sable hue, seemed to become loftier and more imposing on either side, as we advanced. I was now all the better situated for a full view of nature, being no longer cooped up in the canopied sledge of Nijni-Novgorod. The one I had now was entirely open.

At daybreak we came in sight of the Baikal. As the constant and violent winds in these parts sweep the snow from the surface of the ice, the frozen surface assumes nearly everywhere a bluish tint resembling, in some degree, smooth water.

The scene was striking. Deep, deep below our feet, reposed a bay, in the hollow between two chains of mountains, and then, beyond, the lake suddenly expanded, and extended as far as the eye could reach, to the right and left and before us, its endless ice-clad bosom.

"There at last is Lake Baikal!" I exclaimed with enthusiasm at the startling spectacle. "Monsieur," said Pablo, jumping up from his seat, "Has no one, indeed, then told you? You must call it *the sea;* otherwise it will be angry and cause some evil."

This superstitious fear revealed, at once, the character of my new companion. Ignorant and of weak intellect, he had borrowed something his fear of the unknown had prompted him to accept as a revelation of truth regarding it from every people he had lived among, probably with other characteristics. He had thus, I think, acquired from the Germans and Poles, a little melancholy, from the Turks and Arabs, servility, and from the Russians and Siberians, superstition; for his honesty and simplicity, I think he was indebted to none; it was native.

We descended to the shore of the lake by the south side of the mountain. The snow, that had melted during the previous day, had frozen again during the night, and formed at every step a slippery surface.

The sledge shot first in one direction, then in another, in a way to inspire terror, for the route was constantly on the ridge of a precipice. We were, indeed, sometimes so near it, that the yemschik had his legs, now and then, dangling over the brink of a frightful abyss. A sharp clack of the whip, keenly felt, once gave a sudden diversion to the direction of the vehicle, and we were then miraculously saved from an appalling pitch. The yemschik, unfortunately, was over-confident, and, when we had escaped so far, was too ready to believe that all danger was over. He had neglected, just before our arrival at Baikal, to give a required sudden turn to the sledge by administering a sharp cut to the horses, consequently, one of the skates of the sledge passed over the edge of the road, and the entire vehicle and its contents instantly followed; we rolled out, Pablo and I, into a ditch five or six feet deep and almost perpendicular, with all our rugs and baggage huddled together; a pretty kettle of fish. Pablo was too terrified to speak, and probably thought it unnecessary to remind me of the anger of the sea, now only too evident.

A short time after this *divertissement*, we arrived at a stage. The posting master dissuaded me from continuing my journey by land. "The road is not only longer," he said, "but, as you well know, dangerous also, whilst the ice over the Baikal is extremely thick and not likely to crack anywhere." We followed his advice, and trotted away over the ice.

Pablo was most ridiculously alarmed every time I spoke of *Lake* Baikal, and tried to charm away the danger by saying, "The sea! the sea! the sea!" On the right and left towered, over our heads, the two chains of mountains I have just mentioned, closing in the southern extremity of the lake, whereon we had just entered; and before us nothing could be seen, as far as the horizon, but interminable ice.

I was completely lost in admiration of this striking spectacle—such a one, I think, as is unequalled in the whole world. I had seen nowhere else in Siberia so complete an example of the mighty, triumphant effects of winter as this remarkable sea of ice, and in no other part of this climate, have I seen light assuming such magnificent warm tones. In the evening particularly, when the crests of the mountains were glowing in a rich rosy light, the surface of the Baikal, then in the shadow, reflected an intense blue, similar to that of the Mediterranean. The tint would have led me to fancy that I was off Nice or the coast of Algiers, if the sledge, and especially the accompanying noise of its gliding, had not too forcibly recalled me to actuality. This appalling noise, of which I have already spoken in my first sledging experience over the Oka, was much more disquieting there, however, from the depth of the hollow below. Here it contributed to the wonder of this unique scene.

The night was just closing in when we arrived at the eastern extremity of the bay. We went on land merely to dine and change horses. When we started again on the lake it was nine in the evening, and our yemschik, instead of keeping a north-east course to take us towards the Eastern coast, went due north towards the centre of the lake.

Since I had already many times noticed the deviating course of the yemschiks over frozen water-ways, in order to avoid some pit or some spot of doubtful solidity, I did not at first ask any question, but turned round from time to time, to take a view of the retreating land. Thus occupied, it sank lower and lower in the horizon and at last disappeared altogether from my eyes. The aspect was now completely changed; it seemed as if we were on the open sea, for whichever way we turned we could see land nowhere.

I must confess that, at this moment, I began to feel ashamed a little of my boasting indifference a few hours before. This desolate, inhospitable tract now made me shudder, and I seemed to be all at once inspired with a servile respect for this terrible Siberian sea I had so inconsiderately insulted from the shore.

It was so very seldom I had had occasion to complain of my yemschik during my journey, that I was not by any means disposed to find fault in this instance; I was not long, however, in perceiving he was intoxicated, and that he had led us astray.

The surface was becoming gradually more and more irregular; a few loose or superimposed blocks were distributed here and there; presently these became not only larger, but more numerous. This rough broken way, in fact, was threatening, for the further we advanced the more our new difficulties increased, and it was not long before we were obliged to make our way along mountains of ice surpassing even those of the Tom and the Angara.

The view of these ever-augmenting obstacles would have been disquieting in the open day; but now, in the depth of the night, without an outline of land ever so shadowy to be discerned, and in complete ignorance of our direction, the situation was indeed alarming.

I began questioning the yemschik, from whom I could get no intelligible answer, even with the aid of Pablo.

The poor creature was besotted—paralyzed with fear.

Bewildered with the utter helplessness of our perilous situation, the idea that came uppermost to my mind was, to ask on which side we could the soonest gain the land. The yemschik held out his hand towards the west. I understood at once the fearful plight we were in and was resolved to wait on the spot the break of day. The driver refused to stop at once, making light of my apprehensions, but the matter was so serious that I was obliged to draw my revolver and, presenting it at his head, threatened to shoot him on the spot if he advanced a step further.

It was now about one o'clock in the morning, and I could distinguish nothing but mountains of ice surrounding us on all sides. On examining these hillocks, I found they were built up with blocks of about a foot thick.

It was clear, therefore, that we were suspended over the depths of the lake by a floor of no greater thickness. Could we count on this even, throughout, to bear up the weight of the laden sledge and horses?

Between life and death, between the air we breathed and the bottom of the lake, there was only one foot of ice. We were not only far from human beings, but far from the land they inhabited. Who, indeed, knew where we were? Who would be thinking of us at this hour? Who at this distance could have heard our last desperate cry of anguish, at the moment when the ice, breaking under our weight, would open and then close over us for ever?

The mournful moaning of the wind in the hollows of this glacial wild, interrupted by the ominous cracking of the ice, like the low booming of cannon in the distance, broke the silence of the night. Never had I felt the weakness, the ignoble insignificance of man in a manner so complete and absolute: never had I been so sensible to the imposing might of Nature. I held my breath with awe, for man, in her august presence, would be as meaningless as a grain of sand or the poorest worm, if the moment should come when he was doomed to be crushed in the terrible exercise of her power.

When day at last appeared we could realize,

still more forcibly, the danger of our situation. There were fissures scoring the surface in every direction. Pools of water in certain spots showed that the congelation in these parts, from some cause or other, had only been partial. On seeing myself exposed to so many snares, I understood why the Russian Government had declined assuming any responsibility this year for the safety of travellers. I was abandoned to my own resources and trembled for the consequences, for it seemed I was lost.

In the dilemma I knew not what to do; it was necessary to move, for we could not escape danger by remaining still any longer, and I gave orders to the driver, mechanically, as if spell-bound, to take his course towards the rising sun. We started; no way could have been more prudently selected and, in spite of the element of danger still existing, be more replete with thrilling interest. We were obliged to make many long windings to avoid some crevice or other. The yemschik, now having recovered from the effects of his intemperance, seemed desirous of redeeming his fault, and went on foot alone in advance in peril of his life, to ascertain the thickness of the ice. We were obliged to pull up now and then, as we came near an ominous long streak of rippling water that barred our passage. If we ventured to brave it, we decided to draw back on our steps a little way—*reculer pour mieux sauter*—and then, with the whip smartly applied, aided with wild gesture, hallooing and screaming, to give a mad rattling pace to the horses, we cleared, in the twinkling of an eye, but not without a sickening horror, these treacherous crevices gaping to devour us.

About eight in the morning we caught a glimpse of the land, and soon after it plainly came into sight. The further we advanced the thicker and more reliable the ice became, and every step now raised our long depressed spirits, till, at last, all further danger disappeared. Then, strange to say, I felt a pang of regret to quit the Baikal: for though I had blenched with fear, I could not forget that I was still standing on enchanted ground.

At last, at ten in the morning, I entered the village of Slernaia to reflect over the twenty-two hours passed on Lake Baikal—the most stirring and momentous adventure I have experienced in all my travels.

CHAPTER XV.

LAKE BAIKAL TO KIACHTA

Observations on Eastern Siberia and its inhabitants—Their dream of Independence—Motives that might contribute to independence—Example of the Chinese—The Yakuts and the inhabitants of Kamtchatka.

WHILE breakfasting the following morning at Verchni-Oudinsk, I overheard a singular conversation between three men, who were probably natives of this part, for they declared themselves to be more attached to Eastern Siberia than to the Russian Empire; and these reminded me of the people of Vannes or St. Brieux, who profess to love Brittany more than France. If the empire were in danger or the throne of the Czar threatened, these men would no doubt do their duty and, perhaps, better than many others; but, for all that, it was easy to perceive that this Eastern portion of Siberia was by far the nearest to their heart. "What a beautiful country!—

How fertile it is!" they exclaimed, "we have not only abundance of wheat and other grain, but what excellent wine comes from the Ussury valley. I cannot understand at all why our Emperor lives at St. Petersburg. You will see; our capital, which is so unhealthy, will be abandoned one of these days: then the Court will come and establish itself on the banks of the river Okhotsk."

I do not think that the dream of these simple people is worth consideration, still, at some future period, this feeling might develop into a longing for national independence in a manner much more practical among these inhabitants of the banks of the Amoor, and in this event would not be without significance.

It is not very long since the country to the north of the Amoor has been annexed to the Russian Empire, and, as it was a complete desert before this period, it is not surprising that this region is still only very thinly peopled.

The Amoor river has a course of a thousand leagues, and the Governor General informed me, that on this immense territory there were, including the military and civil service, in all twenty-six thousand souls. But since these inhabitants are natives of the old Russian Empire, and are here as colonists, it is natural they should still remain attached to their native country and their Emperor. In the course of a few generations, however, the people of the banks of the Amoor will not fail to perceive that independence will lead to wealth, and, with this incentive, what efforts would they not make to obtain it?

In short, the corn of Siberia is very often preferred by the inhabitants of Northern Russia to that of Odessa. The cultivators on the banks of the Amoor could supply not only themselves but export grain, and profit largely by the exportation. The valley of the Ussury, which would produce not only wine, but all the fruits of the South, such as oranges and bananas, would create additional riches. The inhabitants of this country would not then be obliged, as they are now, to send to St. Petersburg all the gold they get out of the earth. They might also accumulate wealth from other sources in their land, from the immense deposits of iron and graphite, (for the famous Alibert mine is in this district), from clay for the manufacture of porcelain, the forests, and also the coal of the island of Tarakai. Moreover, the sea of Okhotsk would furnish them with an easy outlet, and communication with the markets of the world, whilst the Russian ships from St. Petersburg, could not leave the Baltic, if opposed by Germany, Sweden, and Denmark, or indeed even by England and Holland.

It will be evident from these facts, that this region, measuring ten or twelve hundred leagues in length by eight or nine hundred wide, has all the resources necessary to form not only an independent state, but one of the richest even in the world. It is not at all unlikely, in the course of a few years, that the inhabitants of this country, hitherto a little overruled and overreached by the Czar, will open their eyes to the tempting advantages within their reach, and attempt to secure them fully by making an effort to gain their independence. It may be objected, perhaps, that the prospect of a revolution in Russia is far too remote for such a movement to come to pass; that the religion is too deeply rooted in the hearts of the people, and, consequently, they have too much veneration for the sacred person of the

Czar to venture to assail him. This is, to a certain extent, true, and what I have related about the sentiments of the assassins towards the Poles, in the prison of Irkutsk, gives some weight to the objection. Still, in Russia, it must be admitted, that the respect for religion —contrary to its form of manifestation in France—diminishes in proportion as the social rank rises. And then, if the respect for religion vanishes, that for the authority of the Emperor will soon follow. In Eastern Siberia, in fact, where everyone is trying to enrich himself and often succeeds, examples among these of this disregard for religion, which I have heard so frankly expressed, are not wanting; and when this will have spread among the multitude, the sacred authority of the Emperor, that keeps this country in subjection, will have lost its hold.

I can give instances of this irreverence, for, while I was at Irkutsk, I happened to ask one of the richest and most important personages there, if the priests were gathered from the peasantry. "Oh, no," he replied. "Then they belong to the upper classes?" "Not at all." "Then where are they recruited?"

"God knows where," he replied, with the utmost contempt, as if they were quite beneath his notice.

Another inhabitant of Irkutsk, in a still higher position, asked me one day, how I had passed my Sunday. I told him that, among other occupations, I had been in the morning, to hear mass by the archimandrite, and in the evening at the theatre, to hear *Orphée aux Enfers.* "Then," added my interlocutor, "you have assisted, to-day, at two *représentations bouffes.*"

I do not affirm that all the members of the Russian aristocracy speak so contemptuously of their religion and their priests: but here, certainly, are two remarks that no Catholic in our country even, without faith and without any apparent respect whatever for religion or authority, would have dared to make.

There is not in Siberia as in European Russia so great a distance between the people and the upper classes. The peasantry, one day, will not fail to notice the manner in which their creed, to which they have always bent the knee in veneration, is treated by their superiors, and will not be slow in claiming the alluring liberty they have discovered in those who should serve as models for their conduct.

It may be objected again, that this patient and submissive character of the Russian people, and the remoteness of the Eastern Siberians from any civilized nation that might set them an example and encourage them, would retard this emancipation.

The Russians, it is true, are so habituated to a state of patient endurance, in which they live; their resignation is so manifested in their conduct, in their forms of politeness bordering on servility, in their music, and even in their amusements, that it seems impossible there should be a great leader forthcoming from among them capable of changing their destiny. Their neighbours, the Chinese, live under a form of Government, perhaps, still less desirable, and, consequently, these two nations seem incapable of ever escaping from the slavery under which they now live.

But the Chinese, it must be admitted, are far from accepting their subjection with as much resignation as their neighbours of the North. Hitherto accustomed to regard the

JOURNEY OVER LAKE BAIKAL.

[*To face p.* 27.

frontiers of their empire as the limits of the world, and ignorant of the means by which liberty is acquired, it is not surprising that they should have submitted to an authority imposed on them from the first by irresistible force. But to change their views completely, they require only to know us, and then this enlightenment will gradually spread among them. They are not indeed very partial to us, but we astonish them, and they study us. They will soon appreciate the difference of condition between the European nations and the people of the Celestial Empire: they will come among us to educate themselves still more; and since the Chinese are naturally intelligent and logical, doing nothing superficially, they will adopt among themselves such of our institutions as appear to them sound, and adapted to secure the prosperity and happiness of a nation.

In this event the example would probably be followed in rich, but unhappy Siberia.

The three men I have mentioned, taking their meal at Verchni-Oudinsk, and who seemed so convinced of the brilliant future of Eastern Siberia, were not long in entering into conversation with us. Pablo availed himself of the opportunity for expatiating on the terrors he had experienced on Lake Baikal. He described them with much emphasis, not forgetting the most trifling incident, and embellished his narrative with a recital of certain feats of personal prowess that had inevitably escaped my observation. I should certainly have cut short so bombastic and prolonged an entertainment, if I had not seen this man take from my store of provisions a bottle of brandy which I had kept for a different object, deliberately fill his glass and then his companions', and calmly continue his diversion, sipping all the time as if he were taking his *kirsch* or *anisette*.

I wondered at this habit of swallowing thus such strong spirit. It was probably the cold of Siberia that induced the habit, for he was not addicted to it at Constantinople. This droll fellow, in gratifying this singular taste, revealed a superstition still more odd. He took a pinch of earth from a kind of snuff-box he kept constantly in his pocket, and throwing it into his brandy, gulped it, as if it had been deliciously sweetened with so much sugar.

When I asked him the reason for this practice, he explained: "This earth has been taken from my native land. If I swallow a morsel of it in this way, from time to time, I am sure of not catching any epidemic disease in the country where I am travelling. If you had known that, before quitting France, you would not have been ill on your arrival at Irkutsk."

Pablo, it may be seen, was a singular creature. Good nature and devotedness were so conspicuous in him, that I congratulated myself on having brought him with me: but I should never come to the end if I were to relate all the eccentricities of this half-cracked, childish, superstitious specimen of human nature.

Before leaving Verchni-Oudinsk and entering on Chinese territory, I ought to say a few words about a few tribes inhabiting Eastern Siberia, many specimens of which I had the opportunity of seeing before quitting this part of the Russian Empire.

The Yakuts are copper-coloured and have long black hair. Their wives are regarded with contempt. They are invariably covered with ornaments, generally of iron, yet artistically worked. The Yakuts are good-natured, honest, and hospitable. Their religious belief is exaggerated to superstition and idolatry. Their priests, in fact, are sorcerers who exercise great influence over this simple people by their practice of magic.

When Müller was here, he desired to see a priestess who, he was informed by the Yakuts, plunged a knife into her body without causing death. The first time, it seems, the operation did not succeed, but the next day, the attempt was renewed, and this time the blow was better directed. She had really plunged the blade into the intestines, and withdrew it covered with blood! "I examined the wound," says Müller, "I saw her take a morsel of flesh, which she cut from the incision and, then grilling it on the fire, eat it. She afterwards dressed the wound with a plaster of larch resin and birch bark, and bound it over with a rag. But there was an incident still more singular. She was compelled to sign a sort of official report, in which she declared she had never plunged the knife into her body before having operated before us; that she did not even intend, at first, to go so far; that she designed merely to deceive us as well as the Yakuts, in dexterously slipping the knife between her skin and her dress; that the Yakuts had never suspected the truth of the spell, but we had watched her too closely; that, besides, she had heard from other sorcerers, when one would strike effectively he did not die after it however little he tasted of his own fat; and that, now being required of her own free will to tell the truth, she could not deny that, until now, she had deceived the Yakuts. The wound, which she dressed twice only, was quite cured in ten days, and, probably, her youth contributed much to this prompt cure."

The city of Yakutsk, in the centre of the territory inhabited by the Yakuts, is considered to be the coldest city in Siberia. It serves as a place of exile. I have frequently heard of a poor poet, who was condemned to live indefinitely in this city, after two years of preliminary imprisonment, for having written a little book unfavourable to the Russian Government, which to me seemed quite harmless. This book is entitled *Sto. délaïti*, "What is to be done"? *

The inhabitants of Kamtchatka are divided into three peoples, whose language and manners are dissimilar. The Koriaks in the north, the Kamtchatdales in the centre, and the Kuriles in the south.

Among the Koriaks,† some are nomadic, others stationary.

The wandering Koriaks have Arab features, and small eyes, shaded with thick eye-brows; they are not so stout nor so tall as the stationary Koriaks; they are also less robust and courageous.

And yet, the nomads despise the sedentary tribe as slaves, and these quietly accept this servility. When a wandering Koriak presents himself to a sedentary one, the latter cringes to him, loads him with presents, and pockets all the disdain and insult hurled at him by his guest, without a word of reproach.

The nomads are very jealous of their wives. They slay them at once when caught in adultery, and sometimes even on a bare suspicion of infidelity. They take offence at

---

* See Note 11. † Krachenninikov.

everything. Their wives must appear sluttish and begrimed, for fear of irritating their husbands with too many luring charms. They never wash nor comb themselves; they never have any colour on their cheeks. " Why should they varnish themselves?" their husbands ask, " unless they want to please others." They therefore, sometimes, hide really good clothing under a bundle of rags.

The manners of the fixed Koriaks are quite different. They receive strangers, in the way mentioned of the Laplanders by Bernardin de Saint-Pierre, and they would kill a guest who would refuse to take his place in the conjugal bed.

The Koriaks, whether vagrant or stationary, like all the inhabitants of Kamtchatka, have no religion. " A chief of these tribes," says Krachenninikov, " with whom I had an opportunity of conversing, had no idea of the Divinity." The Koriaks, however, fear an evil spirit, and sometimes sacrifice to him a reindeer, but without the object of satisfying themselves whether this sacrifice should bring them good or evil.

Could the name of worship be given to a

superstitious custom, very prevalent among the stationary Koriaks, which consists in giving a place in the conjugal bed to stones swathed in clothing? "An inhabitant of Oukinka had two of these stones; a large one, which he called his wife, and a little one, which was his son. I asked him," said Krachenninikov, "the reason of this strange act. He told me that, one day, when his body was covered with an eruption, he had found his great stone on the bank of a river; as he desired to take it, it blew on him like a human being, and, through fear, he cast it into the river. From this moment his malady got worse until the end of a year, when, having gone to search for the stone at the place he had thrown it, he was astonished to see it again at some distance from the spot, lying on a great flat stone with a little one beside it. He took them both, carried them to his dwelling, dressed them, and soon after his malady disappeared. Since that time, he said, I have always carried the little stone with me, and I love my stone wife more than my living one."

This story of Krachenninikov shows to what extent of folly, the need of a belief in a Divinity may drive a man whose mind is neither enlightened nor directed.

The Kamtchatdales have dark skins, broad and flat faces and squat noses.* They have a fishy odour; they exhale also a strong scent of sea birds, and sometimes of musk, caused by their eating of the animal containing it without preparation.†

They live, however, principally on fish, which they cook in diverse ways. The most common consists in cutting several salmon in six parts. They put the heads into a pit to decompose, dry the back and belly with smoke, and the tail and flanks in the air. They then pound the whole together, and afterwards dry this paste, which serves them almost daily for their food. Ducks and geese and eggs preserved in fish fat form also, it is said, a portion of their subsistence.

These people formerly had no other drink than water; and to make themselves a little lively, they used to drink an infusion of mushrooms. Since the Russian conquest they have become acquainted with brandy, and now imbibe a large quantity of it.

---

* Steller. † Abbé Chappe.

The Kamtchatdales have a great passion for dress. The costume of a rich man was formerly made of the skins of the reindeer, the fox, the dog, the marmot, the wild ram, bears' and wolves' feet, many seals and feathers. It required twenty animals, at least, to clothe a Kamtchatdale. Commerce was carried on exclusively by barter. A complete costume was worth about a hundred martens or a hundred foxes.*

But now this singular people have borrowed from the Russians the taste for the clothing material of civilized life, and in a slight degree for the form also. The women have odd whims; they stain their faces with red and white. They are very particular in not showing themselves to a stranger before having undergone a special ablution, and then having been well reddened and tricked out.

In order to obtain fire they use the fire drill, and it is produced by twirling rapidly between the hands a round dry stick passed through a hole in a plank. A bit of bruised dry grass serves as tinder.

The manners of the Kamtchatdales are so

Müller.

very gross, that they resemble the instincts of animals rather than the habits of man. They have no idea of the spirituality of the soul.* Moreover, they have no religion. A single *fête*, called Purifications, fully described by Krachenninikov, consists so much more in dancing and revelling than in prayers and sacrifices, that it would be evidently wrong, I think, to consider it as forming part of any religious system.

The Kuriles inhabit the islands of the same name which stretch, one after the other, between the extremity of Kamtchatka and Japan. These people feel the influence of the civilized nation so near them; still they approach much nearer the inhabitants of Kamtchatka than those of Japan. They dwell in tents, like their neighbours on the north, and live on fish.

The Kamtchatdales and the Kuriles differ, however, on many points. A Kurile wife, when unfaithful to her husband, dishonours him. He then challenges his adversary, and they have a duel with clubs. He who challenges is the first to receive, on his back,

---

* Steller.

three blows with a club of the thickness of a man's arm. And then he returns as many to his enemy; the combat continues in this way, till one of them demands pardon or succumbs to the number and violence of the blows.

The Kurile mothers have a very cruel practice. When they have two infants at a birth, they kill one; and yet these people are gentle and humane. They respect old age, they are attached to their kindred, and form friendships.

CHAPTER XVI.

KIACHTA TO MAIMATCHIN.

The tarantass—Tea merchants—Their competition—The Sienzy—Aspect of Maimatchin—A dinner at the Chinese Governor's—Preparations for crossing the Gobi desert.

WE found quite a change in the state of the road after leaving Verchni-Oudinsk. The sledge, in the course of a few hours, being no longer supported with a smooth thick layer of snow, its skates occasionally came in contact with the earth below, and this increasing the friction, considerably retarded our progress. This at last produced so much jolting that, on arriving at the first stage, we were obliged to abandon our sledge and proceed in a *tarantass*. This vehicle, in which the Russians travel in summer, has no other spring than that afforded by four birch poles resting on the axles of four wheels. I do not know any kind of locomotion, excepting the Chinese mule palanquin, more uncomfortable than the tarantass, and yet, the jolting apart, I was delighted the first time I found myself mounted on this vehicle. The country was still for the most part covered with snow, but here and there I caught a glimpse of uncovered spots: the land that had been lost to sight since quitting St. Petersburg, the land of Siberia, in fact, which, although I had passed over fifteen hundred leagues of this country, strictly speaking, I had not yet seen. Here it was a rich soil apparently favourable to agriculture, but of so dark a colour that it must give a more gloomy aspect to the neighbourhood of the villages in summer, than the spotless snowy shroud in winter.

As we went on our way, we noticed a great difference in the people; they were more singular-looking and of a type more Oriental: the villagers, the yemschiks, and even the posting masters, were nearly all Buriats. We now often passed Chinese, in carriages or palanquins, clad in silks, red, blue, and in fact of every colour; still more frequently Mongols perched on camels, or mounted on frisky little horses, all of them capped alike with a yellow turban lined with fur, and wrapped in a full cloak, made of the skin of the white deer of the Gobi desert, folded across the chest. At last, on the 27th of March, at nine in the morning, I caught sight, from the top of a hill, of the village of Kiachta, at the end of which stood up two enormous yellow posts that marked the frontier of the Celestial Empire, and the entry into the town of Maimatchin.

I went straight to M. Pfaffius. "I had no idea," he said, "you would have been so long in coming from Irkutsk." I related to him my adventures of the Baikal. "The little caravan of tea-merchants which you were to join, left here yesterday morning. But you will lose nothing by it, for there will be another caravan leaving here in a week. You will then have plenty of time to make all your preparations to accompany it to Pekin, and we shall have the pleasure of your company here all the week." I went to announce this news to Ivan Michäelovitch Nemptchinof, who was so highly delighted, and offered me, with so much courtesy, the hospitality of his father's house, that I shall never forget the occasion.

Ivan Michäelovitch's father,* with whom I

---

* See Note 12.

lodged at Kiachta, is a cousin of the Nemptchinof I have already mentioned as one of the three proprietors of the richest gold mine of Trans-Baikalia. Not feeling disposed to risk his fortune in gold-hunting, so often precarious, he preferred devoting himself to the tea business, and has acquired in it an immense fortune.

The flourishing state of the tea trade by caravan is due to two causes : first, the great consumption of tea in Siberia and Russia, and particularly in Russia, where it is the necessary part of their meals : secondly, to its free entry into Eastern Siberia, which the Czar has accorded to his Eastern subjects. Since the customs' duty is considerable on the tea imported by Odessa, it follows that nearly all the tea that is drunk in Russia passes through the hands of the Kiachta merchants, and not without leaving in them a great many roubles.

These merchants are a little frightened, just now, by the appearance of a competition, the success of which, still doubtful, it is true, would ruin them completely. This rival enterprise would have for its object the conveyance of tea by sea, from the mouth of the Yang-Se' to the port of Vladivostok, and thence to Irkutsk, by the Ussuri and the Amoor rivers. If this communication were established, there is no doubt that tea could be sold very much cheaper than at present, for the overland carriage, through Mongolia and the Desert of Gobi, is very expensive; but the undertakers of the new project would be obliged to make so considerable an outlay from the commencement, that it is feared the failure of it would be decisive before a single chest could find its way by this route to Irkutsk.

In order to render the carriage as low as possible, they would propose to embark the tea at Han-Kow, the great centre of the plantations of South China, on the banks of the Yang-Se', and disembark it only at Nertchinsk on the Schilka, immediately within the government of Irkutsk. But to attain this object, it would be necessary to scoop out a canal, between Vladivostok and Lake Hinka, where the Ussuri takes its source, a very mountainous region; and besides, to construct steamers small enough to pass into a canal, and, at the same time, large enough to resist the waves, often formidable, in the China seas. The idea is certainly ingenious and even remarkable; but if the capital of the new company is important enough for the establishment of this maritime route, its success is not doubtful. In any case, the rivalry is interesting, and I daresay that some of my readers, already informed of this gigantic commercial enterprise, will be curious to learn its results.

The Chinese who inhabit Maimatchin were not slow in ascertaining if Monsieur Nemptchinof had a *Sienzy* really lodging in his house, that is a man from the extreme west. As specimens of this race are rather rare in Northern China, and the curiosity of no women in the world can approach to that of Chinese men, all the inhabitants of Maimatchin wanted to see me.

According to the Russian custom, all the crannies of the window frames where I was were puttied, although the cold had almost taken its departure, but the doors were wide open; I could not, therefore, escape from the endless crowd of visitors, that came to see me. There were, at least, forty or fifty at a time, in the three little rooms that formed my suite. They scrutinized my most ordinary gestures and movements, pounced on all my writings, felt my beard, which appeared to them as something monstrous; for they are not accustomed to see, on their own faces, nor generally even on those of the Siberians, anything but moustaches; and then they wanted to hear me speak my language. Getting repeatedly quite exhausted from their persistent and indiscreet persecution, I remonstrated sharply, and finding this ineffective, I lost all patience and swore at them like a trooper; but it was all to no purpose, for their ears were evidently so pleased with these euphonious expressions that they often begged me to repeat them to the new comers that nothing might be lost.

The Governor could not resist the temptation to flow with the stream. His visit interested me. He was clad in a robe of cloth of gold. His cap was surmounted with a blue ball, the mark of his dignity. Two long peacock feathers hung from the back of this cap. This Governor was accompanied by two Chinese officers and a Mongolian prince. The latter was costumed like all other Mongols; except that his chest was completely covered with a profusion of ornaments and amulets in silver and coral. A cousin of Ivan Michäelovitch, M. Solomanof, acted as interpreter. "I ought legally to oppose your entry into China," said the Governor to me; "the Russians only have a right to enter by land into the Celestial Empire. I shall, however, wink at it. Ask M. Pfaffius merely for a tea merchant's passport, as a Russian subject, in case you should have any difficulties with the Chinese authorities you may meet on your way." The interview ended by his inviting me to dine with him the next day; an invitation I accepted with pleasure, and we parted cordially like old acquaintances.

Maimatchin is the most singular city in the world, inasmuch as it is peopled with men only. The Chinese women are not only forbidden to leave their territory, but even to pass the great wall of Kalkann and enter into Mongolia. This rule will hinder, for some time to come, any modification of the Chinese character. However numerous the emigrations may be, foreign influence will never be very great over men born in Chinese territory and educated there till manhood in all the customs and prejudices of their own over-extolled country. All the Chinese of this border city are exclusively traders, and they accumulate money, till their trading with Europe through Siberia has created a sufficient fortune, to enable them to return to their native cities and live there in ease with their families. Their dwellings indicate their prosperity. They are separated from the streets by a clay wall, rather ugly, it is true, but surrounding, generally, a very elegant-looking house, before which are gambolling those sleek, plump-looking curs with unusually big eyes, such as are pretty faithfully represented on Chinese vases and screens. It very often happens that objects thus represented to us, which we regard as grotesque caricatures, are, in fact, with their faults of perspective, rather than of form, true images of objects of the country.

The main part of the houses of Maimatchin is divided into two compartments, and that which is behind is raised. Fires are kept up under this great platform, which is covered with mats, that serve as seats by day and beds by night.

Opposite the door a niche is generally seen, where the domestic idols, unaccustomed to attitudinize to profane eyes, repose behind an ornamented blind.

The walls of the reception room are lacquered in red or black, or sometimes, even covered with figured silk, according to the taste and wealth of the proprietor. The apartment overlooking the court, is generally of light wood, perforated and carved, and over these openings coloured paper is stretched. The light, sifted through the artistically carved wood-work, and then casting its diverse shadows on the coloured transparency, produces something of the graceful effect of stained glass.

I was deeply interested with the novelties of these gay interiors, as might be supposed, and I passed here many hours, called, first to one apartment, then to another, to partake of the liberal and courteous entertainment, abounding in pastry and preserved fruits.

It is quite a misconception we have in Europe generally, to confound the edifices designed for worship with the high towers usually dominating the villages. These towers have nothing of a religious character: they are simply landmarks in the vast plains of Central China. They are, therefore, not seen in mountainous districts, as in the neighbourhood of Maimatchin for example.

The idol temple of this city is beside the Governor's house. It is approached by three successive courts, surrounded with sunk wooden galleries, painted in various colours.

In the first, rise three little structures, covering a gigantic *tam-tam*, and two gilt monsters. In the second, stands a theatre, so disposed, that the doors of the temple being open, the idol may contemplate the spectacle, which, to me, seems to constitute an essential part of the religious ceremony. The third court is covered, and serves as a vestibule to the temple specially so called, containing idols of the most grotesque character. The door of this temple is charming: it is of carved open wood-work, richly gilt. There are three sanctuaries: the centre one is devoted to a gigantic idol with monstrous features. I remarked the ferocious look of this figure: he had fierce eyes; his beard, composed of natural hair, descended to the waist, and he was robed in yellow silk. Twelve statues in the attitude of prayer were bending before him. A mass of ornaments, of all kinds, encumbered this sanctuary: immense chandeliers of wrought iron, swords, gilt lances, lighted tapers and lanterns. The god, on the left of this one, was conspicuous with his three eyes and scarlet robe : it is this one that penetrates the most secret thoughts. For this reason, no taper was lighted before him, his clear-sightedness requiring no adventitious aid. The god on the right was decked in a green robe.

I took care not to neglect the invitation the Chinese Governor had given me. At the appointed hour, I punctually presented myself: I met there several I was acquainted with, and, among them, my old travelling companions living at Kiachta, whom my host had the good taste to bring together here. We took our places on the estrade I have mentioned, squatting in groups of three or four round several low tables.

The cover for each guest consisted of a little plate, a liliputian cup, and two sticks. The little plate is not intended to receive the portion of any dish offered to the guest: it contains merely some hot, black vinegar, an indispensable sauce, incessantly renewed by the servants, and into which one steeps each mouthful that he has directly taken from the dish between his two sticks.

When the mouthful thus seasoned is disposed of, the two little sticks are at liberty to seize right and left, on their points, some savoury *hors-d'œuvre*, placed in saucers around the central plate. They consist principally of marine plants,—black mushrooms cultivated on the birch-trees, scented herbs, preserved eggs —the albumen of which, by some process, has turned black—and little reptiles artistically cut into spiral forms and otherwise metamorphosed.

I remember, on another occasion, when I was much nearer to the sea, that one of these side dishes was a little bowl of shrimps, served up in some ingenious sauce that seasoned them well without killing them: they are eaten in this way all alive, preference being given to those that afford the best proofs of their liveliness by their repugnance to the sauce.

The only drink, served in cups about the size of thimbles, is hot rice brandy.

All these minute portions and preparations, these graceful tiny utensils, this variety of little dishes, are suggestive of a dinner children give to their dolls. It is a table indeed, that well represents this effeminate race of attenuated hands and pinched feet, a race of feeble appetites and feeble powers, that accomplishes nothing great, unless through a slow accumulation of puny efforts and petty means. The mouthfuls are prepared and cut before being served in the dishes, and each morsel is surmounted with a red almond, to indicate that no one has yet touched it.

The procession of twenty-five or thirty dishes, composing the governor of Maimatchin's dinner, commenced, according to Chinese habits, with the meats, continued with the soups and sweets, and ended with a plate of plain boiled rice, which is invariably presented to the guests at the end of the repast, no one, however, touching it, and apparently having no other meaning than this: " I have now offered you everything I have in my house, and, to continue the hospitality, I have no other resource than to place before you the most ordinary article of diet."

The day for the departure of the caravan was now approaching, and I began to busy myself with my preparations for crossing the Desert of Gobi.

The tea merchants, with whom I was to travel through Mongolia and north China, undertook to furnish us with conveyances, and to arrange with a Mongolian guide to take us as far as the Great Wall.

This journey is undertaken in little Chinese vehicles, kinds of boxes resting on a pair of wheels behind, and supported in front by a draught camel between two long shafts; the box being of sufficient size to permit the occupant to lie down. The vehicle can contain but one traveller; and the camel, which has to bear considerable fatigue—as the reader will subsequently learn—cannot ascend any hill. These animals, therefore, are not employed in the first part of the route in Mongolia, between Kiachta and Urga, because it is necessary to traverse a steep road along a chain of mountains. During this first period, these little vehicles are drawn by oxen. The tedious slowness of their movements, and, besides, the desire I had to precede the caravan to Urga, that I might stay there a little while, induced me not to join my companions from Kiachta, but to proceed as far as Urga in a tarantass. I accordingly left Pablo and my baggage to come by the slow caravan, and I offered a place in my Russian vehicle to M. Marine, one of the tea merchants who was to cross, with me, the Desert of Gobi.

It is astonishing what a heap of objects are necessary when the traveller is going to wander, more than a month, in the desert, far from the aid of his fellow-creatures. He has to think, not only of the necessary provisions, but of an assortment of tools for repairing the vehicles; preventives and remedies for man and beast against possible accidents of the way; presents, indispensable to making friends among the wandering tribes; and, especially, the strange money current among the Mongols, a stock of which is requisite.

These Orientals despise gold and silver, and their business is carried on exclusively by barter. A tea of ordinary quality, called *brick tea*, on account of the form given to it by compression, is the article of food the most appreciated, and the most common substitute for money. One of these bricks would represent about eight or ten shillings.

Needles ready threaded, sugar and brandy, have also an important exchangeable value. I was obliged to furnish myself with many objects at a village neighbouring to Kiachta, at Triosky-Sawsk, where I had an opportunity of visiting the rare collections of M. Popoff.

This *savant* has studied the habits of all the insects of Trans-Baikalia. I noticed, among the lepidoptera, a butterfly of an extremely rare kind, which he calls *Liparis Ochropoda*, and which lays productive eggs without the aid of the male. This fact is attested by some very curious experiments, confirmed by him by repetition, at the gymnasium of Irkutsk, and at Triosky-Sawsk, with complete success. He has seen these produced for three generations successively without access to the male, the last of these being composed entirely of males.*

Our tarantass, containing M. Marine and myself, left Kiachta three days after the departure of the caravan.

---

* See note 13.

We calculated not only on joining it at Urga, but on passing it on the way, and on remaining many days in this city, waiting its arrival.

Mrs. Grant, Miss Campbell, and Ivan Michäelovich, each in a separate carriage, kept me company on the road for about twelve miles. We passed through Maimatchin and entered into Mongolia. There appeared to me very little difference between this country and the desert. Here and there, however, but at long distances apart, might be seen a native encampment, composed of one or two tents fenced around, with a camel, a horse, and a few sheep in the enclosure.

As soon as the day began to close in, the three little carriages accompanying my tarantass pulled up, their occupants being now obliged to return. I am ashamed to say, I had quite forgotten to bring with me, in accordance with the Siberian custom, a stock of champagne, to lay the dust before their steps on parting: I was therefore quite disconsolate. Moreover, the changed aspect of the country, the prospect before me of having no companion who could speak French—for M. Marine did not know a word of our language—the beginning of an existence quite new and unknown to me, added not a little to the emotion and sadness of such a separation.

After the most cordial leave-taking, I continued my journey towards the south, whilst my three friends, fearing that night would overtake them on the road, set off for Kiachta at a full gallop.

A cloud of fine dust of the desert was thrown up by the horses' feet, which speedily veiled them from my sight.

My journey through Siberia, and with it one of its most pleasing incidents, had come to an end.

CHAPTER XVII.

MAIMATCHIN TO URGA.

First Stage in Mongolia—The Mongols—Their tents; their life—How they steer their way in the desert—The Caravan —A Sacrilege—The Russian Consul at Urga—The Koutoukta.

WE felt the cold becoming rather cutting at the fall of night, and we observed the thermometer already several degrees below zero. We therefore resolved to alight at a Mongolian encampment, that we might be able to warm ourselves at the family fire. Besides, M. Marine, like a true Russian, was longing for a cup of tea, and all the utensils necessary for this purpose were with the caravan, far beyond our reach. The tents, near which our yemschik pulled up his troïka, were most picturesquely pitched on the slope of a hill just on the skirts of a little pine wood, and these trees were the last I had the pleasure of regarding for a long time. The night was

A STREET IN URFA.   [To face p. 304.

beautifully clear, and little plots of snow, that had stood out against the thaw of the preceding days, were quite luminous in the silvery rays of the moon. We quickly leapt to the ground and then over the barrier of the paling, and M. Marine and I, without calling out, presented ourselves at the opening of the tent which appeared to be the principal habitation.

These tents are firmly raised on wooden lattice-work, covered with several layers of sheep's skins. They are about three yards in diameter, and are entered by a single, narrow, low opening, which is closed by a sheep's skin hanging before it. Facing this entrance may invariably be seen a little statuette or picture, representing the protecting deity of the family, and, before it, stand seven or eight small vessels or vases, containing bread, salt, bits of wood, camel-dung, tea,—everything in fact necessary to the ignoble, barbaric existence of these poor, rude people.

The tent was occupied by two men and a woman, who were lying around a fire placed in the centre, and which barely lighted with its glowing embers this wretched hovel. We soon discovered that this recumbent attitude was the only one supportable; for the abundance of smoke rendered respiration impossible beyond two or three feet above the ground. This is the reason the Mongols appear nearly black, from having their faces covered with a layer of soot, a coating they are not accustomed to remove. The wife, like all Mongolian women, was covered with jewels. A demi-crown in silver was set on her forehead; two large pins gathered her hair behind her ears, as in Egyptian mummies, and two enormous brooches, also of silver, fastened the ends of it over her chest; the whole being ornamented with variously coloured stones.

These three human beings crouching like tired hounds around a smouldering heap of dried camel-dung, whose feeble and fitful glowing alone lighted up in the gloaming their black eyes and glittering jewels, formed a scene, in which the startled imagination conjured up, from mediæval times, midnight councils of black spirits, looming through "the fog and filthy air." It was one altogether spectral and diabolic. A few hours had indeed transformed my existence, and carried me beyond the pale of civilized life into a desert, where I was doomed to pass many long days and nights, in which there was no retreat but these unearthly abodes. But then, on the other hand, I was well provided with food and utensils; and, as I looked up through an opening in the top of the tent, and gazed on the pale twinkling stars, they seemed to invite me benignly to spread my repast on the desert sand and trust to their unerring guidance over the trackless way.

Our yemschik was not long in following us into the tent: as he was a Buriat, he entered into conversation with our hosts, who seemed pleased to receive us. I tried to make myself intelligible to M. Marine, but did not venture to do so in Russian: the ease, however, with which I made myself understood, gave me a high opinion of his intelligence. The Mongols quickly perceived that signs and gestures were important elements in our conversation, and I was to them, as to the Chinese of Maimatchin, an object of much curiosity. I took care, however, to keep them at a respectful distance, and not to allow myself to be touched by any member of this filthy, fulsome, fetid race, teeming with vermin and covered with corroding sores. There is not, I am sure, any people in the world more disgusting than the Mongols. Water in this region, unhappily, is too precious to admit of its use for any other purpose than drinking. These wretched creatures are therefore putrefying in their wounds: sometimes, in fact, their limbs drop off and they perish piecemeal, inspiring with horror all those who come near them, who can only stand helpless and aghast at such a spectacle of human suffering.

When we had refreshed ourselves and warmed our benumbed limbs, we hastened to emerge from this loathsome hut and to breathe again, under the star-bespangled firmament, the pure bracing desert air. Then we stretched ourselves in our tarantass for our night's repose.

It was about three o'clock in the morning, when our horses had sufficiently rested, and we resumed our way.

During this journey we found ourselves, many times, suddenly surrounded by Mongol horsemen clad in yellow jackets and red breeches, who, having spied a Russian conveyance, had galloped up at full speed to gratify their curiosity. They had long poles rather heavy fastened to their horses and trailing behind them, and these left on the sand a trace of their course.

This precious furrow, playing the part of the little white pebbles of Tom Thumb, prevents them from going astray, and brings them, after many days' wild roving over the desert, unerringly back to their tents. Armed so formidably as they appeared to be, sometimes with a bow and arrows, sometimes with a musket bristling with a spike, and always with a murderous-looking knife, these savage-looking rovers were calculated to fill one with misgiving as to their pacific intentions. After having escorted us for a few moments, and satisfied their curiosity by questioning our yemschik, they started off at full speed, sometimes standing upright on their stirrups, sometimes bending close over the neck of their courser, cleaving the air like the flight of a dart.

The Mongols, among whom we pulled up the next day, were too much like those of the preceding night to render it worth while to say anything about these. I found it impossible, however, to stay under their tent as soon as I discovered what kind of a repast these wretched creatures were crouched around. There was a dead camel lying on the ground at a few paces from their habitation: the cold had contributed no longer to its preservation, and all around there was a most repulsive odour. These poor creatures, by cutting off a slice of this carrion every day, hoped to have meals for some time to come. When I entered under their blackened roof in a cloud of smoke from the smouldering camel-dung, they were greedily devouring, without sauce, salt, or bread, this revolting, putrid mess, fresh from the pestiferous, reeking caldron of broth standing beside their horrible meal.

We took good care, M. Marine and I, not to boil the water for our tea in this pot; we therefore retired from its unsavoury proximity, and breakfasted on some mutton sausages, with which I had provided myself. Then I went to cleanse myself in the snow, a luxury I was, through the thaw, unhappily deprived of a few days subsequently, and, having emerged from it as clean as a new penny, I stretched myself on the ground till the horses had sufficiently rested and were ready to continue the journey.

Whilst thus musing I watched a Mongol, who came out of his tent, mounted a camel, and disappeared in a turn of the valley, singing joyfully all the way. I thought this incident worth the consideration of philosophers who speculate on the sources of happiness. Still, for my part, I would rather be any animal, however limited its enjoyment of life might be, than this jubilant Mongol.

Our attention was fully occupied the next day in searching intently the horizon to catch the faintest trace of our caravan, which we should now have been approaching. Between Kiachta and Urga, there is no marked way, and the traveller simply takes a southern course; obstacles, however, in his path, may cause a deviation of a few miles from the most direct.

We examined minutely with our telescopes the Mongol encampments, the troops of camels, and the least shadowy objects, and took long turns in every direction, with no other result than to discover that our eyes had been deceived by some phantasm, which we had taken for a group of vehicles and camels.

But, at last, two flags, waving in the wind at the head of a caravan, came into view and left us no longer in doubt that it was ours and really close at hand.

One of the flags bore the Russian eagles, and the other, containing a prayer, had been placed there by the Mongol guide as a protection for our journey. I was delighted to see my poor Pablo again, who appeared to me to be looking quite emaciated. He spoke in the highest terms of my other companions of the journey, with whom he was already on an excellent footing. Having heartily saluted and assured them that it would not be my fault if we were not the best friends in the world, and then having patted lovingly the poor ox drawing my empty vehicle, we continued our way.

A few hours afterwards and just as the darkness was closing in we saw, starting up before us, the dark outline of something very strange. On approaching we found it was an idol, quite open to the sky and to the desert, representing probably the deity of travellers. It was made of compressed bread, covered over with some bituminous substance, and perched on a horse of the same material, and held in its hand a lance in Don Quixote attitude. Its horrible features were surmounted with a shaggy tuft of natural hair. A great number of offerings of all kinds were scattered on the ground all around. Five or six images, formed also of bread, were bending in an attitude of prayer before the deity.

We looked slyly and cautiously all around the horizon, and, in spite of the supplication of our timid yemschik, we laid violent hands on the ample treasure. We at first snatched up several offerings, then seized a few idolaters, and finally, seeing no impediment, I wrung off the head of the god himself and threw it into my big bag. Having committed this sacrilege, we scampered off from the desecrated altar with all the precipitancy of guilty consciences pursued by an avenging spirit. I was not long after all in regretting my sacrilege, for the principal booty, the head of the god, crumbled away from the shocks of the vehicle so as to be no longer recognizable.

We were roused the following morning by the sudden, furious scamper of our horses. The driver had fallen asleep and then dropped the reins to the ground: the animals, scared with something clinging to their heels and finding themselves unrestrained, went straight before them, leaping over ditches, earth mounds, and obstacles of all kinds that came in their way. The most vigorous shouting, or the most soothing *trémolos* from the lips of the yemschik, were of no avail; they kept on their mad, *vent à terre* course.

Our driver then, like a true, devoted subject of the Emperor of Russia, as he was, did not hesitate at the critical moment to expose his life, when, in his conscience, it was imperative to save the lives of other subjects of the same Emperor. Whilst we held him suspended by the feet between the vehicle and the horses, he was—hanging in this way—enabled to gather up the reins which had already become entangled around the legs of one of the horses. A violent kick or fling, in this dangerous position, might have fractured the skull of this brave fellow, whose only fault had been the misfortune to have been suddenly overcome with too much fatigue, and whose devotion we did not fail to reward as it merited, when we arrived at Urga.

But our trouble did not end here: we had unfortunately lost our way.

Not one of us knew how long we had been at the mercy of our team and, consequently, how far we had strayed. After going one way, then another by chance, having nothing but the sun for a guide, our Buriat began to despair of finding the right way. In this dilemma, we resolved to ascend a high mountain and scan the horizon all around, but M. Marine and I being of course quite ignorant of the conformation and chief features of the country, the driver alone undertook this ascent. This accident and its consequences caused us to lose a whole day, but when he returned, happily, he was confident as to the route he had to take, and we set off in the same state as the pigeon in the fable, believing this time, our troubles would end with this trial.

We had not proceeded very far before we were most annoyingly stopped by a watercourse. We feared that its covering of ice was too fragile to bear us, and, on the other hand, it was apparently too treacherous to admit of our sounding it. After my adventures on Lake Baikal, I was quite prepared to trust myself over this ice without much hesitation, but, seeing the apprehensions of M. Marine and the driver, I became timid, and yielded to them.

We got out of the tarantass; M. Marine and I first went across on foot, and then the driver, after starting the horses at a gallop, followed us. The resistance of the ice was just sufficient, and the next day, probably, we could not have crossed, for the ice even now split under the weight, spurting up the compressed water everywhere through the inauspicious fissures.

We still had a mountain to ascend before arriving at Urga, and as our jaded horses crept up with difficulty, we got down to relieve them. Our attention was at once attracted by the picturesqueness of the scenery. As we advanced, the valleys around us coming into view, deepened in shadow and narrowed in width ; the crests of the overhanging mountains were beginning to catch the first rays of the rising sun, and fascinated us with their luminous splendour. It called up, in my memory, my former excursions in the Alps and the Pyrenees. I loitered on my way musingly for some time, and tried to abstract my thoughts from actuality; from the perils of my adventure, the remoteness from my friends, and indulged in the illusion that I had before my eyes the snowy cap of Mont Blanc or the Maladetta. But this attractive imagery was soon rudely dispelled by the sight of two or three Mongolian tents on the summit of the hill we had to ascend. These were too forcibly suggestive of the first encampment I had visited to permit me to indulge any longer in a day-dream that I was so near my home. We resumed our places in the tarantass, and our descent of the mountain, across snow-pits and boggy spots, in the absence of any roadway whatever, kept us in perpetual alarm. The valley into which we descended, was strewn with huge stones, and we could not proceed, even at a snail's pace, without being tossed with fearful joltings. This wearying movement lasted five or six hours, and M. Marine became quite exhausted and alarmingly pale from the effects. Towards one in the afternoon, we perceived a grand lamasery gracefully risin on the slope of a mountain, and, in another hour, we at last arrived at Urga, the capital of Mongolia.

The Russian consul, to whom I had a letter of recommendation, does not live in the city, and the reason will soon be apparent. His government has built a fine residence for him in the Siberian style, about two miles distant, and he has been living there twenty years with his wife, protected by two companies of Russian gendarmes, opening his house to travellers, who rarely present themselves, and having beyond this no other incidents to enliven his existence than he can find in the neighbourhood of this city, into which I will invite the reader to enter with me.

The streets are bordered right and left with palisades of trunks of trees, placed upright and strongly bound together, and these are pierced here and there, on each side, by gates of the same material and kind of construction, which give access into courts, where tents, exactly of the same character as those I have already described, are permanently pitched. The Mongols are essentially nomads, and would not, even in towns, live in any other kind of habitation. The governor of Mongolia, the

Grand Lama, the highest dignitaries, live here also under tents. The lamasery, the *Koutoukta* palace, and the prison, alone stand out above the other strange constructions, but since these three principal are raised commandingly on a series of logs one above the other, they break slightly the monotonous aspect of the whole.

The lamasery is tolerably rich in its contents. The principal idol placed in the centre is cast in copper, sixty feet high; and around this are disposed several other personages, also of copper. Niches are also sunk along the walls, and contain other little copper idols: I counted twelve hundred of them. Flags and banners of precious stuffs embroidered with gold adorn this temple, but prevent one, through intercepting the view, from appreciating the general effect. On the right of the principal god a platform is raised for the *Koutoukta*, who takes his place here during the ceremonies. This *Koutoukta* is the favourite deity of the Mongols. He is brought here from Thibet by the Grand Lama of Urga, who goes into this country to search for him, guided probably by the indications of the other lamas of the country. The child lives retired in the recesses of this building, to which they give the pompous name of "palace." Through some strange fatality, a fatality always renewed, this living deity never survives the age of eighteen or twenty years. The cause of this cruel destiny may be traced, I think, to the apprehensions of the government of Pekin, who, jealous of the influence the *Koutoukta* exercises over the Mongol population, fears it might become dangerous if protracted beyond this age. As to the prison, it consists of two enclosures about eighteen feet high, constructed also with trunks of trees.

Such is the external aspect at first sight; the internal life it covers is much more singular.

THE GRAND LAMA OF MONGOLIA.

[*To face p.* 320.

CHAPTER XVIII.

URGA AND THE ENTRY INTO THE DESERT OF GOBI.

Urga—Mongol religion—Praying wheels—Burial ceremonies—The Holy Mountain—My travelling companions in the desert—Departure from Urga—First halt—A Mongolian repast—Easter Eve.

THE thought of death and a future life hovers constantly over this mournful city, and lugubrious religious ceremonies constitute the principal occupation of its fanatical inhabitants. Banners inscribed with prayers are all around the palings surrounding their tents, everywhere fluttering in the breeze; but, as if these were insufficient, certain fanatics stretch a cord around below this row of banners, and suspend oriflammes therefrom covered with pious texts. These stuffs of every colour, as thick as blossom on a peach tree, in lively agitation from the slightest breeze and glittering in the sun, give to this city the aspect of a perpetual fête, contrasting most singularly with the funereal atmosphere one breathes here amid so many obtrusive relics of the dead.

Their chief religious exercise consists in turning round on an axis like a horse in a mill a great drum, crammed with a countless number of written prayers. In the eyes of the faithful, to obtain a turn or two of this miraculous wheel in their favour, is to procure for themselves all the blessings they could hope to attain if the prayers it contains had been turned over on their tongues, or, perhaps,— could they only see the perfunctory procedure of a more enlightened race,—as others are sometimes turned over in a book without a handle. These praying wheels are quite an institution throughout the country. They are seen in the streets of Urga at every thirty or forty paces, and of sufficient size to accommodate a working team of four or five men at a time. Around the lamasery where they are sown broadcast from eighty to a hundred may be counted. Notwithstanding the wheels are as plentiful as fire plugs in civilized cities, and much more accessible when wanted, and, moreover, are as full of prayers " as a pomegranate is full of seed," they are still insufficient for certain Mongols of exemplary piety feeling the need of private devotion, and who make up for the deficiency by turning a little portable wheel in the left hand, whilst their right is fully employed in the public duty of working the big machine of their district. These praying wheels are furnished with two bells, the one having a grave and the other an acute note, which thus indicate by their tone every turn and half turn: an incessant chime is accordingly heard here which contributes very much to the picturesqueness and grotesqueness of this strange spot.

It is not allowed to enter the space before the palace of the *Koutoukta*, either on horse or camel or in a carriage. The rite imposes the duty to approach on foot, but the majority make of it a work of supererogation and only come crouching on their knees.

But among the curious customs of this people, the most singular are the ceremonies that accompany death and the disposal of the dead.

It is a great misfortune in the eyes of the Mongols to die in one's tent: for the entry into paradise is not only closed against the defunct, but a sort of unlucky fatality surrounds, for the future, the dwelling thus contaminated by the presence of a corpse.

As soon as an inhabitant of Urga is seized with a malady considered incurable, and there is no hope of his recovery, he is carried to a chamber, called the chamber of the dying, a kind of funereal building annexed to the lamasery. When the patient is once there, he is in the hands of his priests, who, far from thinking of any remedy for his disease or of giving the least humane assistance, busy themselves merely with saving his soul.

I had the curiosity to enter this abominable hole; but I must admit, I remained there so short a time, that I can give no adequate description of it. I witnessed the lugubrious spectacle of five or six men or women, stretched on carpets on the ground, in the agony of death. But to finish as soon as possible with this gloomy subject, we will now accompany a corpse to its last resting place.

The body is wrapped in a winding sheet of blue linen, but with the face exposed, and carried to a spot about half a mile on the north-east of the town. Arrived here, it is deposited on the ground, and the mourners standing all around begin filling the air with their piercing shrieks. Hardly has this frightful uproar set in than, on looking round, some enormous dogs are seen prowling about, and while these are watching with ferocious eyes, a hoarse croaking is heard in the air, and suddenly ravens and vultures are seen hovering overhead with their sable wings outspread, trembling with impatience. But these hideous specimens of animal life, which nature seems to have strangely adapted to their horrible *rôle* in bestowing on them beaks and claws of blood-red, have not long to wait; for, in about ten minutes, the friends of the deceased, tired of howling, embrace one after the other the feet of the dead and then retire covering their faces. So soon as the spot is cleared nothing can equal the horror of the scene that takes place. The dogs skulk no longer, but advance snarling and growling at one another all the way, whilst the birds voraciously pounce down, filling the air with their sinister croaking. An hour after the ceremony, nothing remains of the dead but the skull and the winding sheet; but he who has been a spectator of this diabolic repast—resembling in every way that of the dream of *Athalie*—has been so profoundly moved, that he will not, for a long time to come, be able to purge his memory of so ghastly a spectacle.

All this side of the town is strewn with skulls and shrouds : it is almost impossible to advance without striking the foot against the one, or getting it entangled with the other. Some lying on the surface and crumbling away, are sometimes carried by the wind to a long distance; others are partially decomposed and lie confounded with the earth. When cyclones visit this district, and the wanderer has the misfortune to encounter their sweeping clouds of dust, he trembles to think what he may be breathing or grating between his teeth.

I returned to the Russian Consul's with my mind quite troubled with what I had just seen : but I found a great distraction in the delightful evening I passed with his family, and in chatting about St. Petersburg and Paris, which my kind hosts knew very well and hoped to visit again soon. I learnt, however, this evening, some sad news : two of the three merchants forming the first caravan, of whom M. Pfaffius had spoken to me with the thought of joining me, had died; one during the journey from Kiachta to Urga, and the other shortly after having left the Mongolian capital. I went to visit the two fresh graves of those who might have been my travelling companions, and I blessed my stars that Lake Baikal had thus retarded my arrival at Kiachta.

The next morning I went to take a walk, with the young interpreter of the Consulate, over a neighbouring mountain, known by the name of the Holy Mountain. It is an object of great veneration, and cannot be ascended otherwise than on foot. It is not permitted to cultivate the smallest plot or to cut a single tree there; so that this is the sole wooded mountain amid the immense bare surface of Mongolia. The inhabitants of this dismal land often leave their homes and retire into the recesses of this wood to meditate here, weeks and even months in gloomy solitude over the vanities of the things of this world, and to enjoy the consolation procured by leading the life of an anchorite. I saw several of these hermits, established in the depths of the wood, occupied incessantly in turning their devotional wheel, and who charitably offered to intercede for us with the *Koutoukta*.

During my sojourn at Urga, I regretted very much my inability to pay a visit to this young divinity. He had died about six weeks before my arrival in the Mongolian capital. I was equally disappointed at not having seen the Grand Lama, who had gone into Thibet, to hunt for another little god. I was all the more sorry, inasmuch as the Russian Consul told me he could, through the Chinese Governor, have enabled me even to approach the feet of the *Koutoukta*. I should thus have been enabled, for a few moments, to interpellate a god on things of the other world. Such a revelation no doubt, if given to the world, would have assured a great success to this book, for the latest novelties in spirit rapping would have shrunk into insignificance by comparison.

Day after day went by, and our caravan we passed on the road, had not yet made its appearance on the horizon. A young Russian had just arrived in a carriage from Kiachta, and had seen nothing of it on the way; I began therefore to get a little uneasy, for I had confided to Pablo not only my baggage, but also my fortune. It will easily be understood that a large sum in *tea bricks*, the only money current in Mongolia, and also in silver pieces, with which I was obliged to provide myself for my future journey in China, constituted altogether cumbersome luggage. I should, certainly, not have acted in this way with everybody, but Pablo was quite an exceptional servant on the score of scrupulous honesty. I had not a moment's uneasiness from a fear that he had fled with the cash: I depended, moreover, on his continual and salutary apprehensions; still, I feared that some evil had visited the caravan, or that Pablo had died, two events, after all, to me not improbable. Fortunately nothing of the sort happened; for, on the fifth day after my arrival at Urga, he presented himself in my room. He at once took my hand and, in the manner of the Turks, pressed it on his forehead, and laid down the key of my carriage like a soldier laying down his sword. Our Mongol guide asked for a day's delay, that he might have time to sell the oxen and buy camels, required for drawing the carriages. I then had time before leaving to become acquainted with my new companions.

M. Schévélof, the leader of the caravan, was about thirty-eight or forty. He was making the journey from Kiachta to Hankow for the seventh time. His complexion was quite yellow from fevers and liver disease contracted in South China. He spoke Chinese and Mongolian most fluently, and was at once our mentor and our interpreter; consequently, if we had lost him on the way, I do not know what would have become of us.

There was also M. Kousnietzof, a young man of twenty, a native of Verchni-Oudinsk, not related to the millionaire I have mentioned, but a young man of the same name leaving his native city for the first time. Like a true Siberian of pure race, he had thick blonde hair that hung down to the middle of his back, and not a filament of down on his chin. Being accustomed to the great boots and full blouse of the Russian national costume, he was not only uncomfortable in the trousers and short coat he had put on for the occasion of his journey into China, but he imagined he was dressed in a manner quite indecent: therefore, to avoid a blush on his cheek, on presenting himself in the drawing-room of the Consul's wife, he had improvised for himself, as he thought in the most becoming manner, a kind of *jupon* with his new shirt, by employing that part the most scrupulously concealed, to cover the indelicate nakedness of a simple pair of trousers.

It would be difficult to find perhaps a more striking, and at the same time a more amusing illustration, of the predominance of conventionalism in the sentiment of modesty.

M. Marine came from Tobolsk, his native city. He was acquainted with Omsk, the Ural, and Catherineburg; he had been once even as far as Perm, and spoke enthusiastically of his distant travels and of what wonders he had formerly seen in the West. His incessant complaining, his slowness and heaviness of manner in body and mind, wearied us a great deal at first, but later we turned all these weaknesses to our amusement, at his expense, and thus this poor sufferer became, I am ashamed to say, the butt of the party.

It was on the 8th of April when I took leave of the Russian Consul at Urga, whose name, I regret, I have forgotten. As he was about to leave shortly for St. Petersburg with all his family, we could wish each other, mutually, *bon voyage*. He accompanied me as far as the gate of his grounds, and, after a cordial hand-shaking, I accomplished on foot the two first *kilomètres* of the five hundred leagues of desert I had to travel over.

On marching thus behind a conveyance, which was to be, for many days to come, my sole habitation, I imagined myself, for an instant, like the *Chevalier des Grieux* attached to a company of strolling players. No one, alas! in the caravan, could complete the illusion by presenting to my imagination, even in the remotest way, the pretty face of *Manon Lescaut*.

M. Schévélof's carriage led the way; it was surmounted with a Russian flag and a Mongolian prayer banner. Then followed M. Kousnietzof's vehicle, and then fourteen camels, carrying the baggage, marching in a line one after the other. Among this baggage there were two tents; one for us, and the

PRAYING MILL AT URGA. (*p.* 322.)

[*To face p.* 332.

other for the Mongols, and besides a set of cooking utensils. And then the rear was brought up by Pablo's carriage, M. Marine's, and my own. We were accompanied by seven natives, who were under a chief on horseback, and these natives, mounted on camels, guarded, each from his elevated position, the portion of the caravan under his care.

We began by threading our way through a fine mountainous country, but scattered all over with huge stones, which, coming in contact with our wheels, gave us a most unpleasant shaking. Towards eleven at night, we halted, but pitched one tent only, intending not to remain long at this spot. This time, we had the luxury of fresh provisions, which we had brought with us from Urga, and, after we had dined, we went to see the Mongols at their repast.

They quickly lighted a fire with camel-dung in the middle of the tent, and having set over it a caldron filled with water, they threw into it a whole sheep that had just been roughly hacked into seven portions without any method. This had hardly simmered a quarter of an hour, when the chief gave the signal to begin.

With their eyes glaring with ravenous impatience, they all, like beasts of prey, rushed around the caldron, and seized each a portion, which they began tearing and devouring, without bread or salt, cracking and crunching the bones between their teeth, and bolting with painful efforts whatever impeded this savage feat of gorging. This enormous quantity of flesh, the whole sheep in fact except the large bones, was despatched with the celerity of a carcass before a pack of voracious wolves, whose feeding, rather than a human repast of the most savage race even, it so strongly resembled.

Since the Mongols have the custom of simply depositing their dead on the ground, they should, from a desire to avoid a similar treatment of the remains of animals, dispose of these otherwise, either by burial or burning. It was the latter process our guides adopted this evening, A most repulsive odour soon filled the tent and compelled us to quit it, and as there was no other retreat than our carriages, we turned into them and slept profoundly.

Our slumbers, however, were of short duration, for we were suddenly awoke by the cries of our men, who were running after one of our pack camels. This poor beast, having probably already experienced the fatigues of the passage of the Gobi, naturally desired to escape from our caravan. Having luckily shaken off, by his bounding, two little chests that were attached to his back, and which happened to belong to me, he had wandered away in the wide desert, or perhaps to the wood on the Holy Mountain, which we had skirted in our route. In short, we never saw him any more, and the accident hindered us from striking our tent this night. Our guide was obliged to go and buy another camel at Urga, and consequently we could not resume our march till ten in the morning.

On the third day we arrived at the foot of a chain of mountains that formed the limits on this side of the desert proper. As the laden camels cannot ascend any hill, our guide hired oxen of the Mongols, who are established on this side of the range to let them for this purpose. It took us four hours to reach the summit, and when I had got so far, I turned to the north to contemplate, for the last time, the magnificent Altái mountains, whose crests covered with snow now shut out Siberia from my eyes; and I bid adieu for ever to its wintry scenes. In this glance I could trace the whole of the wrong route I had just followed, and when I turned to the south, where not a flake of snow was visible, my thoughts brightened with the prospect of spring over the verdant plains of China, which I hoped soon to reach.

We at last entered the great Desert of Gobi, and began a journey which happened to be of eighteen days' duration across this dreary waste.

We stopped but very little on the way, and I wondered how camels, animals that appear so lank and so loose in their framework, could support so much fatigue. We pitched our tents about eleven in the morning, and, while stationary for about two hours, our camels pastured on some sparse grass. When we started the caravan did not stop again till eleven at night.

The night halt, during which the camels slept, did not last more than an hour, and then we went on again without stopping till eleven in the morning.

The centre of the Desert of Gobi resembles the Sahara. It is a sea of sand, over the whole extent of which there is no object whatever to arrest the eye. When a little later we got further into it, and during the four days which it took us to cross the part wholly void of vegetation, our camels accomplished their work as usual without taking the least nourishment. The last day only, several of them stopped and began to lie down, as if to make us understand their extreme fatigue. A few blows with the stick soon set them up on their legs again and, in the end, not one dropped altogether. The horse that our guide had bought at Kiachta, and whose forage of hay and oats was borne by the camels, died at the end of a week, and another, we had bought of the Mongols we met accidentally on our way, shared the same fate. We had here a striking proof, under our eyes, of the superiority of the camel over the horse in supporting prolonged fatigue.

The Mongol leader of our caravan had a thorough knowledge of the desert. During the day he followed, generally, the still visible traces of caravans; skeletons of camels, horses, or sometimes of oxen, which we saw scattered here and there. At night, he kept his eye on a star, as the mariner does on a distant pharos, and marched straight towards it without looking at the ground, like the Magi of the Gospel. Sometimes, however, the sky was covered with clouds and the ground presented no traces of former passages; but these accidents in no way embarrassed him, he continued guiding our caravan towards Kalkann with the calm assurance of a navigator steering his ship towards some port still beyond the reach of vision.

At one night halt, four days after leaving Urga, M. Schévélof reminded us that the next day the orthodox church would celebrate the feast of Easter: "We must," he said, "on this occasion, give ourselves up to some enjoyment." The project was cheerfully adopted. M. Marine ran out and soon brought in some *bonbons*, which he distributed to begin with; and then I said, "I will provide some delicacy for supper," and hastening to my carriage, I quickly selected and brought in a tureen of *foie gras*, a stock of which I had laid in. M. Schévélof opened a bottle of

Crimean wine, and we sat down to a jolly repast.

The Mongols, hearing our merry-making, came and squatted down at the entrance of our tent, and began discussing the delicate qualities of our repast, some vestiges of which they picked up from the ground with avidity. Young Kousnietzof, impatient to contribute his share to the festivity, also left the tent, but instead of returning with some dainty, came in tuning a guitar, which he played delightfully, soothing us with some of the melancholy thoughts of Wassili-Michäelovitch.

This group of five wanderers, squatting around a fire in this little habitation, the sole plot lighted in the midst of the deep solitude and silence of the immensity of the desert, with the party of Mongols grouped in their national costume at the entrance, presented a highly picturesque tableau. The hour of the night, the loneliness of the spot, our remoteness from civilized life and the strangeness of our surroundings, found us in no mood for protracted gaiety, and this soon gave way to silent reverie more in harmony with the solemn incident and the tender melancholy of the

Russian airs. We should certainly, in this mood, have forgotten the hour, if our Mongol chief, more sensible to the exigencies of the desert than to the notes of the guitar, had not suddenly appeared to warn us of the necessity of departure. In a quarter of an hour the tents were folded and packed; we recommenced our march, and the little spot, that had served us as the site of our temporary habitation, no longer presented any mark to distinguish it from the rest of the desert.

CHAPTER XIX.

CARAVAN ACROSS THE DESERT OF GOBI.

A Mongolian Prince and his Court—Prayer turning—Our life in the desert—The sandy plain—Want of water—Lunar mirage—Three executions—A traveller astray in the desert—Arrival at Kalkann and the Great Wall of China.

THE following morning was ushered in with a wind so violent that no one attempted to emerge from his shelter, and, singular enough, this Easter day, which ought to have been passed in rejoicing, disappeared without anyone having sought the society of his fellow travellers. The weather the following day was not better, and we had, in addition, several hail showers that quite whitened the surface of the desert. Therefore, we did not break from our long confinement till the approach of evening, when M. Schévélof descried, with the aid of his telescope, far away, a large assemblage of tents. On drawing nearer we perceived to our disappointment that they were not inhabited by Europeans; for our guide soon discovered that it was a halt of a Mongolian prince, surrounded with his court.

About a score of tents were pitched beside each other, and that of the prince was distinguished by its larger size and by its being enclosed with a kind of wall covered with coarse paintings. Another of about the same size, surrounded with *praying-wheels*, appeared to be the temple of the tribe. On our approach the dogs, that guarded each a tent, set up such a barking and howling that the whole community was stirred up with alarm. Many of the inhabitants seeing, in the distance, we were strangers, came out to meet us from curiosity, and, at the same time, to be assured of our pacific intentions. After an interview between one of these and M. Schévélof, the latter informed us we were to be admitted to the presence of the prince.

The simplicity and bareness of his tent astonished me. There was nothing special to be seen in the interior but a little stove, with a pipe leading from it through the top of the tent. The sole luxury, therefore, of this princely habitation, consisted in a precaution against asphyxia, a danger to which all others in tent life are exposed through the noxious and nauseous smoke. He was squatting on a carpet, and was clad in an ample blue silk robe edged with black velvet, his feet being covered with a kind of black silk boots. His belt, to which were attached all the requisites for smoking and the production of fire, as is usual with the Mongols, was embroidered with silver. His head was covered with a cap of yellow leather, having the border in fur turned up, and surmounted with a blue ball, from which hung a little tuft of hair.

As soon as we entered, he drew from his pocket a little bottle filled with essence of tobacco, which he presented to M. Schévélof. Our leader then withdrew the stopper, to which was attached a minute spoon, took in this a drop of the essence and bore it to his nose, affecting to be highly delighted with the effect, and then, replacing the stopper, passed it to M. Marine, telling him to repeat the same ceremony. When we had, all five of us, gone through this pantomime of simulated joy, for

Pablo did not miss the opportunity of keeping close to my side to share in this novel ceremony, it was necessary to say something. This delicate mission, of course, was the duty of M. Schévélof, who acquitted himself of it with dignity. He then asked permission to visit the temple, and this being accorded, we went to see the lama, who offered to pray to the god to bless the remainder of our journey. As a recompense for this protection of a deity, I presented him with a brick of tea, five needles, and a bit of thread—a recompense in my estimation ample enough, considering the cost of the benediction, however highly cherished might be its effect.

As soon as I retired to my carriage, it was surrounded by five lamas who, prostrated before it, were chanting prayers, each of them turning all the time little *portable prayer wheels*. This comedy was irresistibly ludicrous : the sight of these grave priests, solemnly turning their prayers as a child winds round a toy windmill, was too much for my gravity, and I was obliged to hide my irreverent laughter in the far corner of my carriage. The grand priest, however, soon opened the door without ceremony, to gratify his curiosity with its contents. Not knowing what to do with my visitors, I took a bottle of scent and presented it to their noses, and they were so delighted with the odour that I sprinkled them with it just as the caravan began to march. Their gratitude at this favour was unbounded: they all bowed repeatedly in acknowledgment, and when they were disappearing from my sight, they were being mobbed apparently by the members of the community, who had come up to sniff at their shoulders, so wonderfully odoriferous. This incident was, perhaps—judging from the popular excitement—of sufficient importance to them to be handed down to posterity.

From this time we had beautiful weather, and it became warm also. Our days passed away much in the same way, it is true, but not without pleasure and even merriment at times. When the caravan halted in the mornings, we all came out of our carriages. As we were not in want of water during the first half of our journey, at least for drinking, a discussion usually took place every day, as they were pitching the tents, between my companions, on tea-making. Were they to have fine tea or brick tea? Should they mix with it sheep's milk, wine, or lemon? Should it be prepared entirely in the Mongolian way, that is, with butter, flour, and salt? Many other suggestions, too long to mention here, were made by M. Kousnietzof and even Pablo who, having lived in many lands, had also his methods. When we had all refreshed ourselves, the tents were struck, the camels resumed their march, and, shouldering our guns, we wandered about till five or six in the evening, when we joined our carriages and fell in again with the march of the caravan. Some pursued winged game. M. Kousnietzof never finished the day without having bagged a duck, or a partridge; the latter of a kind common everywhere in Mongolia, but still little known in Europe, with feet covered with hair, not unlike rat's feet.

For my part, I preferred hunting the white deer and bucks, which we sometimes saw in great numbers, but always at a long distance. How many leagues have I not gone out of my way in the hope of stalking one of these animals! On one occasion, in particular, being fully satisfied I had wounded one badly, I was led a pretty dance after it, and I do not know where I should have wandered, if twilight had not warned me that unless I turned back I might lose sight of the caravan, and then go astray in the middle of this desert—the greatest desert in the world.*

M. Marine, through caution or fear of fatigue, did not venture far from the caravan. Sometimes, even, he used to sit at the opening of his carriage, with his feet resting on the steps, and, from this advantageous position, pepper away at everything that came into view, whatever animal it might be, or at whatever distance it might be beyond gun-shot. One day, however, M. Schévélof and I succeeded in stimulating in him the ardour and enthusiasm of a hunter, under circumstances that amused us for a very long time afterwards.

I happened to be walking about half a mile in advance of the caravan, in conversation with its pleasant leader, when we perceived on the ground a dead ermine—unquestionably dead, as its putrid odour proved. We took it up and perched it in a tuft of grass, raising its head and pointing its ears to make it look as lively

---
* See note 14.

as possible; having done this we went to M. Marine to inform him that an excellent opportunity presented itself to have a good shot. Full of excitement at a chance such as he had long pined for on the steps of his carriage, he advances slowly and noiselessly, entreating us not to stir a peg, and to speak only in whispers. He shoulders his piece, aims carefully, fires, and sees nothing escape; clearly he had bagged something at last. "Bravo!" I exclaimed, with a movement as if I intended to secure the animal in a bound; and here the comic part of the incident began. M. Marine stretches out his arm and with a furious gesture stops me. I comply, and he again takes aim with the greatest precaution, whilst M. Schévélof is ready to split with laughing. "Ah! this time he is surely dead," exclaimed M. Marine immediately after the second shot. "But why did you fire twice?" I asked. "I feared I might have missed the first time, and that it might not have heard the report." After this reply we had no end of fun with poor Ivan Ivanovitch.

Shortly after this we came on the great sandy plain I have mentioned that forms the centre of the Gobi desert. The first day passed pretty well : a certain gloom pervaded us, it is true, though we did not pay much attention to it. The second day was more trying. M. Kousnietzof found that they had put a few grains of salt too many in the tea: every one seemed in the humour to complain. The third day was still worse. Wassili Michäelovitch did not even make his appearance in the tent during the morning halt: with the excuse that he had an interesting book to read, he breakfasted in his carriage. We could not have had more agreeable travelling companions, but we all felt the depressing influence of the bareness of nature—the emptiness of space around us.

In the immense solitudes of Siberia there are forests presenting diverse features that relieve the eye with the change of colour or form; on the open sea the waves are constantly in movement, movement that is suggestive of life and consequently engages our sympathy; but here in the desert there is a complete absence of change as well as movement. There is nothing but an endless solitude of silence and rest. Nowhere, perhaps, except in the presence of the dead, or alone among the tombs, of which the desert is strongly suggestive, do we feel so doleful and lonely, such an oppression on the spirits, encompassed as we are by this endless and changeless sandy waste.

As an illustration of the influence of surrounding nature on the mind, we could not resist the gloominess it inspired, and lounged along, moping in our joylessness, one far apart from the other.*

With our eyes cast down, we occupied ourselves in picking up some rare stones with which the desert of Gobi is scattered in certain parts; large agates and many other minerals, unknown to me, quite transparent, and tinged with orange or green; the soil was quite covered with these, presenting a gigantic mosaic.

The Mongol chief declared one morning, that our provision of water was exhausted. "I had reckoned," he said, "on renewing the supply from a pond here that generally contains water, but you see the spot and that it is quite dry." This news, though rather

---

See note 15.

serious, caused a little diversion in the monotony of our existence, and actually made us merry. M. Schévélof and I alone had thought of providing wine, and our stock of it was not large. We had no tea this day, neither with salt, sugar, nor flour; and our tins of preserves had diminished considerably. Filling our glasses with wine, so suddenly enhanced in value, we drank a toast to the prospect of soon finding water.

M. Kousnietzof who, like a true Siberian, would have preferred half a cup of tea to a whole bottle of the most delicate wine, could not accommodate himself very easily to this privation. He was occupied, all day long, in inspecting the horizon around with his telescope, and again resumed at intervals his persevering work at night. "Wada! Wada!" (water, water,) he suddenly calls out, stopping the caravan, and pointing at a spot with a bluish surface near the horizon. In our enthusiasm we all jumped out of our carriages, and began leading the camels that bore the water kegs towards the indicated spot. M. Kousnietzof ran and M. Marine danced with joy, Pablo sang and I followed M. Schévélof, who doubted, and he was the wisest of all. This deceptive blue tint was produced merely by a large bed of salt; so we returned, looking rather *blue* ourselves, to our carriages. The same night, we witnessed a deception of another kind in a lunar mirage. This phenomenon, which appears to be rather rare, is one of the most graceful and enchanting presented by nature. The landscape that charmed our sight was certainly a phantom, for it was far too dissimilar from any real one to be met with in the middle of the desert; and if I had not witnessed it myself, I should certainly have believed, if my companions had faithfully described it to me, that they had been indulging in a flight of imagination. We had before our eyes not only a little lake reflecting the moonbeams from its smooth surface, but we distinguished on its borders the outlines of groups of fine trees, and even some wading birds. Wassili Michäelovitch, who at Verchni-Oudinsk had never even heard of such a thing as a mirage, went leaping towards this little lake, when the Mongols stopped his enthusiastic course by loud peals of laughter. It is probable that this phenomenon, however rare elsewhere, is not uncommon in the Desert of Gobi, since the natives accompanying us appeared in no wise surprised at such a beautiful vision.

Two days afterwards we came upon a little pond of dirty water, quite stagnant, and surrounded with skeletons of all kinds of animals that had come there to quench their thirst and then die. This water, in which I did not venture to wash myself, was welcomed by us as a God-send. The camels that had not drunk for a very long while, and even, till just previously, eaten anything for many days, needed ample rest. We, therefore, made here a long halt. After the repast M. Kousnietzof began giving us some airs on his guitar, and our caravan, that had been as dull as the ditch water, cheered up a little. We were still in the heart of this great solitude, but we were confident that the most difficult part had been passed, and we should now overcome all further obstacles.

Five or six days later we fell in with a few Mongols. Our leader exchanged one of our camels that was jaded for one of theirs fresh and strong: we bought, also between us, a sheep. This day did not pass without some excitement. The new camel had not yet been broken in to any kind of work: it was therefore necessary to begin by piercing a hole through his nose, in order to pass a stick through it for the purpose of taming and leading him. This operation was not performed without difficulty, for it is extremely painful to the animal. And, besides, one of our camels had its foot cracked; this kind of accident happens pretty often at the end of journeys, on account of the protracted fatigue and the hardness of the ground. The Mongols treat it by sewing together the wound, and the suffering of the poor beast may be easily imagined. But the principal business was the killing of our sheep; the first Mongol appointed by our leader for this work refused to obey; he opened his robe, and showing us a little copper idol suspended on his chest, "I am a lama," he said, "and I am forbidden to spill blood, even the blood of animals." Another Mongol undertook the function of a butcher, but he killed the sheep in a strange way. He made a long incision in the abdomen, and then thrust his arm into the wound to seize the heart and stop its beating by holding it fast.

An adventure, of which I was the hero, caused some delay. About an hour after the caravan had resumed its march, after the usual night halt, the tether that attached my camel to Pablo's carriage got loose; and the beast, feeling itself no longer drawn along, stopped altogether. When my camel found himself thus left behind, I was in the rear of the caravan. The Mongols were sleeping profoundly between the two humps of their camels, and, consequently, not knowing that anything was amiss, kept on their course. The reader may imagine my sensations on finding myself quite alone on awaking in the morning. Fortunately I had the presence of mind to avoid going in search of the caravan; for if I had attempted to overtake it I should, in all probability, have gone astray altogether, and, perhaps, in this plight if any natives had observed my weakness and inexperience, they might have shown towards me little benevolence and hospitality. I sat down on the ground before my stupid-looking camel, with a good mind to give him a sound beating: but, fearing he might take flight, I was constrained to treat him kindly, for I dreaded beyond everything to be obliged to stir even a hundred yards from the spot where I had been left, because there I hoped to be found again. This anxious loneliness, happily, came to an end about ten in the morning. At daybreak, the Mongols having perceived my absence, stopped and turned back on the traces of the caravan, spreading out in different directions. I was soon led back, and the caravan hailed my return with joyous shouting. Pablo was quite overcome with joy on seeing me safe again; his fidelity and attachment could not be more strongly manifested.

The surface was now gradually becoming a little hilly, and we were soon surrounded with high mountains. The temperature had become quite mild, and as the moon shone in all its splendour, our journeying was now easy and agreeable. The tents of the Mongols were more numerous, and we met two or three Chinese caravans going to Maimatchin. At last the route, like the way on leaving Urga, was again strewn all over with huge stones, and these enabled our guide to announce to us that three days later we should come in sight of the Great Wall.

When Mongolia is traversed from north to south, the traveller rises gradually, without suspecting it on account of the ease of the ascent, to four thousand feet above the sea-level. On arriving at this culminating point the land is found cut almost perpendicularly to the depth of this elevation, and in such a manner that, to continue the route, it is necessary to descend by a series of zig-zags cut out by the hand of man, the descent of which is as rapid as the most perilous mountain paths of the Alps and Pyrenees. It is along this peaked crest that the Great Wall of China runs. It is not built of brick, like the interior walls of Nang-Kao for example, of which I shall say something hereafter, and which many travellers erroneously take for the true Great Wall. But the true Great Wall that separates, in the first place, Mongolia from China proper, is built of stones laid over each other without cement. Towers, placed at certain distances from each other, are more solidly constructed, and have thus more effectually resisted the wear of time. This wall has the form of capital A open : the others, which I believe are seven in number, unless I passed more in the night without having seen them, form as many transverse bars.

When our caravan, after three days of fatiguing march across the rough stony land I have mentioned, reached the Great Wall of China, it was about six in the morning on the 29th of April. The sun appeared on the horizon, and we could distinguish a series of hills stretching far away into the interior, with the intervening spaces veiled in cloud. We could see these undulations of the Celestial Empire to advantage at the great elevation we had arrived at, and we sat down some time admiring the magnificent spectacle.

My attention was struck immediately by the remarkable difference between the country we had just travelled over and the one we were about to enter. Behind me was a wild uncultivated waste, and before me extended that famous fertile land that bestows annually on its people two crops of corn or rice, and two crops of vegetables. On one side it was an unpeopled desert, and on the other a swarming of human beings numbering probably more than four hundred millions, and whose assemblage of four hundred thousand even constitutes but a village among its populous cities. But a little while ago it was everywhere bleak and barren, and for the future it will be sunshine over rich verdant lands. Thus much for the most striking advantages on the side of China, to which may be opposed others on the side of Mongolia. The air of Mongolia was pure and invigorating; that of China will be nauseating and unhealthy. The soil was covered with a sand so coarse that the most violent winds were unable to raise it: the soil in future will be composed of a dust so fine that the least breeze will lift it in clouds, impeding the sight and respiration. The Mongols were hospitable; the Chinese will be hostile; the mere circumstance of being there constitutes an offence in their eyes, and one they would punish if they dared. It would be difficult to find two neighbouring countries more dissimilar than China and Mongolia in the nature of the soil and in the character of the inhabitants. The Great Wall, which has separated them in the past, does not seem by its ruin to bring them nearer to one another in the future. If I were asked which of these two peoples I prefer, though it is difficult to compare a civilized with a savage race, I should reply: "The Mongol is superior to the Chinese in honesty and disposition; but the latter to the Mongol in talent and ingenuity in the arts."

We descended on foot the zig-zags that lead from the Great Wall to Kalkann. The natives formed in two rows to see us pass. They came from all parts, even from underground; for they live in caves like the caverns of Touraine, which they have scooped out of the rock in the side of the mountain. The women with their little feet walk with difficulty, and holding a child by one hand make use of the other as a balancing pole to maintain their equilibrium. M. Schévélof got into a rage two or three times with these people, who pressed in around and would not get out of the way to let us pass, and yet we were only in the rural part. Five hours after passing the Great Wall we came to the bottom of the valley, which narrows here almost to a gorge. The aspect of the country is picturesque. A little rivulet, which occasionally swells out in width to fill the whole valley, meanders along, sometimes at the foot of an enormous rock, sometimes lost in a thicket of verdure. Everything is pretty and graceful, but strange in form and arrangement. I recognised here the models of Chinese landscapes I have seen in France, and which I had always taken to be imaginary compositions. Thus in the midst of this valley, formed between two great hills of majestic dark rocks, rises abruptly a pointed granite mound, on the top of which is built a temple: a little further, an enormous red rock is suspended, in a manner incomprehensible, on the apex of a cone of earth. The whole of this singular bit of nature is variegated and enlivened by trees, irregularly disposed here and there, freshly decked in their vernal dress.

If the reader will picture to his fancy this landscape, peopled with men of effeminate look with long pig-tails, and women with painted faces presenting the appearance of wax figures, he will form some idea of the country we traversed in descending from the Great Wall of China.

CHAPTER XX.

FROM THE GREAT WALL TO TCHAH-TAO.

First view of China proper—Last Russian hospitality—The Palankeen—The streets of Kalkann—Travelling along the Great Wall—The Secret Societies—Chinese Art—How order is maintained—Origin of the tress—How the titles of Chinese nobility become extinct.

WE were hospitably received in a Chinese house belonging to a Russian, a friend of M. Schévélof. This house was charmingly situated out of the town, on the other side of the brook I have just mentioned, and, consequently, in view of the mountain we had lately descended surmounted with the irregular outline of the Great Wall.

It was the last Russian house into which I entered, and not the least agreeable. During my leisure in the day I went to ramble about this strange country and among the still more strange people.

I lounged also many hours on the balcony

of this house, where I took refreshments, agreeably occupied in contemplating the scene around me. I shall never forget these days of *far niente* passed at Kalkann after the long monotonous passage of the Gobi without stages and almost without repose. I was approaching at last the goal of my travels— that city of Pekin, towards which I had been almost daily moving for the last seven months. I was indeed in China at last, and all my surroundings forcibly impressed me with the novelty of my situation. I was never tired of watching every object, every incident, from my observatory, and when evening closed in I quitted it with regret.

Then we retired to a distant room. Wassili Michäelovitch, as well as a young inhabitant of Tientsin who happened to be visiting Kalkann, played on the guitar, and, in listening to the melancholy notes of their melodies, I recalled to memory the far-reaching steppe of Omsk and its changing aspects, the perilous night adventure in the snow on leaving Tumen, the savage grandeur of the frozen Angara, the terrors of the lonely Baikal, Mrs. Grant and Constantine—all my adventures in

Siberia,—in fact, that now, with the rigours of an Arctic winter, were things of the past. The remembrance of all these incidents I cherished with that genial sensation that is experienced when we find ourselves safe at the end of a series of perilous adventures, provided they leave behind no ill consequences, but, on the contrary, a feeling of congratulation that we have so happily escaped them.

But what a contrast was this past to the present! It was not simply a change of country and people, but a change of the face of nature; for the trees had put forth their tender leaves and vied in brilliancy of tints with the verdure of the ground, and the whole was bathed in the genial beams of the warm spring sun.

Still it is the destiny of a traveller, who has before him a long journey to be accomplished without delay, to be always on the move. On the morning of the 3rd of May, therefore, we had five palanquins brought up for our accommodation. They are a kind of litter without wheels, furnished with two long shafts projecting before and behind and supported by these on two mules. The mule in the rear is not put in without some trouble, it being repugnant, apparently, to these animals to go into the shafts head foremost; they are, therefore, generally obliged to have their eyes bandaged during the operation.

The palanquin with mules is the most disagreeable vehicle I have ever travelled in: in the first place the greatest care is necessary to keep yourself quite in the middle, inasmuch as the least movement on the one side or the other disturbs at once the adjustment of the harness. In the second place the two mules do not step together or move in harmony, and consequently there is a continual pitching and jolting in every direction, producing as much sickness and distressing fatigue as the movement of the sea.

Our host would accompany us beyond Kalkann; we, therefore, began our journey afoot, going through the city from end to end. We went inside the fortifications, which consist of crenulated walls very solidly built, and from these we had a good view of the streets.

The attention is arrested at once by the swarming of the population. The Arab bazaars, the most thronged even, can give no adequate idea of such a circulation. The noise of all this is quite equal to the concourse. Every shop-keeper considers it his duty to stand in front of his shop to praise his wares. He calls out to the passer-by, to invite him to come in and buy, and, as every one strains his voice to make himself heard over his competitor, it may easily be imagined what a hurly-burly would greet the ear on penetrating further into the city.

Mule drivers, palanquin leaders, mandarins' coachmen or carriers, scream also with all their might to have the way clear. Conjurers and tumblers are exercising their profession all along the streets, some violently beating their drums, others blowing their bamboo pipes with all the vigour at their command to arrest attention. But the concert of sounds is not yet complete; children being drubbed are squalling, and awkward people, that cannot escape from being crushed, are screaming: petty traders are violently quarrelling with their rivals, and then comes the growl of the tam-tam, marking, from time to time, the hour or the intervals on the bourse. An early morning at Billingsgate, or at the Halles in Paris, is quite peaceable in comparison with the obstreperous precinct of a Chinese town. Our ears were greeted with this uproar for an hour without cessation in passing on our way from one end to the other. M. Schévélof turned round to me many times with a wearied look, and exclaimed : " O Mongolia ! calm of the desert, how precious thou art, and how I regret thee! " We arrived at last at the limit of the town, passed through another gate, and were in the country again, but Chinese country without solitude and silence. We took leave of our host, and a quarter of an hour afterwards we were swinging in our five palanquins, anxious to look out, but, following the advice of Mr. Schévélof, we closed our curtains and tried to escape from persecuting curiosity.

When night had quite closed in I opened the three windows of my palanquin, one on the right, one on the left, and the other in front, and was thus enabled to contemplate at my ease the magnificent scenery amid which we were travelling.

We had entered into a narrow and precipitous ravine: it was indeed so narrow, occasionally, that the palanquin had only just room to pass. Massive rocks rising perpendicularly were starting on our vision on all sides. It was clear we were now travelling along the crest of a mountain range, for gaps suddenly appearing here and there opened to view fearful precipices that made the head swim. The wind was blowing violently all the evening; and clouds flitting quickly over the face of the moon gave, through the fitful movements of light and darkness, a most fantastic aspect to this bit of nature.

We fell in with a second wall, built also of stone like the first, but in a better state of preservation: we travelled some distance over this wall, and our mules sometimes approached so near the edge that they made us tremble. The rear mule is especially disquieting to the traveller unaccustomed to this mode of locomotion, this one being obliged to follow blindly the leading of the other; but, unlike the leader, unable to pick its way with the same liberty, and being drawn along at the same time over the ground, which is hardly visible; but at the moment the foot is ready to fall, might very easily take a false step and draw everything with it over the precipice. In several places the Great Wall, along the top of which we were travelling this night, turned suddenly in its course at a right angle; and as our mules had the detestable habit like those of the Alps to follow invariably the edge of a precipice, it resulted that while the leader was turning these angles the rear mule must have marched in a line which would, if prolonged a few feet, have led over the brink of the declivity. In order, however, to accommodate their course to each other, as the rigidity of the shafts compelled them, a struggle invariably took place between the two, and, inevitably, at the most critical spot, during which the poor traveller found himself unpleasantly suspended a moment over the angle of the fearful escarpment.

After a journey of sixty *lies*, about twenty English miles, not without exciting moments, but still in contemplating a phase of nature unique, perhaps, in the world, we arrived at Suen-oua-fou. No sooner had we passed the fortifications of this village than our mule drivers began uttering constantly repeated cries. There is no country more infested with secret societies than China. Every inhabitant of this empire makes it a point of honour to belong to one or two of them. The cries of our mule leaders were the rallying signals of those to which they were attached. I wondered what was the cause of this warning, but did not discover it.

The hotel at which we stopped was disposed like the houses of Maimatchin, already mentioned: there was merely that difference between the two which there is in France between an inn and a palace. One thing in particular deserves notice; it is that throughout China, even in the most humble dwellings, art may be recognized, not merely in the general arrangement, but even in the minutest details. The tables that are placed on the estrade of every room, the stools, the little cups out of which rice brandy is sipped, the small teapots, the slender eating sticks, have all an artistic form or look. It is very often singular, and even occasionally a little farfetched, but everywhere may be witnessed the predominance of artistic ideas, and every object is interesting to examine. After the meal—a miserable low tavern repast this time, and sadly adapted to the demands of European palates—we soon stretched ourselves to sleep, like the Chinese, on the estrade where we had just dined.

The next day, the 4th of May, we passed over a charming country; the loveliest I have seen anywhere, except in some parts of Japan. We followed constantly the course of a rivulet only a few yards wide meandering along the foot of a wall-sided cliff, the top of which was crowned with large trees that formed a bower over the stream and dropped from their spreading branches long festoons of verdant tufty creepers, coming down to caress lovingly the bosom of the brook. We continued our way through this attractive country for at least sixty *lies* more, and at last arrived at an immense village, called Ti-mih-gnih, about eleven in the morning, where we breakfasted. This, like all Chinese villages, was fortified, and had outgrown its fortifications from time to time, for there were several lines of enclosure one within the other. It may surpass in size Toun-cheh-ouh, with its population of 400,000 souls. It took us an hour to cross it.

Perhaps the reader may wonder how good government is ensured among such masses of human beings, and may suppose that an immense army is requisite for the emperor to maintain his throne and his dynasty. Order is secured almost without an army, and by means of a secret police and the rigorous application of the law by those who are responsible for its maintenance. The father of the family answers with his head as a gauge for the conduct of his children; the mandarin of the third class likewise for the order of his district, etc. On the other hand, the father has the power of life or death over his children; and the mandarin likewise over the members of his district. In case of conspiracy, therefore, it may be suspected what takes place. The father of a family, fearing the repressive power of the mandarin, sacrifices his children immediately he knows they are guilty. Before revolution can reach so far as the imperial palace, all the members of the administrative hierarchy must have steeped their hands in it with the conviction that they have all thereby exposed their lives. Such an event, therefore, is highly improbable. This explains also how many travellers have been witnesses of twenty or thirty executions at a time, as they have described in their narratives. If a mandarin admonished of a grave crime in his district spares a single accomplice, he is responsible to his superior : he generally prefers, then, to sacrifice a few lives, and thus be on the right side for the safety of his own head, to running the risk of overlooking a single guilty one.

It is quite intelligible that with such summary, arbitrary proceedings, the Chinese government does not desire Europeans to penetrate into its empire. They are, in short, an imbecile race, who are so besotted as to share the hatred of their government towards us and sacrifice the missionaries we send there rather than profit by them to obtain their liberty.

On leaving Ti-mih-gnih the valley opened considerably. The wind became so boisterous that it caused our mules to yield to its force, even so far as to expose them to the risk of being blown over the edge into the river. After a third march of sixty *lies* we reached Chah-tchen. The evening passed away in the most disconsolate manner. The palanquin journey and the Chinese *cuisine* superadded, had indisposed us severely. M. Schévélof, M. Wassili-Michäelovitch, and Pablo did not even rise from their palanquins. M. Marine and I only slept on the inn platform.

We were startled out of our slumbers in the middle of the night by the report of fire-arms in the court. We leaped up in a hurry, convinced that one of our companions, and probably young Kousnietzof, who had two guns and a revolver, had been the victim of an accident. Our fears were, however, immediately calmed on seeing our friends in a deep sleep. The discharge of fire-arms had taken place undoubtedly in the street. A Chinese man or woman had perhaps received it full in the chest, an incident much too trifling to interrupt one's slumber in this country.

We started early the next morning, and having done fifty *lies* through an uninteresting country we stopped to breakfast at Hrouaé-laeh-sien.

The Chinese villages, just the same as the Arab villages, are very much like one another.

I was never tired, however, at every halt of regarding this bustling movement, quite exceptional and unknown in our western cities, even the most commercial, such as London, San Francisco, or New York. How many types presented themselves in reality now! types I had seen formerly only in albums, or on folding screens. The street porter balancing on his shoulder a pole of exaggerated length, with little round cards hanging from each end covered with dragons or some fantastic figures; children with puffed-out stomachs and three little tails of hair hanging from their shaven crowns, one above the forehead and the other two dangling near their ears. The constant shaving till the age of twelve or fifteen gives to the hair of the back of the head an unusual vigour when it is wanted to form a fine pigtail.

The habit of adults of preserving but a single long tress behind, dates only from the conquest of the Tartars and the establishment of their dynasty. The conquerors being Mahometans, and consequently fanatics, endeavoured to impose the Koran throughout China. They did not succeed in this object, but an edict promulgated by the Emperor, requiring the head to be shaved in the Arabian manner, preserving merely a little tuft of hair on the crown of the head, commonly called the *Mahomet*, continued in force. But as the Chinese are artistic in everything they do, they transformed the ludicrous little tuft of the Arabs into a long thick silky tress. This *coiffure* is, moreover, perfectly consistent with the climate and the nature of the soil. It is so in this way; the dust is so fine, and consequently is so copiously raised by the lightest breeze, that it is necessary after the least travelling, or in Pekin after even an ordinary promenade in the streets, to get into a bath so soon as one reaches his home. Now all the Chinese without exception have abundance of hair, and if they were to keep it all on their heads, it may easily be imagined what care and trouble it would demand to cleanse it, and if neglected, particularly by those whose occupations compelled them to remain constantly in the open air, what foul, dusty mops they would have usurping the place of head-gear. Exported and sold too, in such a condition, these shorn chignons would evidently be less presentable to the ladies of England and France, to whom China sends so many cargoes of these delicate *objets de luxe*—the only valuable remnants probably of so many decapitated criminals.

They can, on the other hand, very easily keep their pigtail free from dust, and as spruce as a skein of silk, either by hiding it under a cap, or by letting it hang under their clothing. The peasants, who are obliged during summer to work in the open field, use this tress to fasten large wet napkins over their heads as a protection against the fierce rays of the sun.

It is astonishing, moreover, on entering China—a country we in France have too long ridiculed—to see what industry pervades the people in everything they do, and especially in their agriculture, which, however much it may be favoured by the richness of the soil, is nevertheless indebted for its prosperity to the industry of the people.

With regard to this question I will refer to a social organization well worth notice. When a Chinese has merited by his services a title of nobility, his son in due course inherits merely the title immediately inferior, and the nobility thus descends, diminishing in rank in the family from generation to generation until it becomes definitely extinct, unless one of its members render some service to his country and thus regain the title originally granted to his ancestors. No one, certainly, has more veneration than I have for old French families and ancient titles; but I should always desire to have good reason to esteem the men that are honoured by them as much as I respect the bare names and titles themselves. The ingenious Chinese institution gives an ever active emulation to the nobility, a desire all the stronger to render a service to the country, since the title is always fading away, because it is thought more dishonourable to suffer this inheritance to become extinct by those who have enjoyed it, than never to have merited a distinction at all.

CHAPTER XXI.

TCHAH-TAO TO PEKIN.

An exciting incident—The Pass of Nang-kao—Picturesqueness of the gorge—A young married couple—The levy of taxes—Toun-cheh-ouh—The last solitude—Entry into Pekin—Arrival at the Legation.

AFTER having travelled over fifty *lies* since leaving Hrouaé-lach-sien, we arrived at Tchah-tao. This village is picturesquely situated at the foot of a little mountain that carries the third wall—here a brick wall. As we arrived rather early, and our inn was near the gate of the town, we went to take a walk along the ramparts, which consist of a great brick wall four or five yards wide. I was much astonished to see there two cannon without carriages, lying abandoned as useless lumber. Can it be true that cannon existed in China long before we had any notion in Europe of the properties of gunpowder? But it is quite certain that no European expedition has penetrated so far as Tchah-tao. These bronze cannon unfortunately bore no inscription, nor even any mark that might indicate their origin.

During this promenade M. Marine thoughtlessly threw a stone from the ramparts, which happened to hit a dog below. The proprietor of the animal turned round in a rage, and seeing that the projectile had been thrown by a European, tried to excite the crowd to take vengeance for such an outrage. The opportunity was only too well appreciated, and we were followed by more than five hundred persons, in our retreat to the inn, hooting, and showing a disposition to rush on us. M. Schévélof made a sign for me to retire with Pablo into some obscure corner, and mounting on the platform began addressing them to pacify their anger.

"We are not Europeans," he earnestly remonstrated. "We are Siberians; look at our passports; the two peoples are brothers, and you cannot doubt our friendly sentiments." A few Chinese who spoke Russian, of which there are instances everywhere here, replied in this language; the affair then came quietly to an end. Pablo and I did not venture out of our hole till this mob was dispersed, and M. Schévélof advised us on account of the adventure to quit the village at day-break.

This day we were to go through the famous passes of Nang-Kao, between the village of Nang-Kao and the portion of the Great Wall the nearest to the capital—an attraction that no tourist to Pekin disregards. Dreading the shocks of the palanquin in so mountainous a country, and desiring to enjoy as much as possible the grand scenery at our ease, we jogged along on asses, from Tchah-tao to Nang-Kao. About an hour after we had left the village, and having passed the brick wall I have mentioned, we arrived at the pass, the entrance of which is very narrow, and is closed by a fourth wall.

The approach is by zigzags in the declivity similar to those we passed between Mongolia and Kalkann, and then, after crossing a fifth wall, one enters into a narrow gorge extremely picturesque. The Chinese doubtlessly must have formerly regarded this spot as the most formidable entrenchment against the Mongols. In a gorge that can only be approached by an escarped road, and protected by two walls surmounted with crenelated towers and fortresses, there were certainly the means of an obstinate defence for a long time, even against an enemy very superior in number. When the tourist has arrived at the bottom of the valley the route is continued amid remarkable sites constantly varied. I will mention one only that struck me more than the others by its originality and its charming aspect.

The pass at this spot may be from about twelve to sixteen yards wide.

The little river of Nang-kao occupies the whole width of it, and scatters its waters amid scores of rocks. Our little donkeys were obliged to leap from one to another to clear the passage between. The two walls of rock forming the gorge overhang the river, and come so near to one another at a certain height that they admit through the opening but a few rays to light up, in a mysterious gloom, this sort of natural grotto. The Chinese have scooped out a little temple in the face of one of these rocks about ten yards from the ground.

It is reached by steps cut out on the wall of the rock, having the appearance of a natural causeway. The entrance of the temple is ornamented with sculptured wood painted red and gilded, with lanterns and all sorts of suspended ornaments. Nothing can be more charming, or gayer and prettier, and at the same time more Chinese than this little nook, which is all at once a valley, a grotto, the bed of a rivulet, and a sanctuary. Once in my life only have I desired to be an idol. Happy the god that dwells in such an enchanting spot!

I was quite astonished on emerging from this little temple to find on the other side the walls of the rock sculptured in the Egyptian manner, and kinds of modillions, as in the land of the Pharaohs.

The remainder of the pass of Nang-kao is also very fine, but resembling too much many similar my readers must have frequently seen in their travels, to render it worth while to describe it here.

But I may say briefly that it resembles the entrance to the gorges of the Trent, Roland's Breach, and the valley of the Chiffa in Algeria; what may be seen and admired very often in mountainous countries. I should mention, however, a village gate, a kind of triumphal arch in stone, sculptured, sunk, and covered with dragons and fabulous monsters in such a way that it may certainly be reckoned among the *chefs-d'œuvre* of Chinese art.

We crossed in due course the two last walls of China, or, to speak more correctly, the two last buttresses of the Great Wall of Kalkann, and arrived at Nang-kao. I was delighted to hear myself addressed in French on entering this village by the Chinese mule drivers and sedan carriers, and to see written on the walls of the inn warnings in French to travellers, such as this: "Défiez-vous du maître de l'hôtel, c'est un hardi voleur;" signed "Un officier de marine compâtissant envers les étrangers;" and many similar.

The reason was, Nang-kao is often a place of rendezvous for the *personnel* of the embassies at Pekin; and the tourists who visit the capital never omit going to Nang-kao and the tomb of the Mignes, returning by the Summer Palace and the Great Bell. It is the established excursion, just as to see the Mer de Glace of Chamounix or the Righi of Lucerne.

After we had resumed our palanquins to take our way to the village of Kouan-chih-lih, M. Schévélof said to me: "We are obliged to reach as quickly as possible the south of China, and consequently to take the road to Toun-cheh-ouh and Tien-tsin. We have just decided on not going to Pekin; still, you are not far from the capital here, and the time is come to separate and say adieu." "I will go with you to the next stage, Toun-cheh-ouh, and from there to Pekin," I said, unwilling to part till absolutely necessary. In truth this sudden announcement of a separation, the prospect of finding myself alone with Pablo in an unknown country, among people that seemed hostile and to whom I could not make myself intelligible, inspired me with misgiving and almost fear. The reader will see what curious result this decision led to from what follows.

At the moment of starting we saw coming into the court of the inn a palanquin borne by two men. It contained, therefore, some aristocratic personage; for in China such a mode of locomotion is permitted only to persons enjoying a certain dignity or holding a certain rank in the hierarchy. The horse and the mule palanquin may be used by everybody; the carriage, and especially the carriage having the axle far removed from the shafts, as well as the palanquin borne by men, are reserved for the aristocracy.

We, therefore, approached this privileged vehicle as soon as we saw it enter into the court of our inn, and presently there descended from it a lady apparently rather pretty, if one might say that a lady could be pretty under a thick coat of paint, with the disadvantage of extraordinary *embonpoint*. What I specially remarked was the apparent absence of feet. Under the ankle the leg ended in a point like the end of a stilt or a wooden leg.

The poor woman, whom this conformation indicated as a member of the high class, and as one to be admired and envied by all fine connoisseurs and people of the most refined taste, could not take a single step, even supported between her two servants. She was carried from the palanquin, to be laid down like anything else unendowed with power of movement, on the platform of a distant

MY PALANQUIN. [*To face p.* 386.

room. M. Schévélof was informed on questioning the palanquin men that she was the wife of a great mandarin, on his honeymoon tour.

We saw the happy husband arrive a few minutes later; it will be sufficient to say he was just like the governor of Maimatchin, already mentioned. These Chinese husbands of high rank should be free from any anxiety on the score of their wives *running away* from them, and at the same time be perfectly satisfied with the important guarantee they hold for obedience to their lord and master.

As the distance is very great between Kouan-chih-lih and Toun-cheh-ouh we left as early as two in the morning. On leaving Nang-kao we left the mountains also, to enter on the plains of Pekin. The country, therefore, was not what would be called picturesque, but it was so well cultivated, so green, so well wooded with fine trees, so cool, from the numerous canals cutting it in every direction, that I was never tired of regarding it, and the sight was all the more grateful to my eyes after the perpetual snow of Siberia and the monotonous desert of Mongolia, in spite of the picturesqueness of their mountain scenery.

After having travelled over sixty *lies* we halted a short time at Lih-choui-tziao, and then resumed our way. We easily passed the Chinese custom house of Tum-bah, thanks again to the ability of M. Schévélof. Wherever the Chinese impose a tax it is difficult to escape it, and to the collection of taxes the law of responsibility extends also. The sovereign says to the grand mandarins, " I want so much money from your government." The grand mandarin says to his subordinate, " I want so much from your province," taking care to double the sum for security. The mandarin of the second class exacts the same from the mandarin of the third class, in each case doubling through precaution ; and the mandarin of the third class announces to his district that he must raise such and such a tax, again doubled no doubt through being over zealous.

Such an organisation doubtlessly is burdensome to the tax-payer, but since so much is extracted, this is precisely what seems to me an incontestable proof of the great riches of this country. In spite of these abuses, misery and destitution are apparently not very prevalent. During the whole of my sojourn in China, there were hardly eight or ten who came to me begging, whilst in Egypt, a country reputed rich, one is constantly assailed with packs of beggars dinning in one's ears: " Backsheesh," " chavaga."

It was about four in the afternoon when we entered the immense village of Toun-cheh-ouh, on the banks of the Pei-ho.

We were entertained at the house of a young Chinese full of health and *embonpoint*, reminding one a little of the exaggerated round figure of Mr. Punch, but a thoroughly good fellow, and one fond of good living in every way. He served us a dinner *à la russe*, which I found to my taste, after the detestable *cuisine* of the Chinese cook-shop.

Immediately after this repast my companions went to embark for Tien-tsin, and I accompanied them as far as the river. On the way M. Schévélof gave all the necessary instructions to my host to enable him to provide for my safe journey on the morrow to Pekin.

When these tea merchants arrived at the port, they entered into one of the barges moored to the shore, in the middle of whose decks is raised a construction for passengers, resembling somewhat that of the Venetian gondola. We wished one another good-bye and pleasant journeys, and off they went. These merchants in departing from my sight dropped completely the curtain between me and the Empire of the Czars, and I turned mine eyes from Siberia, a country over which, in spite of its fertility and auriferous riches, a bird of prey seemed to be continually hovering. Therefore, on seeing the last ties that held me, though only remotely, to this unfortunate land of exile and sorrow cut away, I felt relieved from an oppression, notwithstanding the singular position in which I found myself among these bulb-shaped Chinese. I could say nothing whatever to my host. Even Pablo's talent in expressing himself in pantomime became quite insufficient to penetrate the limited intelligence of the Buddhist with whom I was lodged. I could not close an eye the whole night on account of the repeated attacks of an army of fleas, that annoyed me with their scouts in every quarter, drawn out probably by a change of diet in which they revelled ; and again on account of the night watch, whose duty it was to make a row to frighten away thieves, according to the Chinese custom, which I first became acquainted with at Krasnoïarsk. The next day my host could not provide me with a palanquin before one in the afternoon. I was, however, very glad that he had even so far complied with the instructions of M. Schévélof, for if he had been disposed to keep me at his house some time, I really do not know how I could have managed to have got out of it again. Just as I was going away I gave a trifle to one of the servants: the master perceiving it called all the servants together, who came and knelt before me and touched the ground with their foreheads. However familiar a European may be with Oriental manners, he can never regard without a pang such a spectacle of slavish humility. I jumped into my palanquin as quickly as possible, and took leave of my host, not in offering my hand, which is not in accordance with Chinese custom, but in pressing my hands together, and moving them two or three times in a line perpendicular to my chest. I understood, with satisfaction, that this obliging man recommended my mule driver to conduct me to the

French Embassy; then we started, Pablo and I, towards the capital of the Celestial Empire.

Whilst I was journeying under a burning sun over this road, covered with thick dust, in the abominable vehicle called a palanquin, three young horsemen, whom I shall present to the reader, galloped by without drawing rein between Tien-tsin and Pekin.

The distance is thirty-two leagues, and they would accomplish it in a day. They had, certainly, no time to lose. Having left Tien-tsin at four in the morning, they had stopped an hour in a village to breakfast and change horses: at the time I was leaving Toun-cheh-ouh, they had just begun the second stage. In order to go from Paris to Pekin, these three young French travellers had not braved the hardships of a Siberian winter, nor the monotony of a sledge, nor the discomfort of a Chinese vehicle; and yet their adventures were as interesting as mine. They had been through India: they had been received in the palaces of the nabobs of that country, far more attractive I should say than those of the gold hunters of the North: they had hunted wild beasts in Ceylon and Java, chased the elephant in the virgin forests of Malacca, and continuing their hardy course, they thought it a mere trifle to do thirty-two leagues a day, intending, if circumstances admitted of it, to resume their journey at the same speed.

The first of these three young men—one of my best friends, who, whilst we were travelling a few miles apart on the plain of Pekin, I thought was in Paris—was the Baron Benoist Méchin; his two comrades were the Viscomte de Gouy d'Arsy and Monsieur Guillaume Jeannel. They arrived at the legation as I came in sight of the fortifications of the capital of China.

At this sight I felt quite a glow of enthusiasm. The longer one has had an object in view, and the more efforts he has made to attain it, the greater is the joy on reaching it at last. It is difficult to find anything grander and more boldly constructed than the first wall of Pekin. It is a wall of imposing elevation, crenelated, and perfectly regular. Here and there fortresses are raised above principal gates, rising to three or four stories, and roofed in green porcelain, that glitters in the sun. The gates are of bronze, and gigantic: they are closed at night, and at certain hours of the day.

I did not enter the city without feeling a thrill of emotion. I had to pass over some irregular space scattered over with low, unsightly habitations; then I entered into the populous quarter; finally, under a dome of foliage I perceived a wooden gate, elegantly sculptured with two marble lions, above which I could read, "Légation de France." I had at last accomplished my journey from Paris to Pekin overland.

When I entered into the salon of M. de Geoffroy, who was the Envoy Extraordinary of France in China, all the *personnel* of the legation were present to do honour to the three young travellers I have just mentioned. I shall never forget my entry into this hospitable salon, where I found so much courtesy and affability. The palace was quite an Eden. What happy days I passed there! I slept at last in a bed, a luxury I had not known since I left Nijni-Novgorod: I lived *à la cuisine française*, and I spoke French with French people. But the reader will feel more interested in a description of Pekin and its people, which I shall attempt in the next and last chapter.

CHAPTER XXII.

PEKIN—DEPARTURE.

The Marble Bridge—The Tartar City—Objects of Art—Japanese lacquering—Interments—The Observatory—The Imperial Palace—The Temples—The four harvests—Kinds of tea—Departure from Pekin—Tien-tsin—The sea at last.

THE following day we went first to pay our respects to Monseigneur de Laplace, the bishop of Pekin, who was then residing at the Mission of the Pères Lazaristes.

To get there we had to go over the marble bridge, which is one of the local wonders. This bridge rises in a saddle-back over a pond, I might say a little lake, and this is surrounded by the gardens of the Imperial palace. Unfortunately, the profusion of aquatic flowers with which this pond is so gay during summer were not yet in bloom, still we could, at least, admire the picturesque view from the marble bridge.

Mounds undoubtedly artificial, but called

here by the grand name of mountains, rise in waving outline around this piece of water. They are covered with rare trees, surmounted with kiosks. and those little constructions which we call pagodas. Pavilions are raised on piles above the water. The soil is covered with grass and creeping plants, that stretch along the ground and fall into the lake. The whole is delightfully cool, shady, and attractive, and laid out with unusual refinement of taste.

The Mission of the Lazaristes is built in the middle of this charming spot. All the fathers wear the Chinese costume, and I found it odd to call *Révérends Pères* these men in *papooches*, and adorned with pigtails as long as those of the Chinese: it is true their tresses are false, or nearly all false, but they would scarcely be supposed to be factitious unless seen very near.

The finest part of Pekin is that surrounding the palace: it is known by the name of the Tartar city. The great merchants and the most famous dealers in curiosities live here, and carry on their business as well.

The houses have simply a ground floor and no other storey; but their façades in the streets are of wood sculptured and gilt. The thickness of the ornamentation is considerable, and the carvings are sunk into it with a delicacy quite Chinese in its way. I do not know what one of these house fronts would be worth in France. Let the reader fancy a whole street lined with such shops glittering with gilding under a brilliant sky, and revealing, tastefully disposed in their interiors, embellished with these rich frames, all the wonders of Asiatic fairy-land.

I am sorry to be obliged here to undeceive, perhaps, my readers with regard to the fine Chinese collections which they imagine they possess at home. I am far from saying there are not in Europe admirable specimens of Chinese art. But, generally, all the articles offered for sale in England and France come from the southern cities, from Canton, Hong Kong, and Shanghai, and consequently are the productions of second-rate makers. Pekin art is almost everywhere still unknown, and it will easily be understood why it should be so, when it is remembered that Europeans are not allowed to carry on business in the capital of the Celestial Empire. Our last expeditions have not procured us any more liberty in this respect. The specimens of the art of Pekin are, therefore, almost exclusively bought by tourists on their visits, who do not dispose of them by way of trade. There may be seen in France, it is true, enamels in cloisonné work, but they give no idea of the marvels of the kind of work tourists may admire in the temple of Pekin. But there are entire panels much less known, representing landscapes, produced by the application of lacquer to porcelain; screens, wherein dyed ivory is applied to open-carved woodwork; or lacquered folding screens with ornamentation produced by the coloured transparent stones of Mongolia. The latter kind of work presents objects of incomparable beauty, and one is never tired of admiring them. There are also vases in uniform enamel, generally blue with designs in white, level with the surface, having a most graceful effect. This kind of vase is not rare at Pekin, and yet very little known in Europe.

Whilst I am describing the art of the extreme East, I should like to enlighten the reader a little on Japanese lacquers, though

I intend drawing my notes of travel to a close at Tien-tsin, and to say nothing of those Japan islands—a sojourn dear as a souvenir of pleasure and joy. All the productions to which we in France give this pompous title of *laque au Japon*, consist merely of surfaces of varnished wood. In the true lacquer, on the contrary, the drawings in bold relief are composed of pure gold, and the ground-work is covered with adventurine reduced to a powder before application. Objects in true lacquer command therefore, in Japan, exorbitant prices.

I one day asked at Yeddo the price of a cabinet resembling pretty much those that are become now so common in France, and are generally sold with us for two or three hundred francs. The dealer demanded twenty-five thousand francs for it. A little square box of about four inches each way, of genuine lacquer, is worth, in Japan, from eight hundred to one thousand francs. I shall not enter into the subject of Chinese porcelain, because this alone would form matter for a volume: besides, I did not remain long enough at Pekin to become well acquainted with this delicate department of Chinese art, more difficult to master. I will simply mention two kinds of vases in porcelain which appeared to me much esteemed. The one sort is ornamented with large Chinese figures, having in the middle a medallion representing some scene in character with the surroundings. The other is covered with designs in bold relief, also of porcelain, and coloured. These two kinds of vases, it seems, originated three or four hundred years ago, and are worth generally from four to seven hundred francs. What are known also as pretty little thin cloisonné enamels, date also from about the same epoch, and fetch considerable prices in China. These cloisonné enamels are rather rare in Europe. They may be recognised by their designs being more sunk and less regular than in those relatively modern, and especially by certain parts of them, where the transparency of the enamel permits the copper on which it is laid to be seen beneath.

As I have just mentioned, the streets of the Tartar quarter are lined with shops, exposing in their fronts the beautiful articles just described. In the roadway the throng of people is even greater than in the villages I had passed through.

The crowds of people on foot are obliged to stand aside constantly to make way for the palanquins of the grandees, borne by men; the two-wheeled carriages of the mandarins, who may be seen through the black or green *persiennes*, wrapped in their long robes of embroidered silk; the horses, the camels, the travelling palanquins with mules, then the marriage and funeral processions. The latter occupy a considerable space, and stretch over five hundred or a thousand yards, according to the dignity of the deceased. The poor carry in the line of procession parasols, poles surmounted with hands in gilt wood, and all kinds of amulets. Then follow the objects that belonged to the defunct; his horse, his carriage, in which is generally set up an effigy in wax representing his features, and if a mandarin, wearing his court costume. At last is seen the coffin, made of oak about two and a half inches thick, and placed on a catafalque. The great bier is borne by at least forty or sixty men. The relatives dressed in white, the mark of mourning, precede the coffin, throwing flowers in the way, burning incense, and going through a ceremony of respect to the dead every eighty or hundred steps. For this demonstration the procession comes to a halt. They spread on the ground a white cloth, and the mourners, prostrating themselves entirely face downwards, strike their foreheads on the ground. This part of the ceremony finished, they get up and the procession proceeds, with these interludes, to some land belonging to the deceased, where the coffin is deposited on the ground in the open air and left there without burial. When the coffin decays they form a tumulus of earth around it, but it is never put into a grave. The spot remains ever afterwards sacred, and can be used no more for cultivation.

It may be imagined what an immense extent of valuable land the Chinese lose through this custom. It is known what many quarrels it also leads to in the towns along the coast inhabited by Europeans: the subject has been too often discussed to make it worth while to say anything about it here.

Among the great concourse of people in

the Tartar city may be seen a multitude of conjurers exercising their wonderful feats in the open air.

Their dexterity is surprising; for they execute their tricks among the spectators without the convenient aid of tables and boxes with false bottoms, which are such valuable adjuncts in theatres. Some of them perform even dangerous feats: they leap head-foremost through a cylinder placed horizontally, bristling with nails and pointed blades. I should never come to an end if I were to describe everything that obtrudes itself on the sight in these wide streets of the Tartar city. Nowhere else can be seen such a varied and picturesque kaleidoscope as here meets the astonished eye.

Unfortunately, side by side with these marvels, one turns with disgust from other sights repulsive to European civilization. All along the streets vast holes are sunk for a purpose it would be embarrassing to explain. There is no city in the world so noisome, and I can easily understand why the *personnel* of the legations prefer remaining shut up four and five months at a time in their fine residences and grounds, to seeking any recreation in such a polluted atmosphere.

We visited the observatory, constructed by the Chinese under the direction of the Jesuits. The scientific instruments to be seen there are admirable. They are made of bronze, supported on feet of the same metal, in which all the fancies of Chinese art have been lavished. The contortions of these mountings, composed of dragons and grotesque monsters, produce a striking contrast to the regular forms of the spheres, the parallel lines and astronomical figures which they sustain at a great height in the air.

I have seen at Pekin, in the temples of the Mongolian lamas, or of the priests of Buddha, splendid enamels and objects of great value; but I have never found in China, nor even in Japan, where bronze is, certainly, turned to better account than in the Celestial Empire, anything so artistic, in the strict meaning of the term, as the apparatus of this observatory. The taste of the Chinese it must be admitted is very questionable. One may admire, especially, the colours of their porcelain, the soft hues of their ancient enamels, and the harmony of the tints in their embroidered stuffs; but in their designs, in the forms of their objects and personages, many faults and even repulsive monstrosities may be noticed. But the instruments of the Pekin Observatory are, in my opinion, above all criticism. Fancifulness certainly abounds therein, but it is only within just bounds: the supports I have just mentioned are so slender, so delicately worked, that they seem quite foreign and distinct from the spheres they sustain, and these indeed produce the illusion of being maintained by their proper force like real celestial worlds.

Before quitting this spot I took from the top a panoramic view of this immense capital, and the prospect extended over a considerable distance. The golden roofs of the merchants' houses of the Tartar city were glittering with splendour in the sun; then I remarked the not less brilliant green porcelain roofs of the fortresses rising above the chief gates, the blue porcelain roofs of the pagodas, of the Temple of Heaven, and of the Temple of Agriculture, and then, particularly, the Imperial palace, covered with yellow porcelain.

The Imperial palace of China is the abode of mystery; a mystery no one can boast of having penetrated. It is a little spot, unknown and deserted, amid these teeming millions of human beings—a recess into which no European has ever entered, and wherein only a very limited number of Chinese can penetrate once in the twenty-four hours, and then only in the darkest hours of the night.

The audience which the Emperor gave a few years ago to the European ministers, and which made a considerable sensation, did not take place even in the palace. The Son of Heaven did not deign to show himself here to the ministers but in a pavilion so far removed from the mysterious palace that it is plainly visible from the marble bridge.

Many reports have circulated in Europe regarding the private life of the Emperors of China, and the internal regulations of the palace. M. Berthémy, the French minister in Japan, whom I had the honour to meet at Yokohama, and who had previously been in China for many years, said: "All that has been retailed about the interior of the Imperial palace of Pekin can only be a mere fable, for it is impossible for anyone to know anything about it. The only thing that seems to me likely, because it has been declared to me by all the mandarins, is that the Emperor is subjected to a severe etiquette, and that he would be immediately assassinated by his own guards if he attempted to set it aside."

The sight of the yellow roofs of this palace produced on me a deep impression, and on reposing at my ease at the Embassy I compared in my mind the existence of this poor Emperor, a slave to etiquette, to our good king Saint Louis showing himself to his people and administering justice under an oak in the Bois de Vincennes. How many unhappy there are in this world in all the scales of the social hierarchy !

I shall say little of the Temple of Heaven, and of the Temple of Agriculture, because they are not interesting. The first especially is unworthy of the exalted name it bears. It is in an immense park surrounded with walls, in which chapels and pretty pavilions, covered with blue porcelain, are distributed, and where a subdued light penetrates through blinds composed of little tubes of blue glass placed parallel. A platform of white marble is raised in the middle of the park, and it is here the Emperor occasionally comes to offer with his own hand sacrifices to the Divinity.

The curious portion of the Temple of Agriculture and its precincts is a field where, every year, on a certain day, the Emperor, holding in his hand a plough, makes a furrow along the ground, as if to give an example to his subjects. The remainder of the field is afterwards ploughed by the mandarins. This ceremony shows how much agriculture, the principal source of the wealth of the country, is honoured in China. With their two annual harvests of corn, the Chinese succeed in providing bread at a moderate price, and by exporting their tea and their rice they draw gold into their country from all parts of the world. Their method of cultivation very much resembles the Egyptian system. They divide their fields into little squares, around which water is conducted for irrigation to all parts. This water flows from numerous canals winding through the country, and is supplied by contrivances worked by Chinese labourers like the Egyptian *shadoufs*. For the cultivation of rice the little squares are surrounded with an embankment high enough to maintain over the field a sheet of water several inches deep. The land thus disappears completely. When I visited the rice fields in the month of May, the seed, lately sown, hardly sprouted above the surface of the water.

The tea is a little shrub, a foot and a half to two feet high. The leaves are gathered from May to August, according to the species, and also according to the quality required. There are in China growths of tea as there are in France growths of wine. The nature of the soil and the different kinds of plants produce the varieties known to the trade. The most esteemed kind is known by the name of yellow tea. It is the ordinary drink of the Emperor of China and the Emperor of Russia.

This tea is so valuable, that in Siberia, in certain even rich families, I have sometimes seen one cup of it only made in my honour, whilst my hosts deprived themselves of it by reason of economy. It would not be interesting here to enumerate the different growths, because they are not known by their original names. The various kinds are named in

France according to the mode of gathering: thus pearl tea is from small leaves gathered at the beginning of spring, soon after their formation. The *thé à pointes blanches* is made of a mixture of leaves and flowers. The white points are merely the dried flowers of the shrub; this is the reason this kind is the strongest. One of the commonest kinds is the brick tea, which I have already mentioned as serving for money in Mongolia; and finally the commonest tea, which through some preparation I am ignorant of presents an odd appearance. It has also the form of a brick, but it is quite black, and neither a stalk nor a leaf can be seen in it, as in the other bricks. On looking at it, it might be supposed to be a block of coal or peat. This tea is sold for a mere trifle, and is a great resource for the poor of Siberia as well as China.

The intelligence and skilfulness of the Chinese are everywhere apparent, and they know how to turn these advantages to account in everything. They have also brought to great perfection the art of sail-making. I am not acquainted with all the systems adopted in France, but in mentioning the lateen sail (*la voile latine*), which bears the name of our race, I mention, I believe, one of the inventions of Europe. But this lateen sail in swelling out excessively under the action of the wind does not at the same time utilize all the force this moving power is capable of imparting. Besides, in squalls, the handling consists in slackening the rope that ties it below. The canvas flapping then at the top of the mast imparts a pitching or tossing to the boat that may be very dangerous. This method of sailing is, therefore, imperfect. The Chinese sail is, on the contrary, held in by a series of parallel bars, and thus constantly opposes an even surface to the play of the wind. Then, with the aid of a pulley at the top of the mast, it can be lowered to any degree. In this way the Chinese may, in the most violent squalls, still have a sail spread that offers little, much above the deck, for the storm to grapple with, consequently exposing in no way the ship to danger.

I might quote many examples of this ingenious and practical mind; and in travelling through China I have conceived the highest opinion of the intelligence, the cleverness, and the perseverance of the Chinese. There is only one thing wanting to these people: a government that will let them know there are other nations in the world besides the Chinese; that these nations have also a civilization, from which it would be judicious and especially profitable to borrow certain inventions. But the day will come, and perhaps it is not afar, when the Chinese will immigrate into Europe, as they already immigrate into Japan, California, and Peru; they will form at Marseilles, Paris, and London more important quarters than the depôts of Shanghai, Macao, and Saigon, and foreign commerce will take an expansion unknown with this nation.

The majority of the French people believe the intelligence of the Japanese is very superior to that of the Chinese. It is a serious mistake. The Japanese resemble us very much in their character, and that is the reason this people pleases travellers. They are gay, enterprising, boastful, disputative, and a little revolutionary. There is in Japan an actual pretender, and consequently among the Japanese partisans of such and such a family, and, perhaps, even republicans more or less democratic or socialistic. The French, therefore, like the Japanese, and on the other hand the Japanese admire the French. They create a little army in which they adopt our costumes; nothing is more singular than to see a *chasseur de Vincennes* mounting guard in the streets of Yeddo. They construct little railways, little telegraphs; but in the end these things are not serious, because in the first place there is not, nor can be, anything serious in these people; these applications of our inventions are insignificant because they are confined to a little tongue of land very narrow along the sea, beyond which it is impossible for Europeans to penetrate. The interior of Japan is absolutely closed to us, whilst we are perfectly free to travel from one end of China to the other. It is, therefore, I consider, quite an error to suppose that Japan is marching towards civilization. The existing transformations are limited to a very minute portion of the territory, and consequently have no significance.

The Chinese government does not permit to its people either telegraphs or railways, or anything that is European; but the day when the Chinese, through some much desired revolution, will have obtained these concessions from its government, it will not only apply our inventions with judgment but will perfect them, and perhaps we shall be astonished one fine day to learn from the Chinese the means of uniting on railways the highest speed with the greatest security. To impose on the Chinese a new form of government, or on the existing government a new constitution, is what our last expedition there should have taken in hand, instead of destroying the Summer Palace, a piece of work repugnant to my feelings to dwell on.

A little lake, surrounded entirely with marble galleries and covered with miniature islands, in the middle of which are displayed the most charming pavilions in the world ; a large range of steps in porcelain, rising to the top of the hill of Wan-tcho-chan, and two little temples in porcelain,—these are the remains of the marvels that once astonished the wondering sight in this palace and surrounding park.

I took leave of my kind hosts at the Legation of Pekin, whose hospitality and attentions I shall never forget, on the 18th of May, and went to Tien-tsin by the course of the Peiho.

M. Rystel, then at the Consulate of Tien-tsin, entertained us very agreeably the time we were obliged to wait for a boat, and at last, on the 24th of May, I embarked for Shanghai with my three young companions already mentioned. I could not make up my mind to leave Pablo at Tien-tsin, and I, therefore, took him with me. The poor fellow was so faithful and devoted, and never ceased expatiating with tears in his eyes on the *far niente* life he had enjoyed, with so much good living, at the Embassy of Pekin. On going to sea at the mouth of the Peiho I was overcome with rapture. For this great sea is all one, and, in washing the shores of every land it touches, it brought me nearer to my native land; its waves caressed as lovingly the beaches of Trouville and Biarritz as the cliffs of the gulf of Pei-Chi-Li.

My fatiguing travels over the Siberian steppes and the Desert of Gobi were decidedly at an end, and I now had before me the prospect of my friends and my home.

My readers, perhaps, will wonder what could have induced me to have undertaken so wearisome a journey: I had imagined the bright side of it only then, but now I have seen the other I can advise them not to follow my example; for though there are many novel, grand, and striking scenes of nature, accompanied with much exciting adventure, still they are not to be enjoyed in so rigorous a climate as that of Siberia in Winter without incurring much hardship, and even a certain exposure to a considerable share of danger.

NOTES.

NOTE 1, CHAP. II., PAGE 22.

Whenever the degree of temperature is mentioned in the course of this narrative, it is according to the *Centigrade scale*, although it is calculated by the Réaumur thermometer, and no other, in Russia. 5° Centigrade are equal to 9° Fahrenheit : but since the freezing point in the Centigrade thermometer is 0, and in the Fahrenheit 32°, in converting one scale into the other, care must be taken to add or deduct this difference in calculating above or below freezing point. It will therefore be seen that when 18° below 0 in the Centigrade scale are reached—a point nearly equivalent to zero in the Fahrenheit thermometer—the latter is quite inadequate to indicate the intense cold of Siberia, where, in certain parts, as at Yakutsk and Tomsk, it is said to reach 58° Centigrade even, in some winters. This temperature would be equivalent to 105° Fahrenheit below freezing point, disregarding the irrational descending scale below this mark, and supposing the graduation to continue instead from freezing point with augmenting numbers. But Gabriel Fahrenheit contrived his thermometer for Dantzig, and evidently not for Siberia ; for the lowest point, zero, has no scientific basis, no significance whatever in the phenomena of heat, and represents merely the extreme cold registered at Dantzig in 1709, a degree of cold which must have been surpassed there subsequently by many degrees, and even in Paris by at least 15°, once in the winter of 1871 during the siege, and more than once during the rigorous winter of 1880. We seem to be more attached to this Dantzig thermometer than the Dantzigians themselves, who, probably, have long ago adopted the more rational scale of Réaumur or of Celsius, more rational at least so far as they are graduated each way from freezing point. Perhaps a change may come about when we begin to dine at 18 o'clock instead of 6 p.m.—W. C.

NOTE 2, CHAP. VII., PAGE 127.

Siberia, it appears, judging from an account of a correspondent of the *Times* at Tumen, published November 20th, 1883, is quite *un pays de cocagne*, so far as provisions are concerned, sparkling champagne of course excepted. The prices of some articles of food at Tumen are given as follows:

"Geese in autumn cost fivepence a'pair, and are frozen in numbers to be sent west to Russia and east to Irkutsk; grouse in summer, being a delicacy, cost threepence a pair, and good fish, such as sterlet and nelma, from three-halfpence to twopence-halfpenny per pound. Sheep are scarce and not much eaten, but beef in autumn costs from fifteen to twenty pence the pood, or about a halfpenny per pound."

In spite of the cheapness of provisions and labour, travelling appears to be, at least to the foreigner, very expensive in Siberia.—W. C.

NOTE 3, CHAP. IX., PAGE 165.

Some interesting experiments on seeds and plants have recently been made by a Norwegian *savant*, Professor Schubeler, with the view of demonstrating the beneficial influence of prolonged sunlight on vegetation during the long summer days of the north. Some of these experiments were as follows: dwarf beans taken from Christiania to Drontheim, being less than $4°$ further north, gained more than 60 per cent. in weight; thyme brought from Lyons and planted at Drontheim gained 71 per cent. It appears that the grain grown in northern latitudes is much heavier than that grown in more southern lands: on the other hand, seed taken from Norway and sown at Bresslau greatly diminished in weight the first year. As the differences of soil, moisture, temperature of the ground and air, and other disturbing elements have to be duly accounted for, these experiments do not appear to be sufficient to establish the fact that the increase of weight was *wholly* due to increased sunlight. Perhaps experiments for comparative results will be made under similar conditions, except those of the duration and quantity of sunlight, and such experiments, more in accordance with the principles of experimental science, would, if made, be more satisfactory.—W. C.

NOTE 4, CHAP. XI., PAGE 188.

It does not appear, however, that wolves are always so peaceful and harmless. From a police report it seems that, in 1875, 161 persons, and domestic animals to the value of £2,500,000, were killed by wolves in European Russia: their depredations in Siberia could not probably be easily calculated. In 1882 it is reported that 278 human beings were killed by wolves in British India.—W. C.

NOTE 5, CHAP. XII., PAGE 213.

The following are a few clauses from the Russian penal code that came into operation on the 1st of May, 1846, and will show how far religious intolerance is carried in Russia. Certain clauses relating to corporal punishments, the abrogation of privileges, and the right of suzerainty are omitted, because the decree emancipating the serfs renders them null and void.

"Sec. 196.—He who abandons the orthodox faith for any other creed, Christian even, is to be handed over to the ecclesiastical authorities, in order to be admonished and enlightened, and that his case may be judged according to the rules of the Church. Until he returns to the orthodox faith, the Government *takes steps* to preserve his children, under age, from corruption: a guardian is placed over his estates, and *he is forbidden to reside there.*"

"Sec. 197.—He who shall attempt, either by word of mouth or writing, to draw orthodox believers into another creed, shall be condemned:

"For the first offence, to be imprisoned for one year or two years in a house of correction; for the second, to be incarcerated in a fortress for a period of four to six years; for the third, to be sent into exile in the government of Tobolsk or Tomsk, with imprisonment for one or two years."

"Sec. 198.—If the parents. who are legally obliged to bring up their children in the orthodox faith, shall bring them up according to the practices of some other creed, Christian even, they shall be condemned to imprisonment for one or two years; their children shall be entrusted to parents of the orthodox faith for their education, or in default of such persons, to guardians nominated by the Government."

"Sec. 199.—He who shall hinder anyone from following the orthodox faith shall be condemned to be imprisoned for three to six months: and if he shall have used threats or violence or practised annoyance, he shall be confined for two or three years in a house of correction."

"Sec. 200.—He who is well aware that his wife or his children, or any persons legally under his *surveillance*, intend to abandon the orthodox creed, and does not attempt to dissuade them from it, or take such measures as are authorised by the law to prevent them from doing so, shall be liable to an imprisonment of three days to three months; and if he is orthodox, he shall be subject to ecclesiastical punishment."

This law therefore obliges a man, *even if he is a Roman Catholic*, to denounce his wife and children of the orthodox faith and act with rigour against them.

"Sec. 202 —Members of the clergy of the Christian sects. convicted of having taught the Catechism to orthodox children, *although it should not be proved* that they intended to beguile them, will be liable: for the first offence, to be removed from their spiritual charge for one to three years; for the second, to forfeit entirely their charge, and, after having been imprisoned for one to two years, to be placed continually under the *surveillance* of the police."

With regard to the grave question of mixed marriages, the tenth book of the laws, among other vexatious regulations, stipulates that: "If one of the two contracting parties is orthodox, the priest can only give his benediction to the marriage when he shall have obtained from the heterodox party a formal engagement in writing, that he or she shall not attempt to gain over the other to his or her religion by allurements, threats, or other means, and that *all their children shall be brought up in the orthodox faith.*"

Marriages between members of the Catholic and of the Orthodox faith, celebrated only in a Catholic church, are declared null and void.

NOTE 6, CHAP. XIII., PAGE 225.

The exiled Poles, at present even, can only carry offensive weapons with the permission of the military governor.

NOTE 7, CHAP. XIII., PAGE 226.

In Siberia, poor people, who travel enormous distances afoot, in order to pray at a tomb or the image of a saint, are often met with. It is not a rare occurrence for peasants to attempt to undertake a journey thus as far as Jerusalem. There are many, indeed, that abandon their project on the way from sheer fatigue, but not from want of courage. A few are sometimes known to accomplish even this formidable undertaking.

NOTE 8, CHAP. XIII., PAGE 229.

Many Siberian animals that are white during winter, resume, in the summer, furs of a colour which we habitually see here. The ermine is a changeable fur, and becomes yellow during the warm season. A summer ermine is almost worthless in the eyes of a connoisseur.—*The Author*.

These, no doubt, are instances of the *protective colours* observed by Darwin and Mr. Wallace.

"A common Indian and Sumatran butterfly (*Kallima*) disappears like magic when it settles in a bush; for it hides its head and antennæ between its closed wings, and these in form, *colour*, and veining, *cannot be distinguished from a withered leaf* together with the footstalk."—*Wallace.*

" With animals of all kinds, whenever colour has been modified *for some special purpose*, this has been, as far as we can judge, either *for protection* or as an attraction between the sexes."—*Darwin, Descent of Man.*

The white furs of the animals, liable to become the prey of others amid the snow, are obviously a protection from observation; and likewise in summer, some other colour presenting a diminished contrast with surrounding nature, would have the same effect.

Perhaps this adaptation of colour to surroundings may extend also to certain animals, which would otherwise become extinct if they did not enjoy the facilities it conferred in the capture of their prey when they are placed at a great disadvantage. The Polar bear, for instance, requires no protection from its enemies, but favourable conditions, probably, for approaching its prey unobserved. It seems reasonable to conclude that animals of either class favoured with a colour that enables them either to escape from their pursuers, or, on the other hand, to approach their prey, have, in the struggle for life, the best chance of a prolonged existence, and consequently of leaving the most numerous offspring to perpetuate the race. Though colour is one of the most varying eatures of animals, it is, whether changing or permanent, beginning to be recognised no longer as capricious or accidental, as we have hitherto usually regarded it, but as the consequence of the survival of the most highly favoured in an endowment conducive to the preservation of the species, a discovery on which the continued observations of naturalists are ever throwing fresh light.—W. C.

NOTE 9, CHAP. XIII., PAGE 231.

This is a small fruit resembling that of the dog rose. A beverage is made from it by infusing the berries for a fortnight in some brandy with sugar, which is not disagreeable to the palate.

NOTE 10, CHAP. XIII., PAGE 240.

In England, in the time of Henry VIII., Sable was probably adopted by wealthy people as a distinctive mark of their social position ; otherwise, why should it have become an object of legislation and have been prohibited by the Statute of Apparel (24 Hen. VIII.) to be worn by any under the degree of an earl ?

It will, no doubt, be seen from this diverse and often singularly-extravagant appreciation of furs in Russia—and occasionally not so much for their beauty and elegance as for their rarity and great money value—that it is the lucky possessors who are admired and envied in these luxuries, because they are the means of proclaiming and parading so effectively their opulence ; and the vain, exulting in this special homage to their exaggerated self-importance, cheerfully buy the gratification at their own appraisement, and thereby give to these furs an exorbitant value.

It might be contended that a single caprice of this nature is insufficient to prove the existence of a passion for the display of wealth, and that such instances must necessarily be rare because the furs are rare.

But it has significance enough to deduce from it its pervading character. The vain, it is true, can be vain only of what they possess ; but to suppose these to have undivided possession of the folly, as well as exclusive enjoyment of the highly-prized furs, would be to take no account of the admiring multitude and the envious, without whom the vanity of others would clearly have no *raison d'être*—no visible existence ; for the price of these special badges or symbols, these admirers, the public in fact, so materially sustain, is precisely the measure of the public estimation.

It seems therefore reasonable to infer that the sentiment is general.

Then when a caprice becomes *à la mode*—" the proper thing to do "—a powerful fresh stimulus is added to the folly, and the feverish desire " to be in the fashion " may develop the passion into a mania, whether its special objects be badges of wealth, bibelots, tulips, or bric-à-brac, and

> "Thus does a false ambition rule us,
> Thus pomp delude and folly fool us."

But a desire to fall in with the fashion would alone be insufficient to explain the extraordinary price of blue fox feet fur; for a fashion to become a rage must first take the form of an epidemic—a condition rigorously excluded by the very restricted number of possible possessors of the coveted object. And so far as beauty is concerned, however beautiful this fur may be, its beauty would still far less account for the price. That the Russians consider it beautiful, is likely enough, for beauty to most people is purely conventional, and much more readily perceived through the ears than the eyes. Few, perhaps, would contend that the beauty of pearls and diamonds is at all commensurate with their price, and yet those who recognise the exaggeration, might not readily perceive that nearly all their value is derived from the esteem they command as badges or insignia of wealth and competence. If beauty has no objective existence—and there is no evidence that it has any other than as a sentiment or idea—it can have no money value at all in a beautiful object, simply because it is not there, but in the brain of the beholder; and this would, perhaps, explain why so many seem insensible to its influence, and again, why it appeared to Goethe to elude the grasp of definition. How often we vainly imagine we secure it in acquiring some charming *tableau de genre* or bit of old china, some rare gem or inimitable enamel, and, at the end of a few months' familiarity with it, are disappointed at finding that it no longer rouses the enthusiasm we felt on first beholding its wondrous beauty! And yet, ever fondly clinging to the illusion that it is an intrinsic part of the object, we continue the pursuit like the chase of the beautiful blue-winged butterfly of Kashmeer, described in *The Giaour*, and not rarely find at last that—

> "The lovely toy so fiercely sought,
> Hath lost its charm by being caught."

But it exists only in the mind, which feels no satisfaction in the constant indulgence of a single emotion, and it may, as in pearls and diamonds, be enjoyed for itself alone, without material possession, as gratuitously as the surpassing beauty of a splendid sunset. Nor would, perhaps, the exigencies of fashion—which may be fully met by imitations so deceptive as to elude ordinary detection—raise the price of the real much beyond the fictitious gem, unless the fashionable were as scrupulous as ladies were in the reign of Elizabeth, who, according to Fuller, " would have as patiently digested a lie, as the wearing of false stones or pendants of counterfeit pearl."

But regarded as insignia of wealth, possession is a *sine quâ non*, and the extravagant price is essential to its object, and the more extravagant it is, the higher the gratification to be derived from it, because this implies increased distinction —the consequence of fewer enjoying a superfluity of wealth. The desire also to acquire a beautiful article of exaggerated value is independent of an appreciation of beauty *per se*, and is principally a purely factitious desire, varying for no better reason than because other people in general by a tacit consensus think more or less of it ; and if society should *agree to think* any object, whether beautiful or not, a convenient vehicle to attract attention to any quality it values, such as wealth, refinement, *haut ton*, elegance, or culture, a *new value* is immediately given to such object, which the rage to acquire may exaggerate to outrageous extravagance. If, for instance, diamonds and pearls had not been taken into favour by princes, from time immemorial all the world over, they might not now, perhaps, have a much higher value than Brighton pebbles or Whitby jet. And if blue fox feet fur had not been adopted by the Muscovite grandees, it might have no higher value than grey fox or squirrel. But it is plainly envy and admiration of riches that the Russian grandees buy, and when they have a relish for the luxury they pay for it as munificently as Lucullus paid for a magnificent supper, who probably thought as little of the epicurean gratification to be got out of a dish of peacock's brains, as these nabobs think of the comfort or elegance to be got out of a cloak of blue fox feet, the sentimental value of which they estimate at the rate of sixteen hundred pounds sterling!—W. C.

NOTE 11, CHAP. XV., PAGE 278.

The author of "Chto dyelat" was Tschernishevsky, who wrote it in the Petro-Paolovsky fortress at St. Petersburg. He had written also several romances during his imprisonment, all of which he had burnt with his own hand. According to his own statement, it does not appear that he was imprisoned on account of anything he had written. In the month of December, 1883, he was living as a free convict under surveillance at Astrachan, and on the 11th of this month, had completed his long term of nearly twenty years of banishment. He gave the following account of his treatment as a prisoner to a correspondent of the *Daily News*, whose interesting letter regarding him was published in that journal, December 22nd, 1883.

"I was always treated by the agents of the Government as respectfully as any man could desire. My treatment was not that of a convict, but, throughout, that of a prisoner of war. The hard labour, of which I have spoken, was for me, as well as for many of the Russian and Polish political exiles, among whom my lot was cast, a name only—it existed on paper, but had no reality."—W. C.

NOTE 12, CHAP. XVI., PAGE 287.

The reader perhaps may not know why, in mentioning the names of certain persons, their family names are preceded by two baptismal names. It is because in Russia courtesy demands that, in addressing anyone, you should add the baptismal name of his father, to which is affixed the termination *ovitch*. Thus Iwan Michaelovitch Nemptchinof means Iwan the son of Michael Nemptchinof. This double appellation, not merely polite, but indeed the most respectful of all, especially when the family name is not added, is so rigorously exacted by usage, that the Emperor, in the public acts, is designated Alexander Nicolaevitch. It is one of the grossest insults to address anyone by his sole baptismal name as we are accustomed to do in our intimacies : it seems that in omitting the name of the father in addressing a Russian you would insinuate that he was obscure and unknown and of illegitimate birth.

NOTE 13, CHAP. XVI., PAGE 301.

The same fact has been remarked by Blanchard (*Animaux articulés*, Paris, 1846), and by Lacordaire (*Introduction à l'entomologie*, tome III, page 383).

NOTE 14, CHAP. XIX., PAGE 347.

The Desert of Gobi properly so called is a little less in extent than the Sahara ; it must not be forgotten, however, that the countries bordering it, especially on the west, are actual deserts.

NOTE 15, CHAP. XIX., PAGE 350.

The depressing effect on the mind of the traveller, produced by the aspect of monotonous scenery, has been noticed by M. Gabriel Charmes, in an excursion in the Auvergne (*Journal des Débats*, July, 1881), who attributes the habitual lowness of spirits of the peasantry to the cheerless uniformity of certain parts of the Cantal, amid which they dwell. As some of these are said to become sorcerers from the prolonged effect, may not the gloomy character of the Mongolian religion be largely attributable to the dismal baldness of their desert ? M. Gabriel Charmes thus describes the mountains of the Cantal and their influence on the mind of the spectator: " I have referred to those great, sterile, melancholy table-lands, that are everywhere met with in the Cantal and the mountainous district of the Puy-de-Dôme. In the spring even, when the long grass is mingled with an abundance of flowers, it is almost impossible to traverse them, and quite impossible to dwell there, without feeling some vague, unaccountable weight or oppression on the spirits, similar to that experienced by those who live on the sea-shore, in sight of the incessant monotony of the waves. The clouds depict on them great dark shadows, which, driven on by a brisk wind, flit past like gigantic phantoms. This perpetual play of shadows and light is the only diversity that arrests the eye in the interminable uniformity. They, therefore, who frequent them a long while, acquire, in course of time, strange habits of mind. It is a very widely spread opinion among the peasantry of the Auvergne, that the cow-herds, who pass most of the year on the lonely hills, actually become wizards. The special fixedness, perhaps, which the contemplation of an unvarying nature stamps on their sight, is the cause of this prejudice. . . . The mind contracts there a kind of natural melancholy, and this seems to dispose it to sadness rather than joyousness." It is not probable that the monotony of the waves produces the same effect, for here we have movement, with which the mind sympathises, and, being thus relieved, does not readily become a prey to melancholy. The sea is very different from the motionless, unchanging desert.—W. C.

Notes bearing no initials at the end are taken from the Original Edition.

University of California
SOUTHERN REGIONAL LIBRARY FACILITY
Return this material to the library
from which it was borrowed.

OCT 02 1989

JUL 14

www.ingramcontent.com/pod-product-compliance
Lightning Source LLC
Chambersburg PA
CBHW022100300426
44117CB00007B/527